MEDITATIONS

ON THE

MYSTERIES OF OUR HOLY FAITH.

HIC MAGNVS VOCABITVR QVI FECERIT, ET DOCVERIT
IHS
Vener abilis P. Ludovicus de Ponte
Soc. Iesu Vallisoletanus, obijt magna cū
opinione Sanctitatis Vallisoleti in Collegio
S. Ambrosij decimo sexto Februarij Anno M.DC.
XXIV. Ætatis suæ Septuagesimo.

MEDITATIONS

ON THE

MYSTERIES OF OUR HOLY FAITH:

TOGETHER WITH
A TREATISE ON MENTAL PRAYER.
BY THE VEN. FATHER LOUIS DE PONTE, S. J.
BEING THE
TRANSLATION FROM THE ORIGINAL SPANISH BY JOHN HEIGHAM.
REVISED AND CORRECTED.

TO WHICH ARE ADDED

THE REV. F. C. BORGO'S
MEDITATIONS ON THE SACRED HEART.

TRANSLATED FROM THE ITALIAN.

IN SIX VOLS.—VOL. II.

Permissu Superiorum.

SAINT LOUIS
LIBRI SANCTI PRESS
MMXXIII

NIHIL OBSTAT
GEORGE PORTER, SJ.

IMPRIMATUR
✠ HENRY EDWARD,
Archbishop of Westminster

*Originally published by
Richardson & Son, 1852*

SECOND PRINTING

ISBN 979-8-8689-0211-6

TABLE OF CONTENTS OF VOL. II.

                                                                    PAGE
PART II.—For Proficients in the illuminative way.
  INTRODUCTION.—On the perfect imitation of our Saviour Christ.
    which is the end of these meditations.
  A.—MEDITATIONS on the mysteries of the Incarnation and infancy
    of our Lord Jesus Christ until His Baptism, together with
    meditations on the life of our Blessed Lady until the same
    time   9
  FUNDAMENTAL MEDITATION.—On the infinite excellence of the celes-
    tial King Christ Jesus our Lord, and of the vocation He
    makes, inviting all men to follow Him   13
  MEDITATION I.—On the decree made by the most holy Trinity, that
    the second divine Person should become man for
    the redemption of mankind, lost by the sin of
    Adam   21
  II.—On God's infinite charity resplendent in this mys-
    tery of the Incarnation, and the great benefits
    received from it   30
  III.—On Almighty God's decree to be born of a woman;
    and on the election of our Blessed Lady for His
    mother: and the singular graces that He granted
    her on that account in the instant of her concep-
    tion   36
  IV.—On the life of our Blessed Lady until the Incarna-
    tion : in which are considered her nativity :—her
    presentation in the Temple—and her espousal to
    St. Joseph   46
  V.—On the time that Almighty God chose to announce
    and execute the mystery of the Incarnation   62
  VI.—On the coming of the angel Gabriel, to announce
    to the Virgin the mystery of the Incarnation :
    and the form of salutation and the removal of
    her fear   69
  VII.—On the angel's annunciation and declaration of the
    mystery of the Incarnation to the Blessed Virgin   82
  VIII.—On the final answer given to the angel by the
    Virgin, consenting to his embassage   90
  IX.—On the execution of the Incarnation ; and of some
    of its circumstances as concerning the body of
    our Lord Christ   99
  X.—On the excellence of the most holy soul of our Sa-
    viour Christ, and of the heroic acts of virtue that
    He exercised in the first instant of the Incarna-
    tion   107
  XI.—On the journey which the eternal Word incarnate
    made in His mother's womb, to the house of
    Zacharias to sanctify His fore-runner St. John
    the Baptist   116
  XII.—On the occurrences which took place in the Blessed
    Virgin's visitation of St. Elizabeth   121
  XIII.—On the birth of St. John the fore-runner of our
    Saviour Christ   138
  XIV.—On the events which happened on St. Joseph's pro-
    posing to forsake the Virgin when seeing her with
    child, and on the revelation made to him by the
    angel concerning this mystery   144

CONTENTS OF VOL. II.

	PAGE
MEDITATION XV.—On the expectation of our Blessed Lady's delivery; and on the preparation for the birth of our Saviour Christ	153
XVI.—On the journey of our Blessed Lady the Virgin, from Nazareth to Bethlehem	159
„ XVII.—On the birth of our Saviour Christ in a stable at Bethlehem	165
„ XVIII.—On the joy of the angels at the nativity of the Son of God: and on the tidings which they related to the shepherds	174
XIX.—On the journey of the shepherds to Bethlehem; and the things occurring to them there, with other incidents till the Circumcision	181
XX.—On the Circumcision of our Saviour on the eighth day	185
XXI.—On the giving of the name of Jesus to our Saviour Christ ..	191
„ XXII.—On the coming of the three kings of the East, to adore the Child; and on their entrance into Jerusalem	199
„ XXIII.—On the departure of the sages from Jerusalem, and their entrance into the stable at Bethlehem, and the occurrences there ..	209
„ XXIV.—On the purification of the Blessed Virgin; and on the presentation of the Child in the Temple	217
XXV.—On the occurrences at the presentation, with Simeon, and Anna the prophetess	224
„ XXVI.—Containing a form of prayer, of applying the interior faculties of the soul, to the contemplation of the mysteries that have been meditated	232
„ XXVII.—On the flight into Egypt	242
„ XXVIII.—On the murder of the holy Innocents: and the return from Egypt	254
„ XXIX.—On the coming of our Saviour Christ to the Temple of Jerusalem, and His remaining there among the doctors	258
„ XXX.—On the conduct of the Blessed Virgin on seeing that she had lost her Son, until she found Him	263
„ XXXI.—On the life led by our Saviour Christ at Nazareth until He was thirty years old ..	275

	PAGE
APPENDIX, containing the twelve meditations on the Sacred Heart of Jesus, translated from the Italian of Fr. C. Borgo	287

MEDITATION

			PAGE
i.—On the ends for which the B. Sacrament was instituted			289
ii.—In honour of the Sacred Heart for its life of beatitude			292
iii.	„	„	life of grace	295
iv.	„	„	life of sacrifice	299
v.	„	„	life of humiliation.	302
vi.	„	„	life of love	305
vii.	„	„	active life	309
viii.	„	„	hidden life	313
ix.	„	„	glorious life	317
x.	„	„	life of consummated sacrifice	321
xi. (*For the Vigil of Feast.*)—Priceless value of the sacred Heart ..	325
xii. (*For the Feast of the sacred Heart.*)—The love of the sacred Heart and our ingratitude.	332
Acts of consecration and reparation to the Sacred Heart ..	336

II.—FOR PROFICIENTS IN THE ILLUMINATIVE WAY.

A.—MEDITATIONS

ON THE MYSTERIES OF THE INCARNATION AND INFANCY

OF OUR

LORD AND SAVIOUR CHRIST JESUS,

UNTIL HIS BAPTISM.

WITH THESE ARE INSERTED MEDITATIONS ON THE LIFE OF OUR BLESSED LADY, UNTIL THE SAME TIME.

INTRODUCTION.

ON THE PERFECT IMITATION OF OUR SAVIOUR CHRIST, WHICH IS THE END OF THESE MEDITATIONS.

1. THE meditations belonging to the illuminative way, of which we begin to treat in this Second Part, have for their subject the mysteries of the Life of our Saviour Christ, from the time of His Incarnation until His death upon the cross. These, as it appears by what has been said in the Introduction of this book, in the fourth chapter, are divided into three parts:—(i.) those of His incarnation and child-hood ;—(ii.) those of His preaching ;—and (iii.) those of His passion and death. After which follows the glorified life, which pertains to the unitive way; to this, also, are highly conducive, the mysteries of the passion, in which our Saviour Christ discovered the excess of His love, as hereafter shown. All these mysteries the divine wisdom ordained, in order that they might be, with a pleasing

variety, the spiritual sustenance of those souls that travel to perfection. Into which souls this sovereign king enters, as into the "cellar of His precious wine." (1) And from these mysteries, as from celestial vessels, He draws the fervent wine of love, and of other ardent affections, with which He cheers, sustains, and inebriates, setting in order charity in them, with that order with which our Lord Himself exercised His acts ; to which He invites and exhorts us, saying : " I am come into my garden, O my sister, my spouse, I have gathered my myrrh with my aromatical spices ; I have eaten the honeycomb with my honey; I have drunk my wine, my milk. Eat, O friends, and drink, and be inebriated, my dearly beloved." (2) Which is to say : " By my Incarnation I come into the garden of my Church, and in entering into the world, I cut the myrrh of much bitterness and mortification, that I suffered in my infancy, with the 'aromatical spices' of most odoriferous virtues. I preached my doctrine, and practised it with as much pleasure as he that eats 'the honeycomb with its honey.' I became so inebriated with the wine of my love, that I remained naked, and upon a cross, being as much pleased with drinking the chalice of my passion as he is that drinks 'wine with its milk.' Therefore, O my friends, and my beloved, prepare the garden of your souls ; for in them I desire to work other three like effects, you yourselves also working them, through my grace, to imitate my life. First of all, cut myrrh, and the 'aromatical spices ' of virtues, that may mortify your passions, and preserve you from the corruption of your sins, imitating herein my purity. Then eat my 'honeycomb' with its 'honey,' meditating upon the excellent doctrine that I preached, figured by the wax of the honeycomb that gives light. But you are not to eat

(1) Cant. ii. 4.   (2) Cant. v. 1.

it alone, but with the imitation of the heroic virtues included therein, figured by the honey, that nourish with its sweetness.—And, finally, 'drink' and be inebriated with the wine of my perfect love, mingled with the 'milk' that I will give you of my divine consolation; with which you will so easily renounce the affections of all earthly things, that you shall, if need be, remain naked upon another cross, to imitate my nakedness, and to love me as I loved you."

2. These are the three principal exercises of well-ordered *charity* in her three estates, of beginning, augmentation, and perfection. And these same in that form and degree prescribed, are the principal ends to which the meditations of the childhood, preaching, and passion of our Saviour Christ are designed; of which the three parts that follow treat. Among these, those of this second part, which are of His childhood, have this excellence, that they move us to love Him with more tenderness, and to imitate Him with more sweetness; because, as in making Himself a child for us, He accommodated Himself, as the prophet Isaias says, (3) to "eat" the food proper to children, which is "butter and honey"; so, also, to those that meditate the mysteries of His infancy, especially to beginners, He uses to give more abundantly the milk and honey of divine consolation, to wean them from terrene, and to animate them to the imitation of His heroic virtues.

3. To attain these ends, we should endeavour, by means of these meditations, to know Christ Jesus our Lord, true God and man, with so certain, proper, entire, and perfect a knowledge, that it may come to understand and penetrate the infinite dignity of His person, and the inestimable riches and treasures of His grace, with great esteem and appreciation of it. For in this knowledge, as is testified by

(3) Isai. vii. 15.

our Saviour Himself, consists " eternal life." (4) And from it, as from seed, proceed the means to obtain it; and with its breath is enkindled, in " meditation," the fire (5) of charity, which enflames us with His love, from which springs fortitude of heart to imitate His life with so great perfection, that, according to St. Gregory Nyssen, (6) a Christian may be called " *alter Christus*," another Christ in humility, patience, and all the other virtues; as we say of a wise man, that he is another Solomon.

4. The *manner* of meditating upon these mysteries, to effect what we aim at, must be to carry our eyes fixed upon four things, (7) and to ponder them with attention.

i. The first is, to behold the *persons* that are introduced in the mystery, with the excellencies and interior affections that are in them.

ii. The second is, to consider the *words* they speak, and the *end* of which, and the *manner* with which they speak.

iii. The third is to behold their *works*, and the virtues resplendent in those works.

iv. The fourth is, to consider what *things they suffer* with all their circumstances, considering the ends of it, and motives to it. Out of all these four things, I am always to draw some profit to myself, animating myself to imitate what may be imitated, with those other affections and colloquies that we spoke of in the beginning of this book. (8)

All this is to be done in every point that the meditation shall have, following the order of the history, as will be seen in its progress. And since among the persons that are treated of in many of these mysteries,

(4) John xvii. 3.   (5) Psal. xxxviii. 4.
(6) Sermone de perfecta forma hominis Christiani.
(7) Ex Patre Ignatio in primo exercitio secundæ et tertiæ hebdomadæ.
(8) In the Introduction, chapt. 1 and 2.

especially in those of the second part, the principal is our blessed Lady the Virgin, we must principally attend to drawing out of these meditations the knowledge and love of her, and the imitation of her heroic virtues, ascending from the imitation of the mother, to the imitation of her Son, seeing she may say to us much better than St. Paul, " Be ye followers of me, as I also am of Christ."(9)

5. To dispose us the better to the desire and estimation of the end that has been spoken of, the meditation following, of vocation to imitate our Lord Jesus Christ, will help very much, as a foundation of these meditations, imagining Him in the likeness of a most excellent king, elected by Almighty God, that should raise up men to make war upon His enemies, inviting His vassals to follow Him, and promising them, that if they accompany Him in the fight, they shall enjoy with Him the spoils of the victory. (10)

THE FUNDAMENTAL MEDITATION.

ON THE INFINITE EXCELLENCE OF THE CELESTIAL KING, CHRIST JESUS OUR LORD, AND ON THE VOCATION THAT HE MAKES, INVITING ALL MEN TO FOLLOW HIM.

POINT I.

FIRST, I must consider that our Lord *Christ is a most excellent king*, elected by the eternal Father to rule and govern men, commanding all to obey Him as their proper king and lawful Lord ; according to that which He Himself said by the prophet David : " I am appointed king by Him over Sion His holy mountain, preaching His commandment."(1)

(9) 1 Cor. ii. 1.
(10) Exs. Patre Ignatio in principio secundæ hebdomadæ.
(1) Psal. ii. 6.

1. Upon this truth, I am to consider first, the infinite charity of the eternal Father in the *election of this sovereign king;* since being resolved to give men a king, He made choice of the best that He could give us : who, on the one side, should be true *man* as concerning our nature, that He might be before us with His example, and treat us with meekness and compassion : and on the other side should be true *God*, and His only begotten Son, that by His infinite power He might remedy and aid us. For as St. Leo the Pope says, (2) "if He had been man only, He could not have remedied us : and if He had been God only, He could not have given us example."

2. Hence I will ascend to consider the *excellencies* of this king, in whom concur all the qualities that can be in a most perfect king, (3) as is manifest by those that are attributed to Him by the prophets. But principally I will consider His infinite wisdom, by which He knows our necessities and miseries ;—His omnipotence to remedy them ;—His mercy in compassionating them ;—His bounty and charity in desiring to redress them ;—His providence in being careful for our good;—His meekness and affability in treating us as brethren ;—His liberality and magnificence in sharing among us His riches, and giving us all that he has, even to His very body and blood ;—His justice and prudence in government, directing us with great integrity and uprightness ; and, finally, His eternity with perpetual constancy in His celestial empire, which will never have an end.

3. And to make myself more entirely affectionate in this, I will make a *comparison* between *earthly kings* and this *heavenly* King : for *they* impose tributes and taxes upon their vassals, and exact them with rigour,(4) He quits

(2) Serm. 1. De Nativitate.
(3) Psal. xliv. 3, &c.   Jerem. xxiii. 5.   Zach. ix. 9.   (4) Is. x. 12.

all those, and lovingly pays their debts Himself: they impoverish their vassals to enrich themselves ;—*He* impoverishes Himself to enrich them with His poverty ; (5) *they* err oftentimes in their government through ignorance, passion, or malice :—He never errs because He is infinitely wise, just, and good ; they impose very heavy laws on their subjects, and yet excuse themselves from fulfilling them ;—He imposes laws very "sweet," (6) and by His own example animates men to fulfil them. Finally, those are temporal kings, that end with death ; and their empires, be they "of gold, or silver, of brass, or of iron, will perish, because they are founded upon feet of clay :"(7) but this King is eternal, and His kingdom shall never have end, because it is founded upon Almighty God.

4. From these three considerations, and from each one of them, I must extract several *affections of praise, joy, and thanksgiving*, with great resolutions and offers to do much in the service of this sovereign King : sometimes to this purpose I will speak to the eternal Father: at other times to this royal King, His Son ; and at other times to myself, exhorting myself to them in this manner.

Colloquy.—O my soul, praise, and glorify the celestial Father, for having given thee a King so potent, so wise, and so holy: rejoice at the good fortune that has befallen thee, to have so loving a King, of whom thou mayest obtain favour and interior friendship. If men make so much account to be the familiars of earthly kings, how much more oughtest thou to account thyself, for being the familiar, and favourite of the King of heaven! O sovereign King! I rejoice at the infinite greatness which Thou hast, for which I beseech Thee to take me under Thy

(5) 1 Cor. viii. 9.   (6) Matt. xi. 23-4, &c. 29.   (7) Dan. ii. 32.

protection : for seeing Thou art He that "ruleth me, I shall want nothing."(8)

POINT II.

Secondly, I must consider *the speech* that this sovereign King makes to all His vassals, persuading them to accomplish the commandment (9) of His Father, saying to them : " My most just will is to make war upon my enemies, 'the devil, (10) the world, and the flesh,' and upon all vices and sins ; and triumphing over them, to enter into the Kingdom of my Father : therefore whosoever will follow me in this enterprise let him live like me, and he shall reign like me : let him imitate me in the fight and without doubt, he shall have part in the victory." And this is founded upon that which the same our Lord said by St. John : "If any man minister to me, let him follow me, and where I am there also shall my minister be :" which is to say, "Whosoever offers himself to my service, must live as I live, and so shall he enjoy the eternal reward that I enjoy."(11)

Upon this vocation I will reason, pondering its *sweetness* and *efficacy*, and the great reasons that are used to move me to hear, and to follow this our Lord.

i. Because He that calls me, is a King of so great majesty, so great a benefactor, and free a Giver, that on a thousand accounts I am bound to His service.

ii. Because the enterprise is just, and much more to my profit than to His, seeing it is ordained to destroy my enemies, from whom I receive so great evils.

iii. Thirdly, because He *goes fighting before me*, and has descended from heaven to give me an example : and is it

(8) Psal. xxii. 1.   (9) Psal. ii. 6.
(10) 1 Joa. iii. 18. " In hoc apparuit filius Dei ut dissolvat opera.
diaboli." ·
(11) Joan. xii. 26.

much that a mean soldier should do that which his captain, and his King does, when as Gedeon, and Abimelech, in saying to their soldiers, "what you shall see us do, do you the same,"(12) were instantly obeyed?

iv. Fourthly, for the assurance that He gives us of victory, and the great reward that He will give us, if we conquer.

v. Fifthly, for the great glory, and honour that will ensue, as well to Him, as to His Father, and to all His vassals.

Colloquy.—O eternal King, I give Thee thanks for the sweetness with which Thou callest us, attracting us to Thy service with the cords of Adam weaved with so effectual reasons. (13) O that all men by Thy divine light might understand them, that all with ardent charity might follow Thee!

POINT III.

Thirdly, I will consider the *divers kinds of men* that are in the world, to whose notice this vocation comes.

1. The *first* is of those that make themselves *deaf* to this calling, who being deluded with the goods of this life, will not follow this King ; considering the ingratitude, and disloyalty of these wretches, compassionating their deafness, and grieving that the number of them should be great; for, as St. Bernard says,(14) all Christians desire to arrive where Christ is, and yet few will follow after Christ : all would have the reward of those that follow Him, but there are not many that will endure the labour of following Him : who in chastisement of their disobedience, like those that were called to the banquet, and excused themselves, (15) never attain to enjoy His sweet

(12) Judic. vii. 17. and ix. 49.
(13) Oseæ. xi. 14.   (14) Serm. 21. in Cant.
(15) Luc. xiv. 18.

society : to whom our Lord swore that they should never more " taste of His supper :" using likewise to them that speech of the divine Wisdom : " because I called you, and you refused : I stretched out my hand, and there was none that regarded ; you have despised all my counsel, and have neglected my reprehensions, I also will laugh in your destruction," (16) chastising your rebellion with death everlasting.

2. The second kind is, of those who are willing to follow this King and to accompany Him in this warfare, *but not heartily*, contenting themselves with keeping His commandments, desiring to remain with their riches, and dignities, and to enjoy the lawful pleasures of matrimony, because they have not a mind to arrive at greater perfection ; like that young man who from his infancy had kept the commandments of Almighty God, and when Christ said to him, that if he " would be perfect," he should go sell what he had and give to the poor, " and come follow Him,"(17) he went away sad, and would not do it, contenting himself with doing what he was wont to do. Although these do what is sufficient for their salvation ; yet, as their imitation comes short, so also their reward shall be short. For it is a kind of coming short for a soldier not to imitate his captain in all that he can, to his uttermost power, when his captain does for him more than he is obliged.

3. The third kind is of those who, with a generous mind, offer themselves to follow this King *in all* and *through all*, observing not only His precepts, but also His counsels, as He Himself observed them; living in poverty, chastity, and obedience; renouncing *riches*, and the lawful *pleasures* of matrimony, and even their own liberty to imitate their Lord perfectly. These are religious men,

(16) Prov. i. 24. 25.   (17) Matt. xix. 21.

who, as they imitate Christ with more perfection, so also they receive of Him a more copious reward; one in this life, which is the "hundredfold," and the other afterwards in "life everlasting." (18)   To this manner of life it were well if we should all of us offer ourselves, not so much for the temporal and eternal interest that ensue, as for the infinite obligation that we have to love and serve this great King; and because, as the wise man says, "it is a great glory to follow the Lord" (19) with perfection; and the nearer we follow Him, labouring to be perfect, as our heavenly Father is perfect, and as is this King and master whom, for our example, He has given us, the greater shall be our glory.   Hence it is, that those who, by a special vocation, have not been called to this kind of life, are to show the good will they have to serve this sovereign King, saying to Him, with the royal prophet David, "My heart is ready, O God, my heart is ready." (20)   Behold me here ready to fulfil Thy precepts, and likewise prepared to observe Thy counsels.   I offer myself for Thy love to follow Thee in poverty, and chastity, abandoning my liberty, and all whatsoever I have for Thy glory, if Thou wilt but vouchsafe to call me to such a kind of life.

4. To these three kinds of persons may be added a *fourth*, which is of those that are called by this celestial King, not only to imitate Him in poverty, chastity, and obedience; but also to be *His instruments to call others*, and by His favour to fight, not only against their own enemies; but also against the enemies of their neighbours, assisting them in their salvation, and inviting them, as Wisdom says, to the "tower, and to the walls of the city;" (21) that is, to the highest Christian perfection. Of this class are those religious whose end is, in imitation of

(18) Matt. xix. 29   (19) Eccl. xxiii. 38.
(20) Psalm cvii. 2.   (21) Prov. ix. 3.

the apostle, to attend, not only to their own salvation and perfection; but also to that of others. And such is the end of our Society of Jesus; for we that are religious in it profess to be the companions of Jesus in this enterprise, and those who are called in this manner ought to be exceedingly contented with their vocation, considering its excellence, and give many thanks to Him that called them, offering themselves with great courage to undertake any labour and journeys whatsoever, whether among Christians or infidels, even to the shedding of their blood, if need be, for the glory of Almighty God, and the salvation of their souls; using those words of the prophet Isaias: "Lo here am I; send me, O Lord, whither Thou wilt, for I am ready to do whatsoever Thou commandest me." (22)

THE CONCLUSION OF THE FOREGOING.

1. By what has been said in this meditation, I infer with what *spirit* we are to enter into the meditations ensuing; every one endeavouring to imitate Christ our Lord most perfectly, conformable to the state that he has chosen; if he be a religious man, following his proper institute with perfection; if he be in a state of continency, or the priesthood, fulfilling all his obligations with integrity; and if he be a married man, despoiling his heart of inordinate affections to the things that he possesses, according to the rule of the apostle, that says: "They also who have wives, *let them be as if they had none;*" "and that buy, as though they possessed not;" "and they who use this world as if they used it not," (23) doing all things in such a manner, that for them they neither lose Christ, nor grow cold in His love and holy service.

2. But those who have not yet chosen a state, and

(22) Isa. vi. 8.   (23) 1 Cor. vii. 29.

desire to make choice of that which is most convenient for their salvation and perfection, their end must be, to regard what our Lord Christ inspires them with to imitate Him in that degree of perfection to which they shall find they are moved. In this they will be aided by the sixth, seventh, and eighth meditations of the third Part.

MEDITATION I.

ON THE DECREE MADE BY THE MOST HOLY TRINITY, THAT THE SECOND DIVINE PERSON SHOULD BECOME MAN FOR THE REDEMPTION OF MANKIND, LOST BY THE SIN OF ADAM.

i. In the entrance of this meditation, and of those ensuing which treat of this mystery, it will not be amiss to imagine Almighty God our Lord Three and One, seated on a throne of infinite majesty, environed, as St. John saw him,(1) with the "rainbow of heaven," the symbol of His infinite mercy, with the three colours of His infinite goodness, wisdom, and omnipotence, with which He governs all things, and has both will, knowledge, and ability to remedy our miseries. Then will I imagine all mankind, and myself among them, through the sin of Adam, prostrate upon the earth, despoiled, wounded, and half dead, as was that poor man who in the way to Jericho,(2) "fell among robbers:" and the three Persons of the Deity beholding them, taking compassion on them, and entering into counsel what means They should take for their remedy.

ii. With this holy representation, prostrate in spirit before this throne, and adoring the most blessed Trinity, I will humbly beseech Him to illuminate me with His divine light, that I may know the *depth* of the counsel that He took for our remedy, in such a manner as may be

(1) Apoc. iv. 3.   (2) Luc. x. 30.

to my profit. And the lovely view of His celestial bow, shall encourage me to go, as St. Paul says, "with confidence to the throne of grace, hoping to obtain mercy, and find grace in seasonable aid."(3)

POINT I.

The first point, and the foundation of those that follow, will be to consider the decree that God our Lord made in His eternity, *for the redemption of mankind,* lost by the sin of Adam,(4) pondering the causes that influenced Him to it ; some in behalf of His infinite mercy, and others in behalf of our own misery, and the lamentable means by which we incurred it.

1. First, I will consider that our Lord having created two sorts of creatures to His own image and likeness, to serve, and to praise Him ; viz.—angels and men—"angels in the highest heaven," and men in the terrestrial paradise ; (5) and having seen that a great part of the angels sinned, and so likewise of men ; He determined to show the terrors of His rigorous justice by chastising the angels, bending against them the bow of His indignation, and throwing them immediately from heaven into hell ; (6) not giving them any time for repentance. But to men, though they deserved the same punishment, He was desirous to *shew the riches of His infinite mercy,* determining to cure them, and to draw them out of those miseries into which they had fallen, by giving them means to obtain pardon of their sin. (7) For in nothing is the mercy of Almighty God so resplendent, as in pardoning sins, and taking compassion on His very enemies : neither were it reasonable that mercy should omit to show itself in a thing that so greatly magnifies it. And thus did He with men, according

(3) Heb. iv. 16.

(4) S. Th. iii. p. 3. p. q. 1. Art. 1 and 2, and q. 4. Art. 1.

(5) Heb. ii. 16. (6) 2 Petr. ii. 4. (7) Sap. xi. 10. and vii. 1.

to that of St. Paul ;—"the goodness and kindness," towards man, "of God our Saviour appeared," in that He hath saved us, not by the works of justice which we had done, but according to His "infinite mercy." (8)   For which every one of us ought to give infinite thanks to this our Lord, considering that being creatures so vile, we deserved to be unprotected by His justice ; yet He took us under the protection of His mercy, rejecting the angels that were much more noble than we.

Colloquy.—O Eternal God, true Father of mercy, with what shall we repay Thee for so sovereign a benefit as this, as that without any merit of ours, Thou givest us a remedy, to obtain pardon of our sins? let the angels that remain in heaven praise Thee for this favour; let men that live upon the earth, acknowledge it, and make use of it: and let my soul melt away in Thy love, singing the multitude, and greatness of Thy mercy, by which I beseech Thee to pardon my sins, aiding me that I may never more return to them.   Amen.

This consideration I am to apply to myself, pondering that Almighty God our Lord, through His mercy, has made a decree to pardon sins, and effectually pardons those that submit themselves ; yet to the rebellious He uses His rigorous justice, condemning them as He did the devils.   And, therefore, I am to endeavour not to resist God's mercy, lest I fall into the hands of His justice.

2. Then will I consider the *causes* that, in some manner, moved the divine mercy to have compassion on our misery.   One was, that Adam, by his sin, not only damaged himself, but also all that descended from him,(9) who were to be born sinners, condemned to death and to perpetual prison, incurring these losses, *not by their own*

(8) **Ad Tit, iii. 3.**   (9) **Rom. v. 12.**

personal will, but by that which they had in their first parent. But Almighty God was so merciful, that His clemency could not permit that His whole work, for one man's transgression, should perish without a remedy ; and that all this visible world, that was created for man, should miss its end by serving the sinner ; He, therefore, resolved to find out a remedy. Whence I will gather two motives to repose my confidence in God's mercy, alleging them as David did, as reasons for which He should remedy my misery.

i. The one, because I was " conceived in iniquities ;"(10) from which originally spring all miseries.

ii. The other, because being the work of His hands, (11) I am neither to be contemned nor abhorred : seeing He hates " none of the things which He has made."(12)

Colloquy.—O most merciful Father, seeing Thou knowest the " dust"(13) of which we, Thy children, were formed, who issued good from Thee, and by Adam were made evil, have compassion on us, remedying the injury done by Adam, and restoring the good done by Thee. My hands have defaced in me the work of Thy hands : let Thine, by Thy abundant grace, repair what mine defaced through my great sin. Amen.

3. Another cause was, that man sinned *being tempted* and seduced by the Devil ;(14) partly for the envy that he had of his good, partly for his rage against Almighty God, desiring to revenge himself on the Creator in the creature, who by Him was so favoured, and in whom His divine image was stamped : upon which Almighty God Himself, moved to compassion, would take to Himself the cause of man, with a determination to save him, that His

(10) Psal. l. 7.   (11) Ps. xcix. 3.   (12) Sapient. xi. 25.
(13) Psal. cii. 14.   (14) Sapient. ii. 24.

enemy might not remain for ever victorious.   And, therefore, He said to him, when Adam had sinned, "I will put enmity between thee and the woman, and thy seed, and her seed : and they shall crush thy head," (15) vanquishing him that vanquished them, and triumphing over him that triumphed over them ;· by which He also gives me hope that He will have compassion on me, and take my cause for His own, seeing the devil ever persecutes me with the same envy and rage ; and so I may say to Him with David : " Arise, O Lord, judge Thy own cause," (16) aiding me with Thy grace to crush the head of the serpent, who always persecutes me, because he abhors Thee.

POINT II.

Secondly, I am to consider the admirable decree made by the most sacred Trinity, *that the second Person*, who is the Son of Almighty God, should *be made man* to redeem mankind, lost by the sin of Adam ; pondering the *causes* that moved Him to this, some in regard of *our* own great necessity and misery ; and others in regard of *His* infinite *bounty* and mercy.

1. First, I will consider how the most holy Trinity, seeing in His eternity many means that He had to save mankind, either by pardoning them by His sole and pure mercy,—or by creating another new man to satisfy for them ; or by imposing this charge on the Seraphim ;—would not make choice of a means that was more easy, nor less perfect ;—nor would He impose the charge of this work on another, but *chose the best means* that was possible, devising that the Son of Almighty God should become man for the reparation of man, in such a manner, that He could not give us a better healer, nor a more powerful remedy, nor

(15) Gen. iii, 15.   (16) Psalm lxxiii. 22.

2

a more "copious redemption," willing that "where sin abounded," there "grace should more abound." (17)

2. To ponder this truth the more, I will consider *what the first man did against Almighty God*, and what Almighty *God does for man;* comparing the thoughts and devices of the one with those of the other. Adam disposed himself with pride to rebel against Almighty God Himself, desiring to usurp His divinity and wisdom, and to have lordship over all things; by which he deserved that Almighty God should abhor and humble him, and should annihilate his perverted nature. But God, in His infinite goodness, was not only willing to pardon this injury, but to that end chose a means most honourable and profitable for man, and most humiliating and laborious for Almighty God; since the divine Word, being of infinite greatness and majesty, even "emptied Himself," as St. Paul says, taking the form of a "servant, being made in the likeness of men, and in habit found as a man;" (18) investing Himself with the mortal and passible nature of His very enemy, joining it to Himself in unity of person, to draw him out of that great misery into which he was fallen through sin, and to exalt him to that high honour and happiness which he might obtain by His grace. For, as St. Augustine says, "God made Himself man to make man God; that, by the virtue of God made man, men might be God by participation." (19)

3. Finally, considering this sovereign decree, I will with great astonishment *admire the infinite bounty* and mercy of Almighty God, which sometimes with Moses I will magnify, saying: "O the Lord, the Lord God, merciful and gracious, patient and of much compassion, and true, who keepest mercy unto thousands; who takest away iniquity, and wickedness, and sin, and no man of himself is

(17) Rom. v. 20.   (18) Phil. ii. 6.   (19) Ser. ix. de Nativit.

innocent before Thee." (20) At other times with the Seraphim, covering with my wings the face and feet of Almighty God, and adoring this union of His divinity and humanity, I will cry out saying: "Holy, holy, holy, the Lord God of hosts, all the earth is full of His glory," (21) through the greatness of His mercy.—And at other times I will give thanks to this our Lord for this so glorious benefit, saying to Him,

Colloquy.—O eternal God, I most humbly thank Thee for this sovereign device which Thou inventedst for my remedy, taking upon Thee my baseness to communicate to me Thy greatness. Grant that I may humble myself to serve Thee, as Thou didst humble Thyself to restore me; and that I may do all that I can for Thy service, seeing Thou didst all that Thou couldst for my remedy. O my soul, do for thy God all that thou canst; for all is but little, considering how much thou dost owe Him. Learn to esteem Almighty God as He esteems thee; and, seeing He has exalted thee to such a greatness, do not thou anything that may be unbeseeming it. (22) Amen.

POINT III.

Thirdly, I am to consider how, in this work of the Incarnation, our Lord God meant, moreover, to discover to us the infinite excellence of all *His perfections* and virtues, employing them with the greatest perfection that was possible, and to our greatest advantage. This may be seen by reasoning briefly on the principal.

i. First, He showed His infinite *bounty* in communicating Himself with the most intimate union possible, uniting His own person to a human nature; and in this manner He joined Himself in kindred with the whole lineage of man.

<hr>

(20) Exod. xxxiv. 6, 7.   (21) Is. vi. 3.
(22) Leo. Serm. 1. de Nativit.

ii. He showed His *charity* in uniting this nature to Himself with so strict an union, that one and the same might be man and God, to the end that all men might be one and the same thing with Almighty God, by the union of love, giving them freely and liberally the thing that He most loved and esteemed, and with it " all " other "things" (23) whatsoever.

iii. He showed His infinite *mercy*, joining it in a wonderful manner with justice; (24) for there could not be a greater mercy, than for Almighty God to come personally to remedy our miseries, and to make Himself capable of sorrow, that He might truly compassionate them.

iv. Neither could there be greater *justice*, than for Almighty God Himself, made man, to pay our debt, suffering, on that account, the punishment of death, which our sins have deserved. Neither could there be greater fraternal charity, than to apply to us men, by mercy, that reward which the God-man merited by justice; giving me an assurance of obtaining all things that are proper for me, seeing our Lord gained them all by justice, and applies to me His merits by His infinite mercy.

v. He also shewed His immense *wisdom* in inventing a means by which to join together things so distant, as are Almighty God and man ; (25) eternal, and temporal ; impassible and passible : and in contriving how to unloose the most difficult knot of our sins, the divine mercy pardoning them without prejudice to His justice.

vi. He showed His omnipotence, in doing for man all that He possibly could to honour, and to enrich him ; for among all the divine works there is none greater, than for Almighty God to make Himself man.

vii. Finally, He demonstrated His sanctity, and all His

<hr>

(23) Rom. viii. 32.   (24) Psal. lxxxiv. 11.
(25) Ex. S. Damasco lib. 3. de Fide orthodoxo a principio.

virtues, imprinting them in Almighty God made man, that He might be a visible *pattern* of them all, animating us by His example to imitate them, and aiding us by His grace to procure them, and no man can be excused for neglecting to do so. For if God love His neighbours, who is there that ought not to love them? If God does good to His enemies, who should do evil to his? If God humble Himself, who should be proud? If God suffer and endure, who should be impatient, and loath to suffer? And if God obey, why should not man be obedient?

2. These six divine perfections, resplendent in this work, should move me to praise Almighty God seven times a day—yes, if I may, even seven thousand times, desiring to love and serve Him, with the greatest perfection possible. For if before Almighty God made Himself man, He required that we should "love Him with our whole heart," and with our "whole soul," and with our "whole strength :" (26) with how much greater reason may He now require of me this degree of love, and fervour in His service? And seeing that works are the proof of love, (27) I am in *them* to demonstrate this my love, endeavouring to imitate those most excellent perfections, that He disclosed in this work : viz.—His bounty, charity, liberality, mercy, and the rest which are imitable, and especially those virtues that this God Incarnate exercised in the world for our example.

Colloquy.—O most blessed Trinity, what thanks shall I give Thee for having discovered in this work, those infinite excellencies which Thou holdest closed in Thy breast? What shall I give Thee, that will not be all too little for so sovereign a gift? How shall I love and serve Thee in return? Behold me here, wholly dedicated to Thy service, with a desire to love Thee,

(26) Deut. vi. 5.   (27) S. Greg. homil. xxxvi. in Evang.

as Thou lovest me : and to imitate those virtues, that
Thou discoverest to me. And seeing Thou hast given
me that which is more, give me also that which is
less, granting me that I may love Thee, for the infinite gift that Thou gavest me. Amen.

MEDITATION II.

ON GOD'S INFINITE CHARITY, RESPLENDENT IN THE MYSTERY OF THE INCARNATION, AND OF THE GREAT BENEFITS RECEIVED FROM IT.

Although all the divine perfections are, as has been
said, resplendent in the decree of the Incarnation ; yet
above them all shines the *charity* of God, on which this
meditation shall be ; leaving the others to the sixth part.
And it will be founded on what our Saviour Christ said
to Nicodemus : "God so loved the world, as to give His
only begotten Son, that whosoever believeth in Him may
not perish, but may have life everlasting." (1) In which
words our Saviour declared three principal things concerning this sovereign mystery ; viz.—i. its *principal
fountain;* ii. *its greatness;* iii. its *ends* and *effects.*

POINT I.

"*God so loved the world.*" First, I must consider the
infinite greatness of the *Person* that loved us, and did us
this sovereign benefit, and the infinite baseness of him
that is loved, and to whom this favour is done, *comparing
the one with the other.*

1. First, I will consider how this sovereign benefit
originated in the *infinite charity* and love of Almighty
God; who, as to His own profit and blessedness, had no
need to love any body but Himself ; since, with only beholding and loving Himself, He is infinitely blessed. Yet

(1) Joan. iii. 16;   1 Joan. iv. 9.

for all this, from mere grace He would love creatures, and do good to them ; only *because* He is good, and to demonstrate in them the riches of His bounty ; according to that of the apostle :—"God, who is rich in mercy, for His exceeding great charity wherewith He loved us :" (2) that is to say ; He loved us, not because He had need of us, nor because we of right merited it ; but only because His mercy compassionated our misery ; and His charity would needs break forth from Him to love others.

2. Secondly, I will consider how God, great as He is, in His infinite charity passes yet *farther*, in desiring so to love the world, such as it is. By " the world " I mean the multitude of men that sinned in Adam, contracting from him the foul spot of original sin, and afterwards, through their own will, fell into grievous actual sins, by which they made themselves unworthy of being loved, and deserved to be most abhorred. Insomuch that Almighty God not only loved men when they existed *not*, and were consequently neither friends nor enemies ; but He loved them also when they were *enemies* and *rebels*, and *unthankful* for other innumerable benefits that he has done them, to discover in this the infinite treasures of His mercy and charity.

3. Thirdly, I will make *comparison* between that which Almighty God does in *heaven*, and that which men do upon earth ; pondering how God loves the world which abhors Him.

The world employs itself in offending God ; and God desires to employ Himself in benefiting the world : in wonder, therefore, with myself at the abominable wickedness of the world, and at the infinite bounty and charity of God, I will say :—

Colloquy.—O God, of infinite majesty, why vouch-

(2) Ephes. ii. 4.

safest Thou to love a world of infinite baseness! Knowing what the world is, why dost Thou not abhor it? Why dost Thou not sink and annihilate it? Blessed be Thy immense charity, in whose bosom is contained the love of so ungrateful a creature. Demonstrate it, O Lord, towards me, in making me to love Thee, as Thou lovest me, and to serve Thee, as Thou dost merit. Amen.

These three things I am to apply to myself, putting myself in the place of the world ; I who ungratefully and forgetfully have abhorred and offended Almighty God ; and yet, for all this, God has not omitted to love me, desiring to do me good, that I might heartily love Him.

POINT II.

"*As to give His only-begotten Son.*" Secondly, I must consider the infinite greatness of the *gift* that Almighty God gave to the world, which was His only-begotten Son. In this I am to consider :—

1. That the love of Almighty God is not a love only of words and fair compliments, but a love *of deed* and of action, doing good to those whom He loves : and the more He loves, the greater benefits He bestows upon the beloved. Hence it is, that to demonstrate the infinite greatness of His love, He gave us the most precious thing that He could give us, which was His only-begotten Son, of equal dignity with His Father, and one and the same Almighty God with Him ; willing that He should become man like us, that within one man might dwell " the fulness of the Godhead corporally," (3) of which all might participate. And for this cause Christ our Saviour, desiring to enhance the greatness of the divine love, said : " God so loved the world, as to give His only-begotten Son :" (4) as if He should say : He could not love it more

(3) Coloss. ii. 9.   (4) Joan. iii. 16.

than to give His Son ; and that not *any* Son ; but His natural and only-begotten Son. And instead of this word "loved," He might have put some other like words, saying : God so esteemed the world ; He so honoured it, He so glorified and exalted it ; He so enriched and pro- tected it, "as to give His only-begotten Son :" and this freely and gratuitously ; for there was none that could merit so infinite a gift.

2. Then will I consider *upon whom* this so precious gift was bestowed ; it was upon a world perverse, ungrateful, and forgetful : upon a world so degraded, that when this great and only-begotten Son of Almighty God came to live in it, "Mundus eum non cognovit :" "The world knew him not ;" (5) neither did it esteem or reverence Him as it ought : neither knew it how to be thankful to Him for the great honour and benefit which it received from Him. And so comparing what Almighty God does for men, which is to give them His Son ; and what men do against Almighty God, which is to offend Him, and to be ungrateful for His gifts, I will greatly admire the infi- nite charity of Almighty God, desiring earnestly to love Him for this favour, endeavouring to demonstrate my love *actually*, that as Almighty God gave me the only Son He had ; so I may give Him the only soul, and the only heart that I have, employing my memory, understanding, and will, with all my senses and faculties to love and serve such a Father, that gave such a Son to such a world.

Colloquy.—O Eternal Father, I give Thee all the thanks I can, for the infinite love that Thou hast borne us, in giving us the most beloved, and precious thing that Thou hadst. I desire to love Thee, as Thou lovest me, giving Thee the most precious thing that is within me. Receive my heart in pledge of

<hr>

(5) Joan. i. 10.

this love, that from this day forward, I may not only love "Thee in word nor in tongue" only, "but in deed, and in truth,"(6) seeking always Thy glory without mixture of anything that is profane.   Amen.

POINT III.

" *That whosoever believeth in Him may not perish, but may have life everlasting.*"   Thirdly, I must consider *the end for which* Almighty God gave to the world this His only-begotten Son, and what infinite benefits redound to men from this gift.

1. In this I must consider how the Son of Almighty God came into the world, (as He gives testimony of Himself, "Ut salvificem mundum,") to save the world with most perfect salvation, which consists in two things :—

i. First, in *taking from it* all things that *cause* it to *perish* and be condemned, pardoning it its sins, delivering it from the slavery of the devil, and from the eternal prison of hell, and from all other miseries that are annexed to sin, and are the cause of men's returning to it.

ii. Secondly, in giving to it the *life* of *grace*, with all the supernatural virtues that accompany it, and, finally, life everlasting.   And in these two things are included innumerable others, which we shall hereafter have occasion to speak of.

iii. And, finally, to crown the goodness of this benefit, Almighty God wills that it should *extend itself to all the men* of the world, of what state and condition soever, without excluding, for His part, any that will believe in Him with a lively faith, who shall not perish, but shall all of them obtain life everlasting.   Now this being so, to me also this benefit is extended; and I may apply all these words to myself, saying, with all truth, God so loved me,

(6) 1 Joan. iii. 18.

that He gave me His only-begotten Son, that believing in Him with a lively faith, I may not perish, but obtain life everlasting.

Colloquy.—O only-begotten Son of the Father, what thanks shall I give Thee, for having come into the world to free us from so many evils, and to heap upon us so many benefits! Thou dost pardon our sins, despoilest hell, openest the gates of Paradise, vanquishest the devil, triumphest over the world, tamest our flesh, cuttest off our perils, comfortest our heaviness, quickenest our works, augmentest our merits, givest us perseverance in Thy grace, and finally crownest us with Thy glory. Without Thee we had nothing of this, and now by Thee we possess it all: for by Thee descend from heaven all the blessings and mercies that replenish the earth. Blessed be the Father that gave Thee unto us for our remedy; and blessed be Thou His Son, that came to save us. Save me effectually, O Lord, that I may not perish, but obtain through Thee life everlasting. Amen.

2. By what has been said in this and the foregoing meditation, it appears that the causes and motives of the Incarnation may be reduced to three heads connected one with another. One, in regard of the *divine perfections*, to manifest them. Another, in regard of our *miseries*, to remedy them. And the third, in regard of the *supernatural riches of grace* and glory, to communicate them. Of these three things we are to weave a strong "threefold cord," (7) with which strongly to bind us to this divine Word Incarnate, which will join us to Him with perfect love; seeing we have so many motives for loving Him, as are the divine perfections that He has discovered to us,

(7) Eccles. iv. 12.

and the miseries from which He has freed us, and the graces and virtues that He has merited for us.

MEDITATION III.

ON ALMIGHTY GOD'S DECREE TO BE BORN OF A WOMAN, AND ON THE ELECTION OF OUR BLESSED LADY FOR HIS MOTHER, AND ON THE SINGULAR GRACES THAT HE GRANTED HER ON THAT ACCOUNT IN THE INSTANT OF HER CONCEPTION.

POINT I.

First, I must consider how Almighty God, having determined to make Himself man, although He might have taken the body of a perfect man, (1) as was that of Adam, yet He would not ; but would be born "of a woman," (2) as St. Paul says, *and have a mother*, as other men had. And this He revealed in the beginning of the world, saying to " the serpent," that " the seed " of the woman should crush his " head." (3) To this determination there were many causes that moved Him, in which He discovered, to our advantage, His infinite charity.

1. The first, that the divine bounty, which so much loves to communicate itself to its creatures, might be dilated more, and to greater grandeur, *in both the sexes of human nature*, exalted a *man* to the infinite dignity of the natural Son of God; and exalting a *woman* to the dignity of the Mother of God, which, as St. Thomas says, is in some sense likewise infinite ; (4) by which he gives us assurance that His intention is to do good to all. For, according to that of the apostle, " there is neither bond nor free; there is neither male nor female;" (5) little nor great.

(1) S. Th. 3. p. q. xxxi. art. 4.   (2) Gal. iv. 4.
(3) Gen. iii. 15.   (4) 1. p. q. xxv. ar. 6. ad 4.   (5) Gal. iii. 28.

2. The second was :—That as our perdition began by a man, and a woman ; so our *redemption should begin* by another *man,* and another *woman;* principally by Christ as being the Head, and our only mediator, and "Father of the world to come :" (6) and secondly, by His mother, as by His assistant in the work of our redemption : to both of whom men should repair for the remedy of their necessities, with that confidence, that they use to have recourse to their own father, and mother. But our Lord Christ would have a mother especially for this, that she might likewise be the mother, and advocate of sinners ; who, if through pusillanimity they should be afraid to have recourse to *Him,* because He is not only man and our advocate, but also Almighty God and a most just judge, they might confidently approach to His blessed mother, to whom it belongs not to be a judge, but an advocate, that she as a mother full of mercy, and pity, might be an intercessor for all.(7)   We may see by this, the great longing that Almighty God has for our salvation, and that we should be confident of obtaining it, seeing He has invented, therefore, means so great, so sweet, and so effectual.

Colloquy.—I give Thee thanks, O Eternal Father, for having given us a Father and Mother of our own nature, by whose mediation we may securely purchase Thy grace. I give Thee thanks, O Divine Word, that it was Thy holy will to have a mother, who should likewise be ours, by whom we should find entrance to the throne of Thy infinite mercy, that we may not be condemned by the rigour of Thy justice. Amen.

3. The last cause was, that it was the pleasure of Almighty God to make Himself a child for us, and to

(6) Isai. ix. 6.   (7) S. Ansel. lib. de excell. Virg. cap. 6.

have a mother on earth *whom he might obey*, and *to whom* he might subject Himself, like other men : to give us an example of humility, and of other virtues, as may be seen in the ninth and following meditations.

POINT II.

Secondly, I must consider the *election of our blessed Lady the Virgin*, to be the Mother of Almighty God ; pondering how the most holy Trinity, among the innumerable women that He saw in His eternity, cast graciously His eyes upon the Blessed Virgin, and made choice of her for those excellencies of which we have spoken in the foregoing point ; that is to say ; to be the Mother of the divine Word Incarnate, and His co-operator in the redemption of the world ;—the Mother and advocate of men ;—and she to whom Almighty God Himself, as He was man, subjected Himself, and obeyed. This election, as say the holy fathers, was the root of the other excellencies of our Lady, of which she always made great estimation, and for which she was ever very thankful, considering that it proceeded from mere grace, without any merit of hers : (8) for when Almighty God made choice of her to be His mother, He might have chosen many other women as well as her, and made them like her. But yet I should rejoice that this good lot fell upon her, and congratulate with her for it, saying to her :—

Colloquy.—O most blessed Virgin, I exceedingly rejoice that thou wast elected for so sovereign a dignity, as to be the Mother of Him whose daughter thou art. And seeing with this dignity, it was granted thee likewise to be the mother and advocate of sinners: show thyself to be our mother in favouring us, and advocating for us, that we may be the

(8) Francis. Suarez, Tom. ii. in 3. p. disp. 1.

worthy children of Him, of whom thou art the mother.   Amen.

POINT III.

1. Hence I will go on to consider, that God our Lord, in His eternity, having made choice of our blessed Lady to be His mother, moreover elected her to be the most excellent vessel of His mercy, with whom He would leave in trust *all excellencies of grace and glory* that were suitable for the mother of such a Son ; and consequently the greatest that could be granted to any one, being but a mere creature ; (9) for which it is said of her, that she is, "Electa ut Sol," "bright as the sun :" (10) for as the sun is alone and singular in his excellencies among all the stars, so the Blessed Virgin was elected to be alone and singular in the gifts of grace among all pure creatures, so that none should even be equal to her.

2. This I may ponder in general, by that saying of St. Paul, that God elected us "ut essemus sancti, et immaculati in conspectu ejus in charitate," "That we should be *holy* and *unspotted* in His sight in charity," (11) in all which the election of our blessed Lady the Virgin was supereminent.

i. For, first, she was chosen to be holy with *all the degrees of sanctity*, and in all kinds of graces and virtues, *that were to be bestowed upon all the other creatures*, and with much greater excellency upon her, than upon any of them.   For, as St. Jerome says, " those graces that were distributed among other saints, were given all together with great fulness to Mary, because of her was to be born the author of all graces, Christ Jesus." (12)   Who as He is the Holy of holies, would sanctify her that was to be

<hr>

(9) S. Th. 3. p. q. vii. ar. 10. Ex. Aug. lib. de Nat. &c. Grat. c. 38.
(10) Cant. vi. 9.   (11) Ephes. i. 4.
(12) Serm. de Assumpt. Tom. 4. Matth. i. 21.

His tabernacle, (13) that among all pure creatures she should be, as it were, the Holy of holies, superior to all in sanctity.

ii. Secondly, she was chosen to be *pure* and *without spot*, with all those degrees of purity that might be found *in a pure creature*, without having any stain of sin, or any trace thereof. For, as St. Anselm says, "it was suitable that the Virgin should be resplendent with such purity, that, next to God, none should be greater, because she was to be the mother of Him that is purity itself," (14) who, as in being God, He has a Father by His divine essence, pure and clean from all sin :—so in being man He would have a mother pure and clean with like purity through special grace, that His earthly mother might in this resemble His heavenly Father.

iii. Thirdly, she was chosen to be holy and immaculate, not in an ordinary degree, but *in the sight of Almighty God* :—that is, in such a manner that she should walk with sanctity and purity, true, and not feigned, not exterior only, but also interior, in the presence of Almighty God ; as well in the presence of His Godhead, contemplating and pleasing Him as a faithful daughter in all her works, as also in the presence of God *made man*, nourishing Him and ministering to Him as a mother ; loving Him in both regards with most enkindled charity, and gathering together by such services innumerable and most notable merits, for which He might afterwards communicate to her His amiable presence and resplendent countenance with greater excellence of glory than to all the rest of the elect. All which proceeded from the infinite charity with which the most sacred Trinity loved her above all, and predestined her to so great a glory ;—The Father, because she was to be the mother' of His own Son,—The Son,

(13) Psal. xlv. 5.   (14) Lib, de Conceptu. Virg. c. 18.

because she was to be His own mother,—And the Holy Ghost, because He was to work in her the conception of this Son, true God and true man.

3. And this is the end of the election and predestination of the Blessed Virgin ; for which I should praise the most Holy Trinity, and rejoice at the glory that hence redounds to her whom I hold for my mother. And seeing God our Lord has also called me, through His infinite charity, to be holy and immaculate in His presence, I am in all this to take for my *pattern* the sacred Virgin, imitating her in the three things that have been declared;—and for my advocate, that she may obtain them for me of her Son ; I, for my part endeavouring, as St. Peter says, with good works, to " make sure " my " calling and election."(15)

Colloquy.—O sacred, and sovereign Virgin, I rejoice that thou art "bright as the sun," in whom there can be no obscurity of sin, but great splendour of grace, and finally the shining light of glory, as far exceeding all the saints, as the sun excels the stars. Do to me the office of the sun, enlightening my darkness, that I may be pure and resplendent " as the brightness of the firmament, shining for all eternity."(16) O ever-living God, by whose charity, without our merits, we were elected to be " unspotted, holy, and immaculate" in Thy presence ; I most humbly thank Thee for having elected this sacred Virgin with so sovereign an election ; for whose sake I beseech Thee to purify my soul from its sins, and to adorn it with Thy virtues, that I may live for ever in Thy presence, and obtain life everlasting. Amen.

POINT III.

Fourthly, I must consider how, the time being come in which Almighty God would make Himself man ; to lay the

(15) 2 Pet. i. 10.   (16) Dan. xii. 3.

first stone of this building, He created the Blessed Virgin, who was to be His mother ; and in the very instant of her conception, He communicated to her most excellent graces, and *singular privileges*, as was meet for such a Son to give to His mother, having chosen her through His own will, and through His great charity, and being most rich and potent to enrich her with the treasures of His grace.

These privileges we reduce to four, and pondering briefly some reasons of them, and in what manner we may participate in them.

1. The first privilege He granted her was *her preservation from original sin*, into which, by being the daughter of Adam, she was else to fall, sanctifying her soul in the first instant of her creation, when He joined it to the body. So that, as God our Lord at one instant gave to the sun being and light, and to the angels and to our first parents, Adam and Eve, He gave conjointly, nature and grace ;—so in one and the same instant, He created and sanctified the soul of the Blessed Virgin, making it bright as the sun, that it might not be touched by the darkness of sin. The reason of this, besides what has been said in the preceding point, was because our Saviour Christ came into the world to redeem men, and to free them from all sin, especially from original. This He might have done in two ways— either by *drawing them out of sin*, after they had fallen into it,—or by *preserving them from* falling into it. And this second manner is much more excellent, for in it is most resplendent the omnipotence and mercy of the Redeemer, because, as before has been said, as there is no greater misery than the foul stain of sin, so there is no greater mercy than so to preserve us from sin, that it may not touch us, so much as for an instant (17.) Hence it is that, for the glory of the Redeemer and of His Redemp -

(17) 1 Part in 6th Meditation.

tion, it was very suitable to use this mercy towards her who was to be His mother ; of redeeming her with the best manner of redemption that was possible ; therefore did He preserve her from the infamy and misery of original sin, honouring and beautifying her with His grace, that the mother might be like to the Son in purity, they being both conceived without sin ; He by *right*, and she by *privilege*; He as the Redeemer of the world, and she as His coadjutrix in the work of the Redemption.

Colloquy.—O Son of the living God, who being born of the Virgin, became man, to make " a glorious Church, not having spot or wrinkle, or any such thing,"(18) I render to Thee all the thanks that I can, that it was Thy good pleasure, that Thy blessed mother, by special grace should enjoy even from her conception, that purity from sin, which the elect obtain in glory. O most glorious mother, I rejoice at the purity with which thou enteredst into the world, shining with the light of grace, as thy Son,—the Son of justice entered. Well mayest thou say in this first entrance, as He said in His :—that thou art ready to "do" the "will" of Almighty God, and that His "law is" imprinted "in the midst" of "thy heart,"(19) which is His grace and His charity. And seeing my Redeemer granted thee this favour, that thou mightest assist Him in His office, beseech Him to apply to me His redemption with fulness, pardoning me my sins committed, and preserving me from those I am likely to commit, with so great a horror of sin, that I may not continue in them so much as a moment. Amen.

And this is the principal fruit that I am to gather from this consideration, that beholding this "unspotted

(18) Ephes. v. 27.   (19) Ps. xxxix. 9.

mirror," (20) the most sacred Virgin, I may imitate her purity with the greatest perfection that I can, remembering what Almighty God said to His people, " Thou shalt be perfect and without spot, before the Lord thy God." (21.)

2. The second privilege was her *freedom* from *"fomes peccati," the root, seed, and food of sin*, which is the rebellion of the flesh against the spirit, and of sensuality against reason ; (22) that the house of her soul with all its inhabitants, which are the faculties, might have perpetual peace and concord, for it was to be the habitation of the Prince of Peace, whose dwelling " place," says David, " is in peace" (23) itself. So that this blessed Lady never felt that interior war, which we all feel, and mourn for ; for her " flesh lusted" not " against the spirit," and the spirit found no difficulty in governing "the flesh ;" (24) the law of the appetites contradicted not the law of reason ; neither did reason labour to subdue the passions of the appetites, (25) they were rather with great pleasure united, and accorded in subjecting themselves to the eternal law of their Lord and their God.

Colloquy.—O Princess of peace, much joy to thee for the interior peace that thou possessedst, without having passed through any conflict or war ; obtain for me, most blessed Lady, that the interior war which I suffer, may be moderated, so that I may somewhat enjoy the sweetness of thy peace. Amen.

3. The third privilege was *her confirmation in grace,* so that in all the time of her life she should never sin actually, either in deed, or in word, or so much as in thought. Our Lord assisted her in all her works with particular providence, that they might all be, as St. Paul

<hr>

(20) Sap. vii. 26.   (21) Deut. xviii. 13.
(22) Ex. S. Th. 3. p. q. xxvii. art. 3. et sequent.   (23.) Ps. lxxv. 3.
    (24) Gal. v. 17.   (25) Rom. vii. 23.

says of the Church, works glorious and pure in the three degrees of purity; that is, "not having spot" of mortal sin, "or wrinkle" of venial sin, "or any such thing:" (26) she shunning not only that which is evil, but also that which is imperfect and less good, choosing always what she held for best, and imprinting in every work the glorious purity which is in the Church triumphant. This sort of purity, in the degree that is possible for me, I should endeavour to gain and ask it of our Lord, saying to Him,

Colloquy.—O Eternal God, that didst *sanctify* the "tabernacle" of Thy mother, assisting immutably "in the midst" (27) of her, and daily with great solicitude didst aid her in all her works, sanctify also my soul; assist it perpetually; and arise early, preventing me with Thy grace, that my works may be pure, "not having spot or wrinkle," or "anything" else that may be displeasing to Thee. Amen.

4. The fourth privilege was her being replenished in that instant with *grace*, and *charity*, and with the other virtues and gifts of the Holy Ghost, *with such plenty* and abundance, that she exceeded the angels and Seraphim of heaven, to the end she might be the worthy Mother of Almighty God, and Queen of the angelical hierarchy, God making her "so much better " and holier "than they," as the "name" (28) was better which He intended to give her of His mother, than that which they had of servants and ministers in His house. So that this sacred Virgin began her course where the angels ended theirs; and, being on earth, had greater degrees of sanctity than those who lived in heaven, excepting what is proper to that state, fulfilling in her that which the prophet David says of "the city of God," that her "foundations are in the holy mountains;" (29) for the beginnings of her life were higher

(26) Ephes. v. 27.   (27) Ps. xlv. 5.
(28) Heb. i. 4.   (29) Ps. lxxxvi. 1.

raised in sanctity than the highest height that ever the greatest saints of the Church arrived at. Oh, what content did the most blessed Trinity receive in beholding the excellence of this child!—The eternal Father rejoiced in having such a daughter.—The Son of God was exceedingly pleased to see *her* so beautiful that was to be His mother; —and the Holy Ghost was full of joy to have such a spouse; whilst all Three entered in her by grace, and dwelled in her with great delight.

Colloquy.—O angels of heaven, that adored afterwards the Son of God, when He entered into the world; come now at this instant to reverence her that is to be His mother, and your Queen! O Queen of angels, I now salute thee in the womb of thy mother, with those words which will after be spoken to thee by the angel Gabriel:—"Hail, full of grace, the Lord is with thee: blessed art thou among women:"(30) for in the first instant of thy conception, thou foundest grace before Almighty God above them all. Beseech Him, blessed Lady, to purify my spirit, to bridle my flesh, to moderate my passions, and to replenish me with His grace, that I may begin to serve Him with great fervour and perseverance, until I obtain the crown of glory. Amen.

MEDITATION IV.

ON THE LIFE OF OUR BLESSED LADY UNTIL THE INCARNATION ; IN WHICH ARE CONSIDERED HER NATIVITY, HER PRESENTATION IN THE TEMPLE, AND HER ESPOUSAL TO ST. JOSEPH.

POINT I.

1. First, I must consider how, the nine months after the conception of the Virgin being accomplished, *she was born* in the house of her parents, to the joy of the whole world,

(30) Luc. i. 29.

according to the saying of holy Church; pondering the joy of the most Holy Trinity in seeing the birth of this His beloved child, by whom He intended to work such glorious things for His own glory and our benefit. And, therefore, it is to be believed that, upon that day, He communicated to the angels of heaven, and to the righteous on earth, and to the holy fathers in Limbo a sort of accidental joy, though all knew not its cause, as a prognostication of the joy that they should receive by the coming of Almighty God into the world, whose mother that child was to be; as the birth of the morning causes a kind of joy and solace in all living creatures, because it is a token of the rising of the sun. For if many rejoiced at the nativity of St. John, (1) because he was the day-star and forerunner of Jesus Christ, many more, doubtless, rejoiced at the birth of the Blessed Virgin, who was to be His mother. And with this consideration, I will move myself to affections of praise and joy, congratulating the most Holy Trinity for the birth of this babe,—the eternal Father, because there is born to Him such a daughter,—the Son of God, because she is born that is to be His mother,— the Holy Ghost, because there is born to Him such a spouse.

Colloquy.—O most blessed Trinity, I congratulate with Thee for the birth of this Thy beloved, impart to me some of that joy which Thou impartest to others; because she was born for me as well as for others.

2. Hence I must likewise collect another motive for great spiritual joy ; pondering that as the *nativity* of the *virgin* caused exultation in the world, because it was a sign of the coming of the Saviour to redeem it ; so also when the devotion of the Virgin is born in the soul, it

<hr>

(1) Luc. i. 14.

causes therein wonderful joy ; being a great pledge that Almighty God will come to visit it and save it.   Here-upon St. Anselm said, that to be much devoted to our blessed Lady, is a sign of being predestinated in heaven.(2) For with devotion to her the effects of predestination enter, she negotiating them for such as are devoted to her. She, as a mother, solicits for us the inspirations of heaven, the vocation of Almighty God, the grace of justification, the victory over temptations, the preservation from falls, the augmentation of merits, the perseverance in grace, and the crown of glory, as in the discourse of the ensuing meditations be seen.

Colloquy.—O sacred and sovereign Virgin, who, by the command of Almighty God, didst "take root" in the "elect" for heaven,(3) fix in my soul such deep roots of thy devotion and imitation, that they may be assured pledges of my eternal predestination.   Amen.

POINT II.

Secondly, I must consider how the parents of this our blessed Lady *gave to her the name of Mary*, by revelation from God as is credibly supposed, who also revealed the name of the Baptist, (4) and consequently with the name, Almighty God intended to declare the greatness of this child, which was very high, and therefore He chose a name, that in different languages should have many signi-fications, because she was born for the good of all.   For Mary interpreted, signifies, " Star of the sea," or " bitter sea :"—" Lady," or " the exalted :"—" illuminated," or " illuminatrix," or " mistress of people."(5)

1.   All this is found in the most sacred Virgin Mary.

i. She is the " *star of the sea*," because she is the light,

(2) Lib. de excellent. Virg. c. 4.
(3) Ecclus. xxiv. 16.   (4) Luc. i. 13.
(5) Ex. S. Bonaven. in specul. B. Virg. Cap. 3. Num. xxiv. 17.

consolation, and guide, of those who sail in the sea of this world, tossed with the great waves and tempests of temptations, and in danger of damnation; and who by the prayers and example of the Blessed Virgin, and by the favours she confers on them, are cheered and fortified, and finding the right way, arrive at the port of salvation.

ii. She is a "*bitter sea*," for divers reasons :—a "sea," for the immensity of celestial graces contained within her, communicated by the liberality of Him that elected her for His mother :—"*bitter*," for the immensity of bitterness she suffered in the passion of her Son : (6) for Almighty God generally makes equal the measures of consolation and affliction, and so He did with this sacred Virgin.

iii. She is a "*Lady*," and "*exalted*" because she was supereminently a Lady, and governess over her faculties and appetites, and over her imagination and senses, commanding all with supreme authority, as already has been said. She is likewise Lady of the angels, exalted above them all ; and is after a manner likewise the Lady of God Himself, she commanding Him when He was man, and He obeying her as a son subject to his mother. (7)

iv. She is the "*illuminated*" or "illuminatrix," because she received from Almighty God great light of celestial wisdom ; not for herself alone, but to illuminate others ; and therefore she was the mistress of the apostles and of all the faithful, as hereafter we shall see.

2. With these brief considerations I will awaken in my soul affections of joy and confidence, and great devotion to the sacred name of Mary, beseeching the Virgin to perform, in my regard, those offices that her name signifies.

Colloquy.—O most sacred Virgin, with much reason I may say, that thy blessed name, like that of thy

<hr>

(6) S. Bern.Hcm. se. ii. in "missus est."   (7) Luc. ii. 51.

Son, is "oil poured out,"(8) for that it illuminates, comforts, heats and rejoices my heart. Pour upon me this so precious oil with a liberal hand;—and seeing thou art the "star of the sea," guide and protect me in my temptations and perils:—seeing thou art a sea of "graces and bitterness," impart them also to me; for it is no less a grace to receive gifts from Christ, than to bewail with bitterness His pains:—be thou my "mistress," illuminating my ignorance, aiding me to be master of my passions, and guide me in the path of perfection, that by the invocation of thy holy name, I may arrive at the top and excellency of it. Amen.

Here also may be considered, how this blessed babe, beginning to have the use of reason, either in the womb of her mother by special privilege, like St. John Baptist; or about three years before she was presented in the Temple, (9) presently began, with great fervour, to exercise those gifts and graces which she had received by those means which will be declared in the fourth point.

POINT III.

Thirdly, I am to consider, how the Blessed Virgin being but of tender age,—it is thought three years old,—by God's inspiration, was by her parents presented in the Temple, that she might there be dedicated and devoted to His divine service, with other virgins that had made the like profession.

In this presentation, we are to fix our eyes on three persons there present.

i. The first was the majesty of Almighty God, who chose this blessed child, and inspired in her this her retiring into the Temple, demonstrating His fatherly providence towards her, in drawing her from the noise and

(8) Cant. i. 2.   (9) Vide Suarez, tom. 2. disp. 3. Sect. 7.

bustle of the world, and attracting her to His house and Temple, because she was to be the house in which He would be Incarnate, and the living Temple in which He Himself would live. And therefore with great love He spoke to her heart those words of the Psalm : "Hearken, O daughter, and see, and incline thy ear ; and forget thy people and thy father's house ; and the king shall greatly covet thy beauty." (10) The Blessed Virgin hearkened to this voice, and inspiration of Almighty God : she saw the favour that was done her in this :—she inclined her ear speedily to obey what was commanded :—she wholly forgot her people, and renounced the house of her terrestrial "father," to accommodate herself to the good liking of her celestial Father, who called her His "daughter." And so much did her beauty increase with this new obedience and humility, that the King of heaven and earth cast His affection upon her, and rejoiced for having elected her to be His mother. Hence I will gather how great a favour Almighty God does to him, whom He effectually inspires and withdraws from the occasions and perils of the world, making him abandon his country and his father's house for His service ; and how great reason we all have to be obedient to such an inspiration when we perceive it ; seeing it is a true sign that Almighty God loves us as His well-beloved children, drawing us like holy Abraham, from the fire of the Chaldeans ; (11) or like just Lot, from the burning of Sodom. (12)

ii. Secondly, may be pondered *the devotion of St. Joachim and St. Anne, the parents* of the Blessed Virgin, who, as holy people, not only did not thwart the good desires of their daughter, but took her by the hand, and moved by the inspiration of Almighty God Himself, offered to Him the only fruit of their womb, returning to Him what He

(10) Psal. xliv. 11.   (11) Gen. xi. 31.   (12) Gen. xix. 12.

had given them ; in which they esteemed themselves happy, that God might be served by their daughter, depriving themselves of her, to give her to Him. And this they did with no less spirit than Anne the mother of Samuel offered her son to Almighty God, (13) because they knew how acceptable this offering would be to Him. Whence I may also learn to offer to God with spirit and fervour, the only and best beloved daughter of my soul, which is *Liberty;* and her principal affection, which is *Love,* to determine to will nothing but what He wills ; and only to love what He loves, offering myself to give Him whatsoever He shall ask me.

iii. Thirdly, I will consider the *devotion of the blessed Virgin herself* in this presentation ; for her parents had no sooner told her that they would carry her to the Temple, but she was replenished with joy, saying that of the prophet David, " I rejoiced at the things that were said to me, we shall go into the house of the Lord." (14.) But on arriving at the Temple, she began to mount the fifteen degrees or "steps" (15) with great fervour of spirit, resolving to ascend by all the degrees of virtue to the summit of perfection, fulfilling that of the prophet David, "Blessed is the man whose help is from Thee ; in his heart he hath disposed to ascend by steps, in the vale of tears, in the place which he hath set "—to this end " they shall go from virtue to virtue, the God of gods shall be seen in Sion." (16.)

Colloquy.—O courageous and blessed babe, whom Almighty God favoured with His aid, "helping" thee "in the morning early,"(17) and to assist whom He was so greatly solicitous, what zealous resolutions makest thou in thy heart! and how well dost thou

(13) i. Reg. i. 24.   (14) Ps. cxxi. 1.   (15) Ezech. xl. 6.
(16) Ps. lxxxiii. 6.   (17) Ps. xlv. 6.

dispose the augmentation of virtue in this place which thou hast chosen for thy habitation? Ascend now happily by these degrees "from virtue to virtue;" for thou hast an entrance by the contemplation of Almighty God, to look into this holy city of Sion.

2. The blessed Virgin no sooner had ascended up into the Temple, than prostrate upon the earth she adored the Divine Majesty, and *presented* and offered herself to His perpetual service ; for her intention was not to offer herself for a year, or for ten, like other maidens, but for ever, with a resolution, as much as lay in her, to serve Him all her life in His holy Temple. O how much was Almighty God pleased with this offering ! With what pleasure would He accept it, and what thanks and gifts would He return to her ! The Virgin might say, " Behold me here, O Lord, I am come into Thy house to be Thy slave for ever ; receive me into Thy service, for I desire no other lot more glorious than to serve Thee." To this our Lord would answer within her heart :—" Let my beloved come into" my " garden, (18) O my sister, my spouse ;" for in Thee I will place my throne ; thou shalt be the sun in which I will consent to fix my habitation, and issue out of it " as a bridegroom coming out from his bride-chamber." (19) Adorn it with the flowers of virtues, for the time will speedily come of celebrating therein my espousals.

3. In imitation of this blessed Lady, I am to present myself before Almighty God, and to offer myself to His service, as His perpetual slave, with a determination never to separate myself from Him.

(18) Cant. v. 1.   (19) Ps. xviii. 6.

POINT IV.

Fourthly, I will consider *the most excellent life that this child led* in the temple.

1. For first, as she grew in age, she *grew in spirit before God*, and *before men.* And, as St. Ambrose, says "she accompanied every step of her body with exercise, and augmentation of virtue, (20) as a shining light goeth forwards, and increaseth even to perfect day." (21). For the Holy Spirit solicited her with His inspiration, and she co-operated with all her power, endeavouring, as says the wise man, "in all" her "works" to "keep the pre-eminence" (22) with the four excellencies :—

i. That in every one she increased in charity and sanctity.

ii. That they were all works replenished with the greatest proof, and fulness of perfection, possible for her strength.

iii. That in every work she used great wisdom and discretion, with singular constancy, until she had effected it.

iv. That she ·mixed with every one great variety of affections and virtues, so as to increase, to augment in all together.

For these four excellencies, the *angels* were in admiration of her, saying—"Who is she that cometh forth as the morning rising, fair as the moon, bright as the sun, terrible as an army set in array?" (23) What is this child that makes her progress "from virtue to virtue ;" increasing like the light of the morning, without staying or turning back ?—Beautiful like the full "moon" with fulness of graces, without any waning?—"Bright as the

<table>
<tr><td>(20) Lib. ii. de Virgin.</td><td>(21) Prov. iv. 18.</td></tr>
<tr><td>(22) Ecclus. xxxiii. 23.</td><td>(23) Cant. vi. 9.</td></tr>
</table>

sun," that there is none in earth her equal? And who is this, that being a weak maid by nature, is most firm by grace, containing within her an army of all virtues, ordered with the order of invincible charity? Thus spoke the angels with affection of admiration; and Almighty God rejoiced in beholding her fervour ; and those who beheld her were edified in seeing so great sanctity in such tender years. But I, both wondering and rejoicing at this, will also humble myself, considering how far I am from it through my negligence and coldness, and desire to get out of it, to imitate her example.

2. Then will I consider how this child *spent a great part of the day* in ascending and descending that mystical ladder of Jacob, (24) which reached from earth to heaven; at the top of which stood the Omnipotent God, and whose degrees, as has been said before, are reading,—meditation,—prayer, —and contemplation. (25.)—She spent one time of the day in *reading* holy Scripture, to the great consolation of her soul, Almighty God opening the meaning of them to her, that she might penetrate and understand them.—Hence, she ascended to *meditation*, conferring with herself on what she had read, searching out new truths which illustrated her soul, and inflamed it with the fire of love and devotion.—Hence she mounted another space by the degrees of *prayer*, desiring of Almighty God with great fervour the gifts of His grace, not only for herself, but for her companions, and for all the people.—And lastly, she ascended to the degree of *contemplation* in which she spent very much time, uniting her soul with Almighty God, from whom she received such incredible sweetness and consolation ; and such extraordinary abundance of celestial gifts, that none can comprehend or know them, but God who gave them, and she who received them ; rejoic-

(24) Gen. xxviii. 12.　　　　(25) S. Bern. in scala claustralium.

ing in that " hidden manna, whose taste no man knoweth but he that receiveth it." (26)   And in these exercises she was visited by the angels who guard this ladder, comforting those who ascend it,—but much more this Blessed Virgin, whose purity was greater than theirs ; for, seeing her ascend up, they spoke with admiration that of the Canticles : " Who is she that goeth up by the desert, as a pillar of smoke of aromatical spices of myrrh and frank-incense, and of all the powders of the perfumer ?" (27) " Who is this young maiden who lives in the desert of this world, and in the solitude of this Temple, and springs up, not like a rod, but like a twig that is small and humble in her own eyes, but most odoriferous and gracious in the eyes of Almighty God, in which she always goes ascending and increasing with the 'myrrh' of mortification, with the 'incense' of prayer, and with the continual exercise of all virtue?"

3. Finally, in descending this ladder, this blessed Lady was exercised in *working with her hands* for the service of the temple, and for the benefit of her companions, mingling her exterior works with prayer; and, therefore, it is said of her, that " the smell of her garments " is "as the smell of frankincense." (28)

Colloquy.—O sovereign Virgin, "rod" that didst spring forth from "the root of Jesse,"(29) and didst ascend to thy beloved, like a most odoriferous spring of perfume; obtain for me, that I also may be little in humility, and careful to ascend by the ladder of prayer, by which thou ascendest, until I unite myself with Almighty God; descending also to exercise the works of mortification in myself, and those of piety towards my neighbours; increasing in all virtues, and

(26) Apoc. ii. 17.   (27) Cant. iii. 6.
(28) Cant. iv. 11.   (29) Isa. xi. 1.

giving to all men the odour of good examples, for which they may glorify God world without end. Amen.

POINT V.

1. I am next to consider how, at this time, this sovereign Virgin made another very new and pleasing offer to our Lord God, which was the *vow of perpetual virginity,* offering it to Him by special inspiration of the Holy Spirit, and with extraordinary devotion. For the greatness of the love that she bore to Almighty God, moved her to desire to deliver her whole heart to Him, and to take Him for her spouse, exercising herself entirely in meditating upon Him, and in pleasing Him, without dividing herself by other things, as those are "divided" (30) who are married. And she, knowing that virginity was more precious with a vow than without it, was not contented with a single purpose of preserving it, but made a particular vow of it; because she always desired to do what was best, most firm, and secure, and that which was most to the glory of God, our Lord. Then was fulfilled that which her spouse said of her, "My sister, my spouse, is a garden enclosed, a garden enclosed, a fountain sealed up." (31) He *twice* called her an enclosed garden, because she was perfectly chaste, both in soul and in body, confirming it with a perpetual vow, which served as a lock for her greater security; adding as guards, humility, modesty, silence and abstinence, for which reason He has also called her a *garden*, to give us to understand that her virginity was not barren, but accompanied with many flowers of virtues, and with excellent fruits of good works ; some that beautify the soul, others that adorn the body, that she might be " sancta corpore et spiritu,"—" holy both in

<hr>

(30) 1 Cor. vii. 33. 34.   (31) Cant. iv. 12.

body and in spirit." (32) Oh, how pleasing was this "garden" to the divine Spouse ! He was well pleased with the view and odour of the flowers of her virtues. He ate of the sweet "fruit" (33) of her good works. He rejoiced to behold it so well "inclosed" with a vow, delighting much in the lock and guards which it had. And, therefore, He watered it with great abundance of heavenly consolations and gifts; making in them a fountain and well of the living waters of His graces, inclosed with His divine protection.

2. From this heroic example of the sacred Virgin, I will draw a hearty desire of chastity, offering myself to preserve it with the greatest perfection that I am able, according to my state, taking the Blessed Virgin for my patroness and protectress in this enterprise, saying to her that verse which holy church sings :—

> " Virgo singularis,
>   Inter omnis mitis
>   Nos culpis solutos,
>   Mites fac et castos." (34)

> " Virgin of all virgins,
>   To thy shelter take us;
>   Gentlest of the gentle,
>   Chaste and gentle make us."*

And, in imitation of her, I will shut up the garden of my body and soul, if Almighty God shall inspire me to it, under the lock of a vow; and if in this manner I cannot lock it up, I will place as sentinels those virtues that guard chastity.

POINT VI.

1. I am then to consider how, the time of the Incarnation now approaching very near, the Blessed Virgin our

(32) 1 Cor. vii. 34.　(33) Cant. v. 1.　(34) In Hymno officii. B. V. M.
*Caswall's Lyra Catholica.

Lady, by revelation from God, was espoused to "a just man" named " Joseph," (35) she being assured that it should be without peril of her chastity, which she readily consented to. Hereupon, I will ponder the *causes* why God our Lord would that His mother should be *espoused ;* in which He discovers the providence He has of those that are His. These were,—

i. To conceal the mystery of the Incarnation, and the child-bearing of the Virgin, until the full time.

ii. He had likewise in it a care of the honour of His mother, that she might not be judged as an adultress.

iii. That she might have one to support and serve her in her afflictions, and to accompany her in her journeyings.

iv. That her Son might have a tutor or foster-father to bring Him up, and provide for Him.

v. Finally, to magnify St. Joseph, exalting him to such a dignity, as to be the spouse of the Mother of God, and the foster-father of the Son of God.

Colloquy.—O most loving Father, I give Thee thanks for the care Thou hast of Thy children and servants, providing for their honour, and for their ease and support—providing a remedy in time for anything which may molest them, and seeking out occasions to magnify them. Happy is he who is under Thy wing and protection. Provide for me, O Lord, who am Thy creature, that I may always be employed in serving Thee, since Thou art always employed in governing. Amen.

2. Secondly, I must ponder the great *faith* and confidence which the Virgin had in Almighty God, that her chastity would not be endangered by her marriage, as also the great obedience which she showed in accepting this

(35) S. Tho. 3. p. q. xxix. Matth. i. 18. Luc. i. 34. 35.

state which she had so earnestly refused, denying her own will, and resigning it to the will of Almighty God. In this I am to imitate her, according to my state, persuading myself, that if I trust in Him with a lively faith, I shall not lose virtue, or consolation, or anything whatever I can desire for my salvation, in reason for obedience to Him. For Almighty God has both knowledge and power how to join virginity with wedlock, contemplation with occupation, and the beauty of Rachel with the fruitfulness of Lia, without the one receiving any detriment from the other.

POINT VII.

1. Next I am to consider the *fervent desire which the Blessed Virgin* had for the coming of God into the world, which so much the more increased as the time of the Incarnation approached, the Holy Spirit inspiring them into her, whose property is, when He will grant anything to the elect, to inspire into them lively desires of it; that, with their desire and prayer, they may dispose themselves to receive it.

2. Besides this, the Virgin was solicited by her own " charity," (36) with the *two most noble acts* of the love of Almighty *God*, and of our neighbour—zeal for the glory of God, and the salvation of souls. For, as she loved God very much, she desired to see Him already made man, the better to know His greatness, to contemplate His marvellous works, and to converse familiarly with Him. Then could she say to Him that of the Canticles : " Who shall give Thee to me for my brother, sucking the breasts, that I may find Thee without, and kiss Thee, and now no man may despise me? I will take hold of Thee, and bring Thee into my mother's house. There Thou shalt teach me, and I will give Thee a cup of spiced wine, and new wine of my pomegranates." (37)

(36) 2 Cor. v. 14.   (37) Cant. viii. 1, 2.

Colloquy.—Oh how happy were I, if I might see Thee in human flesh, sucking at the breast of some woman, and might find Thee out of Thy heaven, conversing visibly with men upon earth, that I might both give and receive of Thee the kiss of peace; then would I converse with Thee, and hear Thy doctrine in this temple, and invite Thee to what Thou most of all desirest, giving Thee my whole love with many affections and acts of charity

3. Besides this, her fervent *zeal* devoured her, seeing the *offences against Almighty God,* and the perdition of men; and, therefore, with many and great groanings, and prayers, desiring of God to come to their remedy. She repeated with great affection the prayers of David and of Isaiah, which the Church uses in Advent, saying to Almighty God, " Stir up Thy might, and come to save us ;" (38) —" Show us, O Lord, Thy mercy, and grant us Thy salvation ;" (39)—" Oh that Thou wouldst rend the heavens, and wouldst come down;" (40)—" Drop down dew, ye heavens, from above, and let the clouds rain the just; let the earth be opened, and bud forth a Saviour." (41)

4. Finally, the *prayers of the Blessed Virgin prevailed* so much with God our Lord, that although the world were so wicked, as we shall soon see, and that mankind in no ways merited this favour, she alone outweighed the demerits of all; and with her merits and prayers was the means of the Son of Almighty God *hastening His Incarnation,* without making any account of the world's unworthiness. O marvellous efficacy of the Virgin's prayer!

Colloquy.—I rejoice, O blessed Lady, that thou wast so powerful with God, as to make Him quicken His steps and hasten His coming : beseech Him also

(38) Ps. lxxix. 3.
(39) Ib. lxxxiv. 8.   (40) Isa. lxiv. 1.   (41) Ib. xlv. 8.

to make haste to come to visit me ; and that I may be worthy of His visitation, invoke the divine Spirit to inspire me with fervent desires of it.　Amen.

MEDITATION V.

ON THE TIME THAT ALMIGHTY GOD CHOSE TO ANNOUNCE AND EXECUTE THE MYSTERY OF THE INCARNATION.

Our Lord God might have chosen three different times to execute the decree of His Incarnation.—(1) The first was the beginning of the world as soon as Adam had sinned:—the second the middle of its duration, which the prophet Habacuc the " midst of the years."—(2) The third, about the end.　But the divine Wisdom made choice of the *first* time to *promise* this mystery as a remedy for sin ; the second to execute it, and of all the rest to *gather the copious fruits* that were to spring from it, ordaining it thus for our good.

POINT I.

First, I will consider that God our Lord, as soon as Adam and Eve had sinned, chose to *reveal to them the mystery of the Incarnation* as the remedy for their sin, and for the punishment that they had deserved for it, to demonstrate in this the greatness of His charity and mercy towards men. (3)

1. This was resplendent in this ;—that when coming as a judge to take account of Adam and Eve for their disobedience, and to denounce to them the sentence of death which they had incurred by it ; He, moreover, as a merciful father, *promises them*, not only to make Himself man

(1) S. Th. 3. p. q. i. ar. 5. &c.　　(2) Habac. iii. 2.
(3) S. Th. 2. 2. q. ii. ar. 7., Gen. 3.

for them, but also to *die* to deliver them from death; intending in this, that by their faith in this Redeemer, they should not mistrust the Divine mercy, nor the pardon of their sins, but that grieving for having offended Him who had showed them so much love, they should forthwith procure it by penance. So that when Almighty God cast our first parents, and all their posterity, out of the terrestrial paradise, He then promises them Him who should open the gates of the celestial paradise. When He loads them with maledictions for sin, He offers them of mere grace, the Author of all heavenly benedictions ; and when they are vanquished by the devil, He assures them that there shall be born of them a man that shall free them from his tyranny.

Colloquy.—O Father of mercies, and God of all consolation, I humbly thank Thee, that "in the midst of" Thy wrath Thou dost remember Thy infinite "mercy." (4) And when all men by the first Adam deserved to be accursed, Thou didst promise us the second Adam by whom we should be blessed. Show, O Lord, this Thy mercy to me, delivering me from the maledictions which I deserve through my sins, and replenishing me with the blessings which Thy Son gained by His merits. O Son of the ever-living God, "Lamb which wast slain from the beginning of the world,"(5) (for then was published Thy death, and true life was given to men who had sinned;)—I humbly thank Thee for this favour which Thou hast done us, and therefore I beseech Thee to apply the fruit of it to me, that being free from the death of sin, I may obtain through Thee the life of grace. Amen.

2. I will likewise ponder the infinite mercy of Almighty God, *in not deferring this promise of our redemption many days,* nor yet many hours ; but even the self same day

<hr>

(4) Habac. iii. 2.   (5) Apoc. xiii. 8.

that Adam sinned, He came to admonish him both of his transgression, and of his remedy. He greatly desires that the sinner, although he sin through frailty, should not remain so much as one day in his sin, on account of the great injury which redounds to him from it, but should presently be converted and do penance. All this I should apply to myself considering how many times our Lord has prevented me by inspirations, when I have sinned, offering me pardon and mercy instead of chastising me with justice, for which I ought humbly to render to Him many thanks, endeavouring to raise myself up immediately by doing penance the very day on which I have sinned. So that, as St. Paul says, I " let not the sun go down" without taking from me " wrath," (6) and pride, and every other sin whatsoever.

POINT II.

Secondly, I am to consider the *seasonableness* of the time which Almighty God chose to execute the decree of His Incarnation, in order to make His infinite mercy the more eminent.

1. Upon this I should behold *the state in which* the world stood when Almighty God came to redeem it, running through the thoughts, words, and deeds, of men, and comparing them with those of Almighty God. which, as the prophet Isaias says, " are as exalted above " them " as the heavens are exalted above the earth." (7)

i. First, I will lift up my eyes to heaven, and behold the most blessed Trinity on the throne of His glory, considering what thoughts He had, and what devices He was then inventing to redeem man, by means of the Incarnation of the divine Word. And as the three Persons of the Godhead, when they would create Adam, said : " Let us

(6) Ephes. iv. 26.   (7) Is. lv. 9.

make man to our image and likeness," (8) so now They said : " Let us redeem man whom we created, repairing the image and likeness that we gave him." O what great delight They took in this decree ! What joy in beholding the time arrived of executing Their determination ! And with what joy did each Person prepare Himself for what belonged to Him to do in this work ! The Father to send His Son into the world—the Son to come and to unite His divine Person with our nature—and the Holy Ghost to work this sovereign union.

Colloquy.—I thank Thee, O most blessed Trinity, that Thou tookest delight to treat of my remedy. O that I might treat with much delight of all that belongs to Thy holy service. Amen.

ii. I will then cast my eyes down to see what was at that time passing *in the world*, considering how it had then reached the deepest abyss of iniquity. The Gentiles were grown to such a height in their idolatries, that they caused themselves to be adored as gods. The Jews were full of hypocrisy, avarice, ambition, and other innumerable sins. The earth was wholly drowned with a deluge of uncleanness and carnalities, it was as the prophet Osee described, when he said, " Cursing and lying, and killing, and theft, and adultery, have overflowed, and blood hath touched blood.'' (9)

iii. Almighty God was *beholding all this* from heaven, for nothing is hidden from Him ; and though this so great multitude of sins provoked Him to great fury, yet they did not cause Him to defer His determination. Rather this most merciful God, as said the prophet Habacuc, was mindful to do us the greatest " mercy " when He had most occasion to be "angry ;" (10) and instead of drown-

(8) Gen. i. 26.   (9) Osee iv. 2.   (10) Habac. iii. 2.

ing the world again with another deluge, or burning it with fire like Sodom, He would drown it with abundance of mercies, and burn it with the fire of His love, giving it His own Son to redeem it.

Colloquy.—O infinite "Charity," whose flames "many waters" of the rivers of innumerable sins could "not quench,"(11) but rather increasing with greater demonstrations of love, did the greatest of all favours to us, who made ourselves more unworthy of it every day, I give Thee thanks, O most loving and merciful Lord, for this love which Thou didst show us; for which, I beseech Thee, though as a wicked wretch I deserve Thy indignation, yet Thou, as a good God, wouldst cease not to favour me with the greatness of Thy mercy. Amen.

2. I should likewise apply this consideration to myself, pondering how it has many times happened, that when I was actually offending God by my deeds, God was then doing me great benefits, and devising to do me yet greater, how, perhaps, to draw me out of the world into religion or the like, for which I must give Him many thanks.

3. Hence I may likewise ascend to consider how much the infinite mercy of Almighty God was resplendent, in having awaited the time for making Himself man, when Judea was in such a state, that men through their wicked life were to abhor Him, and through envy to persecute Him, even to the bereaving Him of His life, taking occasion hence to redeem them by His death.

Colloquy.—O infinite wisdom of Almighty God, how contrary art Thou to the wisdom of the world, seeing Thou seekest occasions to suffer for the redemption of it! O how contrary to this wisdom are the imaginations of my flesh, which flies the occasions of affliction, and seeks the occasions of its own ease!

<hr>

(11) Cant. viii. 7.

Chase away, O Lord, my imaginations, that I may follow Thine, embracing affliction, as Thou hast embraced it for my example. Amen.

POINT III.

1. I am to consider why our Lord deferred His coming into the world *so many thousand years*, especially pondering two causes for my own profit.

i. The first is, because by that time mankind, by the experience of their innumerable and most grievous sins, *knew* the extreme *need* they had of a Redeemer. And as He came from heaven to remedy our miseries, He waited for them to increase and be made manifest, in order that His infinite wisdom and omnipotency might likewise be made manifest in curing such grievous infirmities by remedies well proportioned to them. For this cause when pride was grown to that excessive height in the world, that man would usurp the greatness of God, then would God take the form of man to cure such abominable pride by such profound humility. And when the desire of riches, honours, and delicacies, was most eager and hot, then would Almighty God clothe Himself with poverty, contempt and pain, to cure such an ardent desire of temporal goods, with a contempt of them as ardent.

Colloquy.—O sovereign physician, I humbly thank Thee for having come in such a season to cure our infirmities with such precious medicines. Behold, O Lord, my wounds are much increased, defer not to remedy them, that the greatness of Thy mercies may be manifested in me. Amen.

ii. The *second cause* of this delay was that it is the good pleasure of our Lord, that His gifts, especially when they are very great, should be *esteemed, desired, and solicited, with prayers* and groanings, as the Fathers who were in

Limbo, and the righteous who lived on the earth all this time. And, likewise, by this deferring, He proved the confidence and patience of the just to whom " the promises were made ;" (12) for it is an heroic virtue not to lose confidence, though the accomplishment of the promise should be deferred a long time. Upon which said a prophet, " if it make any delay wait for it ; for it shall surely come, and it shall not be slack," (13) that is, though He delay according to the desire of the heart, He will not delay according to the order of His divine providence, to accomplish what thy necessity requires ; for He will come infallibly in His appointed time, when His coming will much more avail thee.

2. These two causes I am to apply to myself, pondering how Almighty God our Lord sometimes permits His elect to suffer great afflictions and dryness a long time, that they may know by experience what need they have of God's visitation ; that they may be grounded in profound humility, and that, by this delay, the desires of their remedy may increase, and their faith and confidence may be proved ; and that so they may come to make great esteem of the gift of Almighty God, and to preserve it with great care. With this entering into consideration what a great happiness it was to me to be born after this sovereign mystery was executed, to enjoy the graces and gifts thereby communicated to men more abundantly ; my longings and sighs, my desires and groanings, must be to this end—that God by His grace may come to my heart, and visit my soul with abundance of these gifts, insomuch as to take for my name, like another Daniel, " a man of desires," (14) employing them in desiring the coming of Him who took the name of " the desired of

(12) Heb. xi. (13) Habac. ii. 3. (14) Dan. ix. 23 ; x. 19.

nations," (15) nor should I be weary of soliciting it, though it seem to me to be long deferred, since there is no day that comes not at last ; and the more earnest the solicitation, the less the delay, and the greater the reward.

MEDITATION VI.

ON THE COMING OF THE ANGEL GABRIEL TO ANNOUNCE TO THE VIRGIN THE MYSTERY OF THE INCARNATION; AND ON THE FORM OF SALUTA-TION, AND REMOVAL OF HER FEAR.

POINT I.

1. First, I am to consider what passed in heaven when the appointed time was come, in which God our Lord would make Himself man. Imagining how the most sacred Trinity, being on the throne of His glory, desiring to give notice to her who was to be the Mother of the Word Incarnate, determined to send a very glorious embassy, to move her to accept it ; the beginning of which is recounted by the Evangelist, saying :—" And in the sixth month, the angel Gabriel was sent from God into a city of Galilee, called Nazareth, to a Virgin espoused to a man whose name was Joseph, of the house of David : and the Virgin's name was Mary:" (1)

In this embassy I am to ponder,—i. who sends it ;—ii. who brings it : —iii. to whom it is sent :—iv. and for what object, collecting out of all profit to my own soul.

i. He who sends it is the *omnipotent God,* who, without having need of His creatures, of His mere bounty only, and to do good to men, delights to communicate with them, and to send them messages and embassies, using for His ministers herein, such noble creatures as the angels ;

(15) Agg. ii. 8.　　　　　(1) Luc. i. 26.

who, as St. Paul says, are "all ministering spirits, sent to minister for them who shall receive the inheritance of salvation." (2)

And their continual ministry is to ascend and descend that "ladder" which Jacob "saw," (3) bringing down messages from God to man, and carrying up messages and petitions from man to God.

Colloquy.—O God of immense majesty, "what is man that Thou art mindful of him? or the son of man, that Thou visitest him?"(4) Let Thy angels praise Thee for the tender love Thou bearest to man. Amen.

ii. He who brings this embassy is an *Archangel* so excellent, that his name is Gabriel ; that is to say, " Fortitude of God :"—to signify the fortitude resplendent in our Lord who sent him ; and in Him who is to be Incarnate, and in the works the Word Incarnate is to do, and in the ministers He will appoint to publish them ; (5) and whom this ambassador represents ; who in the virtue of Almighty was strong and potent to fulfil whatever He commanded him ; not only in this case which was so glorious, but in any other how humble soever, as we shall see hereafter. For his glory is to do what Almighty God commands ; and in imitation of him I will endeavour, by God's grace, to clothe myself with his fortitude, to accomplish in all things the divine will.

iii. *She to whom the embassy is sent, is a poor Virgin,* forgotten by the world, espoused to a poor artificer, who lived in a little city of such obscure name, that it was hardly believed that "any good" could "come from" it. (6) But she was most holy and pure, and, therefore, so much esteemed by God, that she was preferred before

(2) Heb. i. 14.   3) Gen. xxviii. 12.   (4) Ps. viii. 5.
(5) Greg. hom. xxxiv. in Evang.   (6) Joan. i. 46.

the daughters of the kings and emperors of the world.; for in the eyes of God there is no greatness such as sanctity ; neither ought there to be in mine, for I should only esteem what God esteems.

iv. *The object of the embassy is to require the consent of the Virgin* to be the Mother of God ; for our Lord is of so noble a condition, that though He be an absolute Lord, He will not be served by His creatures in such weighty affairs *without their free consent.* For though to be the Mother of God was a thing very excellent, yet great afflictions were annexed to it ; it was therefore meet that the Virgin should, of her own free will, accept the dignity with the charge, that she might merit the more, and that it might be the more sweet and easy to her. And so likewise, neither will Almighty God enter to dwell in the souls of men by grace, nor exalt them to the dignity of sons of God, if they have attained to the use of reason, without their free consent.

2. Hence, I will pass spiritually to consider this embassy, applying it to myself, and pondering how God our Lord sends *me* every day, invisibly, many embassies with His inspirations ; which, as St. Bonaventure says, are the invisible ambassadors and messengers of Almighty God ; and by them He speaks to me, and manifests His will, and solicits me to give Him entrance into my soul, and to employ myself always in His service. (7) And, therefore, in feeling within myself these inspirations, I must reverence them as ambassadors of God, giving Him many thanks that He vouchsafes to speak to me by them, consenting immediately to all that He requires of me, and beseeching Him to speak to me more often.

Colloquy.—O most loving Father, who solicitest my

(7) Tract. de Septem. don. Spirit. sancti c. vi. Rich. de S. Victor.
S. Ber. Ser. i. de Pentec.

consent with so great love and care, as if that which benefits me benefited Thee; inspire into me what Thou wilt, for I am ready to consent to whatsoever Thou inspirest me with.   Amen.

POINT. II.

Secondly, I am to consider the entrance of the angel to the Virgin, and the form of salutation : pondering—

1. How he took of air a most beautiful body of human shape, and in this form entered the Blessed Virgin's room where she abode, with great *modesty, reverence,* and *gravity,* and with such an exterior demeanour of sanctity, as well declared what she was interiorly ; to instruct us what Apostolical men ought exteriorly to be, who, as St. Paul says, are ambassadors "for Christ ;" (8) and likewise what Religious men ought to be who profess an angelical life ; whose exterior behaviour ought to bespeak sanctity, and to move all that behold them to the same.

2. The angel on entering saluted the Blessed Virgin, not with vain salutations, but with those divine words which Almighty God put in his mouth,—saying to her : " Hail, full of grace, the Lord is with thee : blessed art thou among women." (9)   This salutation, as the saints say, was new, and never before heard of in the world, devised by the most holy Trinity to honour the sacred Virgin, and to declare her rare sanctity and new dignity, as the mystery was new for which it was ordained. For as Christ was a new " man " contrary to the old Adam : so the blessed Virgin who conceived Him, was a new " woman " (10) contrary to the old Eve.   In this spirit and estimation we ought to say, and to meditate this new salutation, pondering in every word the greatness

(8) 2 Cor. v. 20 ; Ephes. vi. 20.   (9) S. Ambr., Beda in Luc. i.
(10) Jer. xxxi. 22.

that it imports, with affections of joy and thanksgiving; rejoicing that the Blessed Virgin has such greatness, and giving thanks to Almighty God for giving it her ; desiring of Him some part of it, and purposing to imitate what is imitable.

" AVE "—" HAIL."

1. The angel, to manifest his love, and the joyful news that he brought, and to assure the Virgin, enters saying, "Ave," which is as much as to say, "Hail," or "God save thee ; peace be with thee, be cheerful and assured ; for the news that I bring is of peace and prosperity."

Colloquy.—O sovereign Virgin, with all the affection of my heart, I salute thee, and say, "Ave," "Hail," "God save thee ;" for by thee began our salvation, conceiving Him who was the author of it: thou hast changed the name of Eve, reversing her miseries, and replenishing us with mercies. The first Eve was the beginning of sin;—*thou* the beginning of grace. By the first, death entered into the world ;—by *thee*, life. The first subjected us to the serpent ;—thou hast crushed his "head." (11) Be of good heart, Blessed Virgin, for the good lot which has befallen thee, and renew my heart that I may daily "sing a new canticle" (12) of praise with new fervour of spirit. Amen.

2. Secondly, I must ponder *the cause why the angel* in this first salutation, named not the Virgin by her proper name, saying :—"*hail Mary*,"—but "hail, *full of grace*, the Lord is with thee : blessed art thou among women." This he did that we might understand, that as Almighty God gave to the Messiah the names of " Wonderful, Counseller, God the Mighty, the Father of the world to come, the Prince of peace ;" (13) so also He gave to the

(11) Gen. iii. 15.   (12) Ps. xxxii. 3.
(13) Is. ix. 6.

5

Virgin new and most glorious names, which, for excellency, are to be attributed to her in the Church ; so that as we call Solomon " the Wise," and St. Paul " the Apostle," so we may call the Blessed Virgin the "Full of grace," or the " Blessed among women." And as the name of the Messiah is " *Emmanuel*," (14) which is as much as to say, " God with us ;" so the name of the Virgin may, for excellency, be " the Lord with thee."

Colloquy.—O most sacred Virgin, let others call thee the rod of Jesse, the gate of heaven, the " house of wisdom," and other like names. I will now call thee, as did the angel, "full of grace," the abode of our Lord, and " blessed among women," and declare to thy glory the greatness signified by these names.

" FULL OF GRACE."

First, I will consider *what fulness this is*, and how the Blessed Virgin was "*full of grace*" with all manner of fulness.

1. She was full of the grace which justifies, full of charity, faith, and hope; of humility, obedience, and patience, with all other virtues; full, likewise, of wisdom, of knowledge, of piety, and the fear of God, with all the other gifts of the Holy Ghost.

2. Her *memory* was full of holy thoughts; her *understanding* of great illuminations from God; her *will* of fervent acts, and affections of love and zeal, with inward and hearty desires of the glory of God, of the coming of the Messiah, and of the redemption of the world. And this fulness she actually had, when the angel entered to salute her; for she was employed in the contemplation of these mysteries, which was in a manner her continual occupation. Besides this she was "full of grace" in her

(14) Is. vii. 14.

works; for they were all works full, entire, and solid, with that fulness that they might have of pure intention, fervour and love, so that God could not say to her, as He said to the bishop of Sardis ; "I find not thy works full before me." (15.)

3. Then will I ponder the *greatness of this plenitude;* for many vessels are full of precious liquor ; but the greater contains the greater quantity: so many saints were full of grace ; but the Blessed Virgin, as says St. Thomas, (16) above all ; for she was a much greater vessel, and her fulness was conformable to the dignity of the Mother of God, which far exceeds the dignities and offices of the other saints ; and by the good use of graces received, she every day enlarged the vessel, and made it capable of others still greater.

Colloquy.—O most sacred Virgin, who is able to recount the fulness of grace which thou hast above all the saints who were filled with it! They were like rivers; but thou, according to thy name, art full like the sea. I rejoice on account of thy excellence. St. Gabriel calls thee "full of grace," for it seemed to him that there was no other that had the like fulness; and that he and his companions, compared with thee, might call themselves empty. I thank Thee, most blessed Trinity, for the fulness of grace which Thou gavest to this sovereign Virgin : by whose merits I beseech Thee to give me some part of them, that the vessel of my soul, though but a little one, may be filled according to its capacity. O Mother of mercy, and immense sea of grace, since " unto the place from whence the rivers come, they return to flow again,"(17) let there issue from thee some river of graces, to fill the vacant places of my soul, that my works may be

<hr>

(15) Apoc. iii. 2.
(16) 3. p. q. xxvii. art 5.   (17) Eccles. i. 7.

"full" and "perfect" before Almighty "God." Amen.

"THE LORD BE WITH THEE."

1. In this third word the angel ascends to the height of the salutation, saying, "*The Lord is with thee*," that is, *He is in thee by excellency in all those ways that He may be in His pure creatures.* He is with thee, not only by essence, presence, and power, as He is with all the just, but with eminency of grace, assisting thee with special grace and friendship, and with close familiarity.— He is with thee in all thy faculties, uniting them with Himself ; He is in thy memory awakening it that thou mayest always remember Him ; in thy understanding, illuminating it, that thou mayest perpetually know Him ; and in thy will, inflaming it, that thou mayest love Him everlastingly.— He is with thee likewise, assisting in all thy affairs with special providence and protection, governing thee with His inspirations, and directing thee in all that thou dost.—He is in thee as in His heaven, in His temple, in His chamber, in His house of repose ; and shortly He will be in thy womb as thy son; and therefore pre-eminently and with fullest declaration I say to thee, "Dominus tecum." "The Lord is with thee."

2. I will also ponder, that the angel says not, "the Lord" *is, was,* or *shall be* with thee; but " the Lord *with thee*," to signify that He was, is, and shall be perpetually with her, as if He should say, from thy creation "God is in the midst of thee," (18) and now is, and will be throughout all eternity. He will not depart, nor be alienated from thee, neither will there be in thee any change that may impair the divine Providence.

Colloquy.—O Blessed Virgin, I rejoice at the great

<hr>

(18) Ps. xlv. 6.

good thou hast in having God Himself with thee firmly, and constantly enjoying His sweet conversation. Beseech Him that He will be with me, through grace, possessing me with such love, that He will never depart from me, nor I from Him, for ever and ever. Amen.

"BLESSED ART THOU AMONG WOMEN."

With this fourth word the angel concludes the salutation, saying, "Blessed art thou among women;"—i. Because thou shalt be free from the curse of barrenness without loss of virginity ;—ii. Because thou shalt be free from the malediction of bringing "forth in sorrow," (19) since thou shalt not conceive with pleasure.— iii. Because thou shalt· be blessed among women; because, as a woman was the beginning of all the maledictions that fell upon men, so thou shalt be the beginning of all "spiritual blessings" (20) that shall light upon them, by the blessed fruit of thy womb, by whom thou shalt crush the "head" of the serpent, and deliver them from those maledictions which his cursed suggestion heaped upon them. For which thou shalt be blessed and praised among all women; and both the angels in heaven, and men on earth, the just as well as sinners, shall give thee a thousand benedictions, for all have a share in thy abundant benediction.

Colloquy.—And I, also, thy unworthy servant, praise, bless, and glorify thee; and rejoice that all should praise, bless, and glorify thee; and I beseech thee to make me partaker of those blessings which thy most sweet Son, our Head, communicated through thee as through the means of His neck, to the Church. Deliver me, O blessed Lady, from the maledictions of sin, and the punishment to which I live subject, that I

(19) Gen. iii. 16.　　　　　　(20) Eph. i. 3.

may bless thy Son, and serve Him, world without end.
Amen.

POINT III.

Thirdly, I must consider the *manner how the Blessed Virgin received this salutation;* for she having heard it, "was troubled at his saying, and thought with herself what manner of salutation this should be." (21.)

1. In this she discovered *four excellent virtues*, in which we may imitate her, viz., chastity, humility, prudence, and silence.

i. She showed her excellent *chastity*, being troubled, as St. Ambrose says, (22) at the sudden view of a man in her chamber, she being alone; for it is the property of a modest, circumspect virgin, to be troubled at any view or word whatsoever of a man; as it is likewise the property of a chaste man, to make "a covenant with" his "eyes," like Job, "that" he *should* "not so much as think upon a virgin." (23.)

ii. But principally she showed her rare *humility*, because at the time the angel entered in the form of man, our Blessed Lady was recollected in her chamber, in deep contemplation of the greatness of God, and the Messiah, and of her who was to be His mother. Through her profound humility, she had a very mean opinion of herself ; and when she heard so strange, and yet so glorious a salutation, she was troubled, not so much at the sight of the angel, as because she found in herself no foundation of such praises, and greatness as he declared.

iii. She showed her *prudence* in thinking well "what manner of salutation this might be," and to what end it might be ordained; and therefore she would not trust her-

(21) Luc. i. 29.

(22) Lib. ii. de virginib: et exhort. ad virg.   (23) Job xxxi. 1 ;

self to answer inconsiderately, till the angel had explained himself somewhat more.

iv. She showed how much she loved *silence*, by holding her peace at that time, and answering only by the exterior demeanour of her humble and bashful amazement.

Colloquy.—O most pure Virgin, how well befits thee at this instant that which thy spouse said, " Thy cheeks are beautiful as the turtle dove's," (24) (a shy and chaste bird), for in them is resplendent the beauty of thy chastity, and the splendour of thy humble wisdom.

v. These virtues of the Virgin are more eminent, when compared with the first woman Eve, who when she was yet a virgin, went wandering, and gazing through paradise, and to the first question which the Evil angel in the form of a serpent, asked her, made answer, and exchanged many words with him : (25) in which she shewed pride, curiosity, imprudence and desire of talking, and other vices, in which we her children imitate her. Considering this I should be confounded, imploring the aid of this "most prudent virgin," that I may follow her on the like occasions.

POINT IV.

The angel knowing the holy trouble and fear of the Blessed Virgin, said to her, " Fear not, Mary, for thou hast found grace with God."

1. In this I am first to consider, that it is the *property of the good spirit to pacify* and calm any *fear* or disturbance of the heart whatever, that it may quietly receive the revelation and visitation of God. And although the trouble of the Blessed Virgin was without any kind of sin or imperfection, yet we may gather from it, with what care the Good angel endeavours to take away those com-

(24) Cant. i. 9.   (25) Gen. iii. 3.

motions which spring from sin, or our own imbecility. And I, for my part, should labour to remove them, lest they hinder the visitations of Almighty God, remembering how Christ our Saviour reprehended Martha, when He said " Martha, Martha, thou art careful and art troubled about many things," when " but one thing is necessary." (26) And this I should ask of my guardian angel, saying to him—

Colloquy.—O most blessed angel, remove from my heart all vain fear, that it may be capable of divine love; appease the disturbance that it suffers in earthly things, that it may contemplate the things of heaven, contenting myself with that one in which consists my eternal rest.   Amen.

2. Secondly, I will ponder that most sweet word added by the angel to persuade the Blessed Virgin not to "fear:" " For," says he, " thou hast found grace with God," which was to say to her, " Thou needst not to fear the devil, nor hell, nor visible, nor invisible enemies : neither hast thou cause to suspect the greatness that I have signified to thee in this salutation ; nor other greater which I shall presently tell thee of : for I declare to thee that thou art received in grace with Almighty God.   And this is sufficient to secure thee ; for hence it follows that thou art "full of grace;" that our Lord is "with thee ;" and that thou art "blessed among women :" for whosoever finds grace with God, what benefits shall he not receive from His liberal hand ?   O happy, and a thousand times happy, is that soul which finds grace with God !   If it be held among men for a high felicity to be in grace with an earthly king, how much greater shall it be to be in grace with the King of heaven?   From that grace proceeds abundance of riches, honours, dignities, and many other temporal benefits which a king bestows upon his favourite;

<hr>

(26) Luc. x. 41.

and yet, sometimes all ends with disgrace ; but from this grace proceeds an abundance of virtues and heavenly gifts which God bestows on His beloved: wherefore it is said in holy Scripture of the great saints, as of Noah, Moses, David, and such like, that they "found grace before the Lord :"—(27) but above all, the most sacred Virgin found much greater, and more familiar grace with Almighty God : even so familiar that she was always with Him, and He with her, even to the containing Him in her womb as His mother.

Colloquy.—O most sweet Mother, I rejoice that thou hast "found grace before God" with such singular favour. And as Queen Esther, because she found grace before King Assuerus, was the cause that her people found the like, and were very much favoured by him ; (28) be thou our mediatrix, that we may find grace before God, and obtain that perfect grace which is eternal glory. Amen.

3. But I must consider very carefully, that although Almighty God does not this favour through the merits of man, but only through His mercy ; yet humility most of all disposes us to gain it, since by humility the Blessed Virgin obtained it. And, therefore, the Holy Ghost said: "The greater thou art, the more humble thyself in all things, and thou shalt find grace before God ; for great is the power of God alone, and He is honoured by the humble." (29) He says that the humble do Him honour, because they attribute to Him the honour and glory of all that they have, for which God honours them much more, and they find greater grace before Him.

Colloquy.—Therefore, O my soul, if like the Blessed Virgin thou wilt find grace with God, humble thyself

(27) Gen. vi. 8.   Exod. xxxiii. 17.   Act. vii. 46.   (28) Esth. ii. 9.
(29) Ecclus. iii. 20.

in all things as she did; for "God resisteth the proud, and giveth grace to the humble." (30)

MEDITATION VII.

ON THE ANGEL'S ANNOUNCING AND DECLARING THE MYSTERY OF THE INCARNATION TO THE BLESSED VIRGIN.

POINT I.

The angel having quieted the holy perturbation of the Blessed Virgin, delivered his message in this manner : " Behold, thou shalt conceive in thy womb, and shalt bring forth a son, and thou shalt call His name Jesus." "He shall be great, and shall be called the Son of the most High ; and the Lord God shall give him the throne of David his father; and he shall reign in the house of Jacob for ever, and of his kingdom there shall be no end." (1)

1. In these words are to be pondered the *greatness* and excellencies of the Son whom the angel promises to the Virgin.

i. That He shall be Jesus, and the Saviour of the world, with greater excellency than all others who had this name, as will be declared hereafter.

ii. That He shall be great above all greatness without limitation ;—great in His divinity and humanity—great in wisdom and sanctity, in life and in doctrine ;—in example and in word ; and, finally, great in power ; because He shall have power over all things, with faculty to make others also great before God, by participation of His greatness.

iii. That He shall be her son in such a manner that He shall be likewise the Son of the most High God.

iv. That His eternal Father shall give Him the throne

(30) Jac. iv. 6.   (1) Luc. i. 31, 32.

and the empire over all the elect, figured by the " throne
of David," and by " the house of Jacob," from whom He
descended according to the flesh.

v. That His kingdom shall be eternal and have no end.

O glorious message ! O most joyful news ! O happy
Virgin to whom such a son is promised : and blessed son
in whom such greatness is contained. Of all which the
angel gave notice to the Virgin, that she might know that
this son whom she was to conceive was the Messiah, promised by the prophets, of whom such great excellencies
were written. Whence I will conceive a great esteem and
love of this sovereign Messiah, rejoicing at each one of
these five excellencies, and calling to mind the five wounds
which He received on the cross, that He may apply the
fruit of them to His elect and to me; for on the cross they
were all made manifest, as will be described hereafter in
the proper place.

2. I will here meditate only, how these greatnesses had
their origin *from the most profound humility* of the only
begotten *Son* of the everliving *God*, which is included in
the first word spoken by the angel to the Virgin : " Ecce
concipies in utero." " Behold thou shalt conceive in thy
womb;" as if he should say, "this Saviour and this eternal
King being so great, yet will so far humble Himself as to
reduce Himself to the smallness of an infant conceived in
the womb of a woman. And from this smallness His
greatness shall have beginning, fulfilling that of the prophet Isaias : ' A child is born to us, and a son is given to
us, and the government is upon his shoulder; and his
name shall be called Wonderful, Counsellor, the Mighty
God, the Father of the world to come, the Prince of Peace;
His empire shall be multiplied, and there shall be no end
of peace.' " (2.)

(2) Is. ix. 6.

Colloquy.—O sovereign Prince, who descendedst from heaven, as "a stone without hands," being conceived in the womb of a virgin without the aid of man; and then camest to be "a great mountain," so as to fill "the whole earth," (3) enlarging in it Thy Kingdom, which is a kingdom without end, I humbly thank Thee for having chosen so strange a smallness to be the origin of so sovereign a greatness. Grant me, O Lord, that I, sustained not by my own hands, but by Thine, may conceive such resolutions in Thy service, that they may increase to very great works of Thy glory. Amen.

POINT II.

The Blessed Virgin having heard this message, said to the angel, " How shall this be done ? because I know not man." (4) As if she would say, " I doubt not God's omnipotency, nor thy promise, but I desire to be informed how I am to obey this commandment, having made a vow not to know man."

1. In this answer, the holy Virgin manifested as well *great wisdom,* as excessive love of virginity ; and therefore with much reason, the holy Church calls her the " most prudent Virgin." For though the promise of the angel was so great, yet she did not immediately yield to it until she might perceive how it would accord with the vow of chastity she had made, to which she was so entirely attached, that she made a difficulty to be a mother, though it were of such a son, with the loss of it. And although she knew by the prophecy of Isaias, that the mother of the Messiah should be "a virgin," (5) yet she would prudently examine the revelation of the angel, to see how it agreed with the revelation of the prophet, whence I will draw a fervent and hearty love of chastity, avoiding, as much as

(3) Dan. ii. 35, 45.   (4) Luc. i. 34.   (5) Is. vii. 14.

lies in me, whatever may be an occasion of impairing it, though it carry with it an appearance of piety and religion. For, in imitation of the most sacred Virgin, I am to examine the spirit which carefully inclines me to a thing, in which there may be danger, fearing lest it may be the spirit of Satan, "who," as says the apostle St. Paul, " transformeth himself into an angel of light," (6) to deceive those who are either very simple, or over-confident, or exceedingly zealous of other men's good, without regarding their own.

2. Secondly, I will consider in these words, since they are the first which we read concerning the Blessed Virgin, *four circumstances* with which she spoke them, in which is portrayed an admirable rule how to *speak prudently ;* for these words were but *few*, and *no more than necessary* in a case of great importance; and in a very humble and decent manner. It seems that the Virgin held firmly in her memory the counsel of Ecclesiasticus, which says, " Young man scarcely speak in thy own cause. If thou be asked twice, let thy answer be short," (7) and to the purpose. In many things be, as it were, ignorant, and listen, holding thy peace, and only asking. All this the Blessed Virgin marvellously observed, in these brief words, which she uttered not till the angel had spoken to her twice. And though she had occasion to enlarge on this question, yet she touched no more than the necessary point, and that with great brevity, declaring the vow of chastity that she had made, with humble and chaste words, but sufficient for the angel to understand her, saying to him, " I know not man."

Colloquy.—O most sacred Virgin, with much reason was the divine spouse pleased with " thy lips," saying, that they were "as a scarlet lace," and " as a drop-

<hr>

(6) 2 Cor. xi. 14.   (7) Ecclus. xxxii. 10, 11.

ping honey-comb ;" (8) for thy words are well guarded, and much pondered, and uttered with calmness, sweetness, and charity. And since this rule in speaking is so pleasing to Him, beseech Him to imprint in my heart, that my words may proceed from it well ordered and ruled.

POINT III.

1. To this question of the Virgin, the angel made answer, saying, "The Holy Ghost shall come upon thee; and the power of the Most High shall overshadow thee." And therefore, also, "the Holy thing which shall be born of thee shall be called the Son of God." (9) In these words may be pondered *three most excellent promises* made by the angel to the most sacred Virgin.

i. First, that this conception should not be by the work of man, but by *the power of the Holy Ghost*, who from heaven should come upon her to accomplish this work. And because the works of the Holy Ghost are perfect, He descended on her with new fulness of grace to dispose her to so sovereign a work.

ii. The second, that the power of the *most High should overshadow her*, preserving her from sensual delight in conception, and forming of her purest blood, the body of this child, as the bird covering her eggs with her wings, gives them life with her heat.

iii. The third promise was, the giving a reason for the other two, because that which was to be so holily conceived should be "the Son of God"—not by adoption, as the rest of the just, but by the union of the human nature with the divine Person, so that He should be holy, not by privilege, but by the power of His holy conception. Oh what an exceeding joy did these three promises cause in the Virgin.

(8) Cant. iv. 3, 11.   (9) Luc. i. 35.

Colloquy.—O most Blessed Virgin, when the angel entered thou wast already full of grace; how much fuller wilt thou be, the Holy Ghost coming upon thee with this new fulness? If *before* our Lord was with thee to govern, protect, and console thee, how much more shall He be with thee now, the power of the Most High coming to overshadow thee? Now mayest thou, O blessed Lady, say by a new title, "I sat down under his shadow whom I desired; and his fruit was sweet to my palate." (10) Thou art seated under the shadow of the Most High, which shall take from thee sensual pleasure in conceiving; and the fruit of Thy conception shall be delectable to Almighty God, pleasing to the angels, sweet to thee, and to our salvation. Much joy to thee, O most pure Virgin, for so great a fulness, so happy a shadow, with hope of so sweet a fruit. And since thou hast this day found so great grace with the Holy Ghost, beseech Him to come anew upon me, and with His power to overshadow me; that, being seated under His loving protection, I may taste the sweet fruit of His divine presence. Amen.

2. Hence, I must gather that as, for the Virgin to conceive the Son of God, it was necessary that the Holy Ghost should come upon her from heaven, to accomplish this work; and that the power of the Most High should overshadow her ; so likewise that I may conceive in my soul the spirit of " salvation," (11) by which to become the adopted son of Almighty God, it is necessary that the Holy Ghost inspire me, and that the power and omnipotence of God overshadow me, tempering the heat of my sensual concupiscences, and protecting me in all temptations and dangers, and in this faith I am to cry to heaven, saying—

<hr>

(10) Cant. ii. 3.
(11) Is. xxvi. 8.   Ex. Fulgentio lib. de Incarnatione Cap. 20.

Colloquy.—O most Holy Spirit, come from on high to my poor soul; sow in it the seed of Thy divine inspiration, that it may conceive within itself the spirit of salvation. O power of the Most High, "protect me under the shadow of Thy wings:" (12) cover me with them in the day of temptation, that the legions of hell may prevail not against me, and that I lose not, through my own weakness, what Thou hast begun in me by Thy grace. Amen.

POINT IV.

To what had been said the angel added: "And behold thy cousin Elizabeth; she also hath conceived a son in her old age, and this is the sixth month with her that is called barren, because no word shall be impossible with God." (13)

1. In these words the angel intended three things.

i. The first, to *reveal to* the Blessed Virgin a *thing that would give her much content,* because of the abundance of her charity; whose property is to "rejoice with those that rejoice," and "weep with those that weep." (14) And as the Blessed Virgin was concerned at the barrenness of her cousin, because of the grief that she thereby received, so she rejoiced at the news of her being with child, because of the great joy that it would give her.

ii. The second was, to *confirm his embassage with some sensible token ;* as if he should say, seeing she has conceived that was old and barren, thou mayest well believe that a virgin shall conceive, for with Almighty God nothing is impossible. He can do the one with as great facility as the other. Whereby we see how it is the property of the good spirit, to chastise the incredulous that require a sign or a miracle with an affection of incredulity, as this St. Gabriel himself chastised Zacharias, (15) because he asked

---

(12) Ps. xvi. 8.   Ps. cxxxix. 8.   (13) Luc. i. 36, 37.
(14) Rom. xii. 15.   (15) Luc. i. 20.

a sign to be assured that he should have a son, himself being old, and his wife barren ; whereas, on the other hand, to those that have faith, He gives a sign, although they ask it not, as He did to our Blessed Lady, the Virgin, to cheer and comfort her, and by the way to confirm her more and more in her faith.   Hence I will gather how much it imports constantly to believe matters of faith ; for to believers our Lord gives interiorly greater signs of His truth, (16) which He denies to the incredulous, according to that of the prophet Isaias, " If you will not believe you shall not understand." (17.)

iii. The third was, that the angel intended to show the fundamental reason of all that had been spoken, adding that glorious word, " that no word shall be impossible with God," (18) which is to say, He can do all that He will, and can accomplish all that He promises ; especially those two miraculous things that I have told thee, viz., that the barren and the virgin shall conceive and bring forth.

. Whence I will collect two other things for my spiritual comfort.

i. That by the omnipotence of God our Lord, any soul whatsoever that has been a long time barren of good works, how deep-rooted soever this barrenness be in it, may be altered and become fertile.   And as barren Elizabeth conceived John, which signifies grace, so it may conceive in itself the fruits of grace, and of benediction which are very gracious and pleasing to Almighty God.   And with this hope, I am to cheer and animate myself to obtain this happy fertility, remembering what is said by the prophet Isaias, and the apostle St. Paul : " Rejoice thou barren that bearest not, break forth and cry that thou travailest not, for many are the children of the desolate, like Sarah,

(16) Joan. xv

(17) Is. vii. 9. juxta. Septuag.   (18) Luc. i. 37.

6

more than of her that hath a husband," (19) or is fruitful like Agar.

ii. That as our Blessed Lady, the Virgin, by virtue of the Holy Ghost might conceive, and have a son which should be worth a hundred thousand ; so those who pro- mise and keep virginity, shall conceive spiritual children, which shall be of incomparably greater worth than any carnal, (20) our Lord fulfilling to them that promise, which He made them by the prophet Isaias, (21) as was declared in the first part, and the 20th Meditation.

MEDITATION VIII.

ON THE FINAL ANSWER GIVEN BY THE VIRGIN TO THE ANGEL, CONSENTING TO HIS EMBASSAGE.

POINT I.

The Blessed Virgin having heard all that was spoken to her by the angel, said to him, " Behold the handmaid of the Lord, be it done to me according to thy word." (1)

1. And here I am to consider what a longing desire the angel had, as he expected the answer of the Virgin; and not only the angel, but the Holy Ghost Himself, her spouse, who spoke to her heart that of the Canticles, " Let thy voice sound in my ears, for Thy voice is sweet" (2) and pleasing to me. And He Himself likewise inspired into her the words she should say, *exercising* therein some most excellent *virtues* wherewith she perfectly disposed herself to be the worthy Mother of God.

i. The first was, great *faith*, giving credit to the words

(19) Is. liv. 1.   Gal. iv. 27.   (20) Matt. xix. 29.
(21) Is. lvi, 4.   (1) Luc. i. 38.
. (2) Cant. ii. 1.

of the angel, and believing that she might be a mother, and a virgin, thinking highly of the omnipotency of God.

ii. The second was, profound *humility*, in the midst of that greatness that was offered, calling herself "handmaid of the Lord;" and consequently judging herself unworthy to be His mother, placing herself as much as lay in her, in the lowest place, as is that of the handmaids.

iii. The third was, great *obedience*, and resignation into the hands of Almighty God, offering herself to fulfil what the angel said, and all whatsoever God should command.

2. O most prudent virgin, who has instructed thee to join with such excellency things so far distant? If thou believest that thou art to be the Mother of God, why callest thou thyself His handmaid? And if thou holdest thyself for a handmaid, why dost thou offer thyself to be the mother of God? What has a mother to do with being a handmaid? And how compatible is a belief of such baseness with a belief of such great highness? and so profound a humility, with so exalted a magnanimity?

Colloquy.—O height of the wisdom of Almighty God! O miracle of His omnipotence! Thine, O Lord, are these marvels, and Thou art He that hast knowledge and ability to join together mother and virgin, handmaid and mother, humility and magnanimity, and the faith of all this with human understanding. O heavenly Father, "Thou" that "hast hid these things from the wise and prudent, and hast revealed them to little ones," (3) and therefore "where humility is, there also is wisdom," (4) teach me to choose with humility the lowest place on earth, and to seek with magnanimity the highest in heaven; joining together the nothing that I am of myself, with the much that I may be by Thy grace. Amen.

(3) Matt. xi. 25.

(4) Prov. xi. 2.

POINT II.

As the mysteries which are included in these words of
the Virgin are numerous, it will not be amiss to meditate
each one by itself, considering the spirit contained in it
for our profit.

" ECCE"—" BEHOLD."

This word " Ecce," " Behold," the Scripture uses to
denote or signify some great thing worthy of much consideration; and the angel used it in the beginning of this
embassy, saying, " Ecce concipies," " Behold, thou shalt
conceive" a son.   And therefore also would the most
holy Virgin use the same in her answer, saying, " Ecce
ancilla Domini," " Behold the handmaid of the Lord,"
for as the angel had a great desire that our Blessed
Lady the Virgin should consider the greatness which
he promised her from Almighty God ; so the *virgin*
had as great a desire that the angel should consider
how mean and lowly a handmaid she was of herself,
and what fervent longings she had to obey whatsoever God
commanded her.   For the humble, when the gifts they
have of God are published, desire very earnestly that the
miseries should be known, which they have of themselves,
that those gifts be not attributed to their own merits, but
to the bounty of Him that gave them, to whom they desire
to be very thankful, and therefore very obedient.

"THE HANDMAID OF THE LORD."

In this word, " Handmaid of the Lord," the Blessed
Virgin declared what low esteem she had always *had of
herself*, ever since she had the use of reason.

1. And although the name of servant or bondman, when it
signifies to serve Almighty God with a "spirit" of "fear," (5)

(5) Gal. iv.   Rom. viii.

and as it were by force, is dispraised in holy Scripture ; yet when servant is joined with love, it is a most glorious name. For the slave is not his own, but his lord's ; he has not liberty to do what he likes, but must do what his lord commands him. He serves him not for salary or wages, but because he is obliged to this service. He labours not for himself, but for his lord, nor does he serve only him in person, but also all those of his house and family, in which he holds the lowest place, and has always that which is worst and meanest given to him.

2. All this the Blessed Virgin our Lady, imagined in herself, when she called herself "the handmaid of the Lord."

i. For she held not herself to be her own, but a thing belonging to God our Lord, and in His possession; as well because He created her, as also because she had wholly dedicated herself to His perpetual service, saying in her heart those words which the prophet Isaias reports of the righteous : He "shall say, I am the Lord's," and another shall subscribe with his hand, to the Lord, and surname himself by the name of Israel." (6) And as the faithful bondman never flies from his master, nor is at any time absent, nor will serve any other master, because " no man can" at once " serve two masters," (7) so the Blessed Virgin never separated herself one moment from the service of God, neither served she any other Lord but God, fulfilling most perfectly that precept, " The Lord thy God shalt thou adore, and Him only shalt thou serve." (8)

ii. In all other things, also, she did not what she list, but what Almighty God commanded, for she had no will of her own, nor liberty of flesh, but was so *fastened to the*

<hr>

(6) Is. xliv. 5.
(7) Matt. vi. 24.   (8) Matt. iv. 10. Deut. vi. 13.

will of our Lord, as if she had no liberty to depart therefrom, esteeming herself as a handmaid, who has her "eyes" always "on the hands of her" Lord, (9) suffering herself to be managed by Him, and to be moved by every beck that He should make.

iii. Besides this, she served not God for salary, or day wages, intending principally any reward ; but because as *His handmaid* she was obliged to it, and took delight in pleasing her Lord. And therefore she had settled in her heart that verity, which afterwards our Saviour Christ taught His disciples : " *When you shall have done all these things that are commanded you, say, we are unprofitable servants ; we have done that which we ought to do.*" (10)

iv. And hence it proceeded, that all whatsoever she did, or laboured to do, she attributed it not to herself, but *to her Lord* : for although it is true that the merit and reward was for her ; yet she attributed all to the glory of God, and not to her own, saying that of the Canticles " *All fruits, the new and the old, my beloved, I have kept for Thee.*" (11) That is, all the works of my life, present and passed, I will that they be to Thy honour and glory, for I will neither live nor die to myself, but *to Thee*, because *I am Thine*. (12)

Finally, the Blessed Virgin esteemed herself not only as the handmaid of our Lord to serve Him, but also to serve all those of His house and family; and therefore she dedicated herself to the service of her parents when she was in the Temple, and of her husband when she was in his company. And much better than Abigail might she have said, what she said to David : " Behold let Thy servant be handmaid, to wash the feet of the servants of my Lord." (13) And with this spirit of humility, she

(9) Ps. cxxii. 2. (10) Luc. xvii. 10. (11) Cant. vii. 13.
(12) Rom. xiv. 7, 8. (13) 1 Reg. xxv. 41.

always chose for herself the lowest place in *the house* of God, and the worst and most contemptible in the world, as hereafter we shall see.

3. All these inward feelings had the Blessed Virgin when she called herself "the handmaid of" our "Lord," and she esteemed very highly this title; for she knew how pleasing it was to Almighty God, who used to call by the same name of "servant," (14) the Messiah His Son, as He was man, and He Himself esteemed it highly, as appears by what is delivered by the prophets.   And if I desire to be devoted to our Blessed Lady, I am highly to esteem myself for this name, and for the spirit which she includes in the saidthings, saying to God with David,

Colloquy.—"O Lord, I am Thy servant : I am Thy servant, and the son of Thy handmaid; for Thou hast broken my bonds.   I will sacrifice to Thee the sacrifice of praise, and I will call upon the name of the Lord." (15)   O God of my soul, I highly esteem my lot in being Thy servant, because Thou createdst me ; and again for being Thy servant, because Thou redeemedst me.   I am the son of Thy handmaid, because by inheritance it falls to my lot to be Thy slave ; but especially I hold myself for the son of Thy handmaid, the Blessed Virgin Thy Mother, by whose merits I beseech Thee to loose the chains of my sins and passions, that being free from this evil bondage, I may serve Thee with liberty of spirit, and may praise and glorify Thy holy name world without end. Amen.

"BE IT DONE TO ME."

It was not without a mystery, that the Blessed Virgin said not to the angel, I will do what thou sayest ; but this word, " Fiat"—" Be it done"—which God our Lord used when He created the world, saying, " Be light made."(16)

---

(14) Is. xli. 8, 9; xliv. 1, 21.   Zach. iii. 8.   [(15) Ps. cxv. 16.
(16) Gen. i. 3.

1. For the Virgin understood that the Incarnation was as well a *work of the omnipotence of God* as the creation of the world ; and that with one " Fiat" of His omnipotence it might be done, though on her part there was no merit of so glorious a thing. Although she accepted it, saying " Fiat," as who should say, " Although there were no need of my consent, because I am the handmaid of Almighty God, and He may do with His handmaid what He will ; and although being but handmaid, I merited not that this thing should be done to me, yet notwithstanding since God will have it so, ' Fiat,' be it done ; for I am pleased with all whatsoever shall please Him." By which we see the sovereign obedience and resignation of the Virgin, founded upon the knowledge of her own, as being nothing, offering herself not to resist the Fiat of Almighty God, as the insensible creatures resist it not, or as that which is nothing resists not, when God says, " Be it done."

2. But that we may the better understand the height of this consenting, we are to consider that she not only fixed her eyes upon the greatness, foretold her by the angel, but also upon *the terrible afflictions* which that Son who was offered to her, was to suffer, which she knew well by the sacred Scriptures, as also that a very great share of them was to light upon His mother ; and yet notwithstanding she accepted this dignity of a mother, with the most heavy charge of that office, and hereupon she called herself " a handmaid," as one that accepted it, not to be served as a lady, but to serve and suffer as a handmaid.

Colloquy.—I thank thee, most sacred Virgin, for this generous offer that thou makest with such great magnanimity of heart. Let the angels in heaven praise thee, and the righteous on the earth, as likewise those that were in Limbo expecting Him. And seeing that all have a share in thy consent, beseech thy Son to grant me such a resignation of myself unto His holy will, that I may resist nothing whatsoever He commands me, nor any affliction whatsoever that He shall send me; but that to all, my reply may be, "*fiat*." "It is the Lord; let Him do what is good in His sight." (17)   Amen.

"ACCORDING TO THY WORD."

It is likewise not without a great mystery, that the Blessed Virgin said not to the angel "Be it done to me as God commandeth or willeth," but "Be it done according to thy word," since in this she exhibited the perfection of her *faith* and *obedience*.

For perfect faith believes whatsoever Almighty God reveals by Himself, or by the means of others: and perfect obedience obeys God in whatsoever He commands, either by Himself, or by the means of His ministers; for "he that heareth" them "heareth" (18) Christ. Although I may likewise contemplate that the Blessed Virgin in this point exalted herself above herself, and above all the angels, and above all whatsoever is created; directing her answer, not so much to the ambassador, as to Almighty God Himself, who sent the embassy, saying to the eternal Father,

Colloquy.—Behold here the handmaid of Thee, O Lord. Be it done to me according to Thy word; not only according to what Thou commandest by this word which the angel delivereth, but according to the desire of that word and speech which Thou speakest within Thyself in Thy eternity, which is Thy only Son, who also desires to be mine. And since it is His good pleasure, so let it be as He commands.

In imitation of the Blessed Virgin, I will also often-

(17) 1 Reg. iii. 18.   (18) Luc. x. 16.

times say to Almighty God with the same understanding that she had, "Behold me here Thy slave, O Lord: be it done to me according to Thy word ; for I am ready to put in practice all, whatsoever shall be ordained me by Thy divine word."

POINT III.

The angel having heard the answer of the blessed Virgin returned to heaven ; "*Et discessit Angelus ab ea.*" "*And the angel departed from her.*" (19)   In this departure I am to consider.

1. *How joyful* and contented the angel was with the Virgin's answer, being full of admiration of her sovereign prudence and virtue, and full of joy for having fulfilled what Almighty God gave him in charge; for these two things are matter of special joy to the angels, and to the righteous : for there is no joy equal to the accomplishing His good "will," and seeing it accomplished by others : for therein, according to that of the prophet David, consists our "life." (20)

2. I am to consider how the angel *departed presently to heaven* without staying any moment more : to give us to understand, that the angels having fulfilled that ministry which Almighty God charged them with on earth, make no tarrying there, but forthwith return to their centre which is heaven : instructing us, especially such as are religious, that having fulfilled our ministries with our neighbours, we make no causeless tarrying among them, but that, forthwith, we retire to our oratory, which is our heaven, to repose with Almighty God.

3. And as we after our human fashion imagine, that the angel entering into heaven, *gave account to Almighty God of his embassy*, and presented himself ready to serve

(19) Luc. i. 38.　　　　　　　(20) Ps. xxix. 6.

again in whatsoever he should be commanded : so we having fulfilled our obligations, are to present ourselves before Almighty God, ready to accomplish whatsoever He shall impose on us anew, or give us in charge according to that of holy Job: "Canst thou send lightnings, and will they go, and will they return and say to thee: Here we are?" (21)

Colloquy.—O eternal, and omnipotent King, make me like one of these celestial lightnings resplendent with Thy light, inflamed with the fire of Thy love, quick in obeying thy holy will, and thankful in returning to give Thee thanks for the accomplishment thereof.

4. I may likewise piously contemplate, how the angel Gabriel being entered into heaven, *related to his companions the excellent humility, wisdom, and sanctity of the Blessed Virgin;* all of them being full of alacrity, that Almighty God had found upon earth a person that was as pleasing, and acceptable to Him, as the inhabitants of heaven: for it is the property of the saints to rejoice, that there are many others, that supply what they want in loving, and serving with great fervour our Lord God, to whom be honour, and glory, world without end.   Amen.

MEDITATION IX.

OF THE EXECUTION OF THE INCARNATION: AND OF SOME OF ITS CIRCUMSTANCES AS CONCERNING THE BODY OF OUR LORD CHRIST.

POINT I.

First, I am to consider, how the Blessed Virgin having given her consent,—in the very same instant, the Holy Ghost formed of her purest blood, a most perfect body,

(21) Job xxxviii. 35.

and created a most excellent reasonable soul, (1) and joined them together with the Person of the eternal Word; God being made man, and man God, (2) and *God being espoused with human nature*, in that virgin chamber: and the Virgin herself exalted to the dignity of Mother of God.

1. In this action we are to ponder *the content of all those persons that are concerned herein;* principally the contentment of the most blessed Trinity to see His promise fulfilled, and to have made this demonstration of His omnipotence, and of His bounty, and charity.

i. Oh how joyful was the eternal Father, for having given us His Son; and with what infinite love He loved this His Son, true God and man ! And how pleased He was in Him above all that was created ! For, as St. Thomas sayeth, Almighty God much more loves Christ alone, than all the angels, and men, and than all creatures together : since He would give " him a name which is above all names," (3) which is the name, and being of Almighty God: and therefore He was much more pleased, and more rejoiced to behold Him, than to behold all the rest of the beings created, or to be created. With this consideration I will rejoice at this joy of the Father, and will be thankful to Him for the favour He has done us: beseeching Him, that since He so much loves this Son, for His sake He will also love me, and grant me His holy love.

Colloquy.—O God, " our protector, behold and look upon the face of Thy Christ," (4) in whom Thou art so much pleased; and since He made Himself like to us in our nature, make us like to Him in His grace. Amen.

ii. Then will I ponder what *contentment the eternal*

(1) S. Th. 3. p. q xxxii. et **xxxiii.**   (2) Joan. i. 14,
(3) 1. p. q. xx. art 4. ad 1. 3. Phil. ii. 9.   (4) Ps. lxxxiii. 10.

Word had to see Himself made man, and with what hearty love He loved that His most sacred humanity, uniting it to Himself, with a purpose never to forsake what once He had taken upon Him: and in respect thereof He desired to embrace, and to put into His bowels all mankind, as His kindred. And therefore I may confidently say unto Him, as Ruth said to Booz : " Spread thy coverlet over thy servant, for thou art a near kinsman." (5)

Colloquy.—O divine Word, true Booz, and fortitude of the Father, seeing Thou hast made Thyself of the kindred of men, spread upon me the cloak of Thy divine protection ; unite me to Thee in faith and charity, and give me the " kiss of peace " with the kiss of Thy " mouth," (6) and embrace me with the " right hand " (7) of Thy omnipotence, that nothing created may be able to separate me from Thy friendship. Amen.

iii. We may likewise contemplate the contentment *of the Holy Ghost*, for having accomplished this work, which is attributed to Him, because goodness and love are proper to this person, and it seems that then He satisfied fully His desire, when He had performed the most supreme work of love that He could. Upon which the prophet Isaias said : And there shall come forth a rod out of the root of Jesse, and a flower shall rise up out of his root. And the Spirit of the Lord shall rest upon Him" (8) For in this eternal Word Incarnate, figured by this rod, and flower of Jesse, the Holy Spirit found rest and perpetual joy, as in the thing that He most loved.

iv. Hence I will pass on to consider the joy of that *most sacred humanity*, when it saw itself exalted to such a greatness; and that from the depth of nothing, it had mounted to the height of the divine essence, saying with

(5) Ruth iii. 9.   (6) Cant. i. 1.   (7) Cant. ii. 6.   (8) Is. xi. 1.

great joy that of the spouse in the Canticles: "I have found Him whom my soul loveth: I held Him: and I will not let Him go." (9)

Colloquy.—O most sacred humanity, I rejoice for Thy joy, and for Thy good fortune; and since Thou art so content with Thy beloved, give us part of that love which Thou hast, that with Thee we also may enjoy it.

v. Then will I ponder the content of *the most Blessed Virgin* in that instant of the Incarnation: for God our Lord gave to her an extraordinary light, whereby she saw the manner how this mystery was wrought in her womb; for when she saw Almighty God made man within herself; and saw herself a Virgin, and a mother, and the Mother of such a Son, she was full of unspeakable joy. Oh what gratitude, what praise, and thanksgiving, and what exultations had she! Oh what a fulness of good did she receive in that moment! For as this visible Sun, as soon as it was created in this world, filled it with its light, and communicated to it its heat, and influences: so the Sun of righteousness Christ Jesus our Lord, in that very instant that He was conceived, and formed in the abbreviated world of His Blessed Mother, filled her with exceeding great light, and celestial heat, with the influences of life everlasting. So that she, who before was "full of grace," was then much more replenished, and heaped up with all graces, and with inestimable joy in the possession of them. (10)

Colloquy.—O most sacred Virgin, I congratulate thee for being the Mother of Almighty God made man. And, since thou likewise beginnest to be the mother of us men, distribute to us that light and

(9) Cant. iii. 4.　　(10) S. Th. 3. p. q. xxvii. art. 5. ad. 2.

joy which were given thee, that we may know, love, and serve Him whom thou hast conceived.   Amen.

2. Lastly, I will ponder the great *reason that we men have to be contented*, to see ourselves of kindred with Almighty God, and exalted to so high a dignity: for which I am to give Him humble thanks, and beseech the holy angels to be therefore thankful to Him, and to get a new, noble, and generous courage, resolving, as St. Leo the Pope says, to live as the kinsman of so great a king, without admitting any thing that may be contrary to this exalted state. (11)

POINT II.

Secondly, I am to consider the circumstances of this Incarnation, as concerns *the body of this being—God and man*, beholding it as a body *mortal and passible;* and the causes thereof.   For according to that which naturally was due to the Person of our Lord Jesus Christ, His body was not to be mortal, nor passible for two causes.

1. Because Christ our Lord was absolutely *free from original sin*, not by privilege, but by *right*, for being the natural Son of God, and for having been conceived not by the work of man, but by the power of the Holy Ghost. And consequently the punishment of mortality, and passibility due to original sin touched not Him: and yet notwithstanding this our Lord, to demonstrate His humility, and charity, was willing to leave the sin, and take the punishment; and without being a sinner, to take, as St. Paul said, sinful flesh, (12) subject to all the penalties, and miseries of sinners, to pay with His death, and with His pains our sins.

Colloquy.—O blessed be such an immense charity, from which sprung so profound a humility! Oh what

(11) Serm. 1. de Nativit.   (12) Rom. viii. 3.

reason have I to confound myself for my pride, since that, contrary to this our Lord, I would have the sin, but not the punishment. I am a sinner, and yet would not suffer the penalties due to sinners. Animate thyself, O my soul, to imitate this example of humility. And, seeing thou hast subjected thyself to sin, be content to suffer the punishment that thy sin doth deserve.

2. The second cause why the body of our Lord Christ was not to be mortal, is for that *His soul was glorious*, and blessed: and so by right His body was to have the four endowments of glory, which He now hath in heaven, which are—clarity, i-mpassibility, subtility, and agility: yet notwithstanding this our most loving Lord was willing to perform this new miracle, and to renounce His right, depriving Himself of the endowments of glory, and investing Himself with mortality, and with ignominy, with all the rest of our miseries, that His body, as He Himself said, might be fit to be a " sacrifice and oblation'' for our sins upon the altar of the cross. (13)

Colloquy.—Let the angels bless Thee, O Lord, and let my soul praise Thee for ever; for the charity that Thou hast shewed in performing miracles to be able to die, and in renouncing all that which might have excused Thee from suffering. Oh, how I am confounded and ashamed, beholding how carefully I fly from afflictions, desiring sometimes miracles to deliver me from them. I desire henceforth rather to renounce all that shall be honourable and delicate; to imitate Thee in suffering, ignominy, and torment; and, since Thou hast given me such a desire, give me also grace to fulfil it. Amen.

POINT. III.

Thirdly, I will consider *the causes why our Lord God*

(13) Ps. xxxix. 7. Heb. x. 5.

was willing to become a babe, (14) and to be conceived in the womb of a woman, when He might have taken the body of a perfect man, as He formed the body of Adam. The causes thereof, omitting those which were enumerated in the third meditation, were these:—

1. "To make Himself," as the apostle says, "in all things like unto men "His brethren," (15) and to oblige them hereby to love Him more tenderly.

Colloquy.—O most loving God, who as a mother bearest us "in" Thy "womb," (16) who has made Thee a babe inclosed in the womb of Thy mother? Thy love doubtless is the cause of this, and the great desire Thou hast to be loved; for that if we should not love Thee for the greatness that Thou shewest, as Thou art Almighty God, yet we should love Thee for the tenderness Thou shewest towards us, as Thou art a babe.

2. The second cause was, *to give us an example of humility*, and to endear this virtue to us, when with the eyes of faith we should see the God of Majesty made a little babe ; and see Him whom heaven and earth cannot contain, contained in the narrow bounds of the womb of a woman. And so comparing the greatness of Almighty God with this littleness, I will break into affections of admiration and imitation, saying to this our Lord:

Colloquy.—O divine Word, who, as Thou art God, art in the immense bosom of Thy Father, and, as Thou art man, inclosedst Thyself in the narrow bosom of Thy mother, clear the eyes of my soul, that, considering the greatness Thou hast in the one bosom, and the littleness Thou hast in the other, filled with wonder at both, I may adore Thy greatness with trembling, and embrace Thy littleness with humility.

(14) Isa. ix. 6.
(15) Heb. ii. 17.   (16) Isa. xlvi. 30.

7

3. The third cause was, to enter into the world, *giving us an example of patience and most perfect mortification,* suffering for nine months a horrid, obscure, and narrow prison, such as the " womb" (17) of a woman, in which this babe was straitened and pressed, not being able to move Himself from one side to another, nor to stir hand or foot, nor to see, nor to hear, nor smell, nor to taste anything. Of which although other babes have no feeling, because they have not the use of reason, yet this most blessed babe having the most perfect use of it, had an acute feeling, and yet with a good will suffered this imprisonment, and this mortification of senses, to free us from the everlasting prison, and to satisfy for the liberty and overmuch laxity of Eve, who going to recreate herself in paradise, beheld the fruit of the tree, and contrary to God's commandment, tasted thereof. And so likewise to satisfy for the liberties and indulgence of my senses, and to animate me by His example to mortify them, and to suffer any shutting up, or straitness whatsoever in my chamber, or bed, or in whatsoever else pertaineth to the pampering of my flesh.

Colloquy.—I humbly thank Thee, O divine Word Incarnate, for this entrance Thou hast made into the world, suffering so strait a gaol, such a horrible prison, and so long and tedious a mortification of Thy flesh, by which I humbly beseech Thee to deliver me from the eternal prison of hell, and from the troublesome gaol of my vices, aiding me to mortify my passions, and with the spirit to restrain the inordinate use of my senses. Amen.

(17) Ecclesia in Hymno—" Te Deum"—Non horruisti Virginis uterum.

MEDITATION X.

OF THE EXCELLENCY OF THE MOST HOLY SOUL OP OUR SAVIOUR CHRIST, AND OF
THE HEROIC ACTS OF VIRTUE THAT HE EXERCISED IN THE FIRST INSTANT OF
THE INCARNATION. (I)

POINT I.

1. I am to consider *the graces and excellencies of our
Saviour Christ*, as He was man, His soul being united
with the Deity, which were immense : for as His fore-
runner said to Him, "God gave Him not His spirit by
measure, for the Father loveth the Son, and hath given all
things into his hand," (2) that is to say, to the saints He
gives them His spirit by measure, and the graces of the
Holy Ghost, as St. Paul says, are divided among them, (3)
some being given to some, and others to others; but to
our Saviour Christ His Father gave His spirit without
measure, for He gave Him these graces all at once, not
only for Himself, but with power to distribute them to
others, giving to every one his measure; (4) for He loveth
Him as His Only begotten Son with a most singular love,
and therefore He communicated to Him such fulness of
wisdom and grace as was fitting for the glory of such a
Son; whereupon His Evangelist St. John said of Him,
" We saw His glory, the glory as it were of the Only begotten of the Father, full of grace and truth."(5) Besides
this, the eternal Word having communicated to this most
blessed soul the principal thing which He had, which was
His own personal essence, it belonged to His honour to

(1) S. Th. 3. p. q. xxxiv. et etiam q. vii. cum seq.　(2) !Joan. iii. 34.
(3) 1 Cor. xii. 11.　　(4) Ephes. iv. 7.　　(5) Joan. i. 14.　.

communicate likewise to it the immensity of those graces and gifts suitable to Him who had so noble a being.

2. These graces we may reduce to seven heads.

i. The first was, immense *purity*, in such sort that He neither sinned, (6) nor could sin, nor err, nor be deceived, nor have any imperfection that might be repugnant to this purity and cleanness of heart; for He was " the Lamb of God," (7) not the earthly but the heavenly Lamb, the most innocent Lamb without any blot, whose coming was to take away the sins of the world, and so by right to free Himself from them all.

ii. The second is, grace of *sanctity*, which incomparably exceeded that of men and angels altogether. And in this measure He had charity, and humility, and obedience, and the rest of the virtues in such a manner, that by excellence He is called " the Holy of holies," (8) in whom the Holy Spirit reposed, (9) filling Him with His seven gifts with an immense plenitude.

iii. The third was, grace consummated, which is *blessedness*, and the beatific vision, for from that very first instant His soul saw the divine essence with greater clearness than all the Blessed together, and in this proportion it loved Almighty God, and rejoiced with unspeakable joy, for which it is said of Him,—" God anointed Thee with the oil of gladness above Thy fellows." (10)

iv. From hence proceeded the fourth grace, which comprehendeth the treasures of the *wisdom and knowledge* of Almighty God, (11) not divided, but altogether, as St. Paul says, that He might know all things created, past, present, and to come, and that nothing might be hidden from Him, as He was to be the judge of all things, to reward the good, and to chastise the wicked.

(6) 1 Pet. ii. 22.   (7) Isa. i. 36.   (8) Dan. ix. 24.

(9) Isa. xi. 2.   (10) Ps. xliv. 8.   (11) Coloss. ii. 3.

v. The fifth is, *the power of working miracles*, without any limitation, merely by His own will, by which He had power to give life to the dead, to heal all that were sick, to cast out devils out of possessed bodies, to command the winds and the sea, and all the elements, subjecting them to His command. (12)

vi. The sixth is, the power of *pardoning sins*, (13) converting sinners, changing their hearts, ordaining sacraments and sacrifices, and distributing among men graces and supernatural gifts.

vii. The seventh is the grace of *being head*, (14) as well of the Church militant as triumphant, (15) of men and of angels, being superior to all, and the fountain of all the celestial blessings, and of all the gifts and graces (16) that proceed from the Father of light, for the good of the mystical body, of which Christ is the head.

2. Hence it is that this our Lord was the first and principal of all the predestinated, for whose sake God also predestinated others, that He might have many companions in glory, but especially that He might be, as the apostle St. Paul says "the first-born among many brethren," (17) like and conformable to Him in the gifts of graces as they were in nature, and so He entered first before all men into this glory, and saw the divine essence, and opened the gates of heaven, that the rest might enter in to behold it.

3. Considering these seven kinds of graces that our Saviour Christ has, and every one of them, I must collect from them several affections, sometimes blessing and praying the eternal Father for the gifts He gave to His Son, as He was man, sometimes rejoicing at the benefits which

(12) Luc. iv. 14, 32, 36, 39.   (13) Matt. ix. 6. et ultim. 18.
, (14) Coloss. ii. 10.   (15) Ephes. i. 22.   (16) Jac. i. 17.
(17) Rom. viii. 29.

this our Lord has, congratulating Him therein,—and sometimes beseeching Him to impart to me something of what He has, for "of His fulness all we have received," (18) and therefore with great love I may say unto Him :—

Colloquy.—O Son of the living God, I rejoice to see Thee "so beautiful above all the sons of men," (19) "white and ruddy, chosen out of thousands." (20) O living and corner stone, how beautiful art Thou with these "seven eyes" (21) of unspeakable splendour, put into Thee by the hand of Thy Father! O Son of man, how well do those "seven stars" (22) become Thee, given Thee for Thy glory, and to impart their light to the whole world. O Word made flesh, "full of grace and truth," (23) since from Thy fulness men receive grace according to their necessities, fill my soul with this grace, that thereby I may be thankful unto Thee, and may merit the reward of Thy glory. Amen.

POINT II.

Secondly, I am to consider the heroic *acts of virtue* which this most sanctified soul of our Saviour Christ exercised in the first instant *towards God our Lord.*

1. For as it clearly beheld the Divine essence with that clearness that has been spoken of, and on the other side beheld the innumerable benefits which without any merits of its own it had graciously received, at the instant very forcibly budded out four excellent affections, like the four rivers that sprung from paradise, that is to say,—i. a most fervent *love of Almighty God.*—ii. a most grateful *thankfulness* for so great benefits.—iii. a most profound *humiliation* in His presence, considering the nothing she had of herself.—iv. a most ready *offer to obey Him* in all that might be His pleasure, desiring that occasion might be

<hr>

(18) Joan. i. 16.   (19) Ps. xliv. 3.   (20) Cant. v. 10.
(21) Zach. iii. 9.   (22) Apoc. i. 16.   (23) Joan. i. 14.

offered her actually to make demonstration of it.   O what sweet colloquies had then this blessed soul with the most Holy Trinity, sometimes with the Father, that united it to His Son, sometimes with the Son, that had it united to Himself, and sometimes with the Holy Ghost, the worker of this union, giving them with the four affections before said, a celestial music of four voices, the eternal Word to whom it was united, as a master of a chapel guiding it therein.

Colloquy.—O divine Word, give to my soul some part of that light which Thou gavest unto Thine, and unite Thyself therewith with the union of charity, that it may make Thee such music as this.   Incline my heart to the lowest with humility : exalt it to the highest with thanksgiving : draw it out at length in spirit with love ; and cause it to act in all things with promptness of obedience, that it may always glorify Thee, and accomplish Thy holy will.   Amen.

2. These four affections I am to exercise in this consideration, pondering with the light of faith the infinite bounty of Almighty God, and the multitude of benefits that He has done me, without any merit of mine.

POINT III.

Thirdly, I will consider the most excellent acts of virtue which our Lord Christ exercised *towards His neighbours.*

1. For first He beheld the sins of men, and the *great injuries* they *did to Almighty God.*

i. For the Devil possessed the world, and hell was peopled with souls; and all this caused Him terrible pain, and grief, partly to see the Father injured whom He so much loved, and whose glory He so much desired; partly to see how men, His brethren, according to human nature, were cast away and destroyed.   And this interior grief was the greatest that ever was or will be in this life, there being in one and the same soul, extreme joy from the view of Almighty God, and extreme sorrow from the view of our sins.

Colloquy.—O Word Incarnate, what a sorrow is this which possesses Thee! If it be an importunate thing to join music with lamentation, (24) why joinest Thou so great joy with so great sorrow? Hardly hadst Thou entered into the womb of Thy mother but the zeal of the house of God had eaten Thee up. (25) Cause, O Lord, that the like zeal may eat up me, tormenting myself with sorrow for having offended Thee, and consuming in me all that may be any occasion to offend Thee. Amen.

ii. Hence I will collect *how great an evil mortal sin is,* seeing that the sin of other men was sufficient to cause such extreme sorrow in a soul so full of extreme joy. And is there not much more reason that I should be very sorrowful for my own sins, since Christ Jesus our Saviour was so sorrowful for them? And He deferred not this sorrow to the end of His life, but had it even in the first instant of it, that I should not defer sorrowing and doing penance for my sins, but should, as soon as I fall into them, be heartily grieved.

2. I will ponder how this our Lord, in that very instant, perceived that it was the will of His Father that He should *be the Redeemer and Mediator of men,* and that He should thus repay the gifts that He had given Him, in loving and redeeming them; and that to this end He had given Him a body mortal and passible, that He might die for them. And in the very instant that He understood this, with a force like that with which He loved the Father, He loved us, and offered Himself to redeem us,

(24) Ecclus. xxii. 6. (25) Ps. lxviii. 9.

and to die for our salvation, being full of joy that an occasion was offered in which He might manifest the love He bore to His Father, and the zeal which He had for His glory, and the good of His brethren. And therefore He spoke to Him that of the psalm: (26) The "sacrifice and oblation" of our elders Thou acceptest not, neither were their holocausts sufficient for the salvation of men, but seeing Thou hast given me a body fit to be sacrificed, I offer myself thereunto with a good will. "Ecce venio, ut faciam voluntatem tuam Deus." (27) "Behold, I come" into the world in this, and in all things, "to do Thy" holy "will," writing "Thy law in the midst of my heart."

3. O how *pleasing to the eternal Father* was this *offer* and will of His Son, since by this, as St. Paul says, (28) "we were all sanctified;" He merited for us grace and sanctification. In thankfulness for this generous will, with which our Saviour Christ offered Himself to be my Redeemer, I will offer to Him a will to serve Him so effectually, that He may dispose me to receive that sanctification which He gained for me ; and, in imitation of Him, I will say :—

Colloquy.—"Ecce venio ut faciam voluntatem tuam Deus." Behold me here, O Lord, ready to accomplish Thy will, and Thy holy law shall be from henceforth evermore in the midst of my heart. This I should have done in the very first instant that I had use of reason, as Thou didst in the very first instant of Thy life. But although I did it not then, I now say, "Nunc cœpi." (29) Now I will begin to serve Thee with a resolution to continue even unto death.

POINT IV.

Finally, the better to know the *greatness of the charity*

(26) Ps. xxxix. 7, 8.   (27) Heb. x. 5. 6.   (28) Heb. x. 10.
(29) Ps. lxxvi. 11.

and obedience of our Saviour Christ in that instant, I must consider :

1. How then the eternal *Father discovered to Him all the afflictions that He was to suffer*, from the time of His Incarnation to His death upon the cross ; saying to Him, " My Son, it is my will that, to redeem men, and to give them an example of all virtue, Thou be born in a poor manger ; Thou be circumcised, and persecuted by Herod and the Jews ; and that Thou be taken, whipped, crowned with thorns, and die upon a cross with great pain and contempt. Therefore, seeing Thou lovest me for my love, and for the good of Thy brethren, accept these afflictions."

1. To this will of the Father, which our Lord Christ calls the " commandment" (30) and precept of His death, He readily answered, *offering Himself with a prompt and ready will to suffer all whatsoever.* And then was fulfilled that saying of St. Paul, that, abandoning the joy of this life, and contemplating the eternal joy of the other, He embraced the cross, not regarding that it was very ignominious. (31) Then, also, with an efficacious will, He drank the bitter chalice of His passion, and was baptized with the baptism (32) of His ignominies and dolours, persevering, as He Himself said, in the bitterness of this drink, and of this baptism, all the days of His life ; until in the end thereof He effectually drank it, accomplishing all that His Father had commanded Him.

2. But His charity and obedience passed yet farther ; for, although that was so much that He was to suffer, yet, not contented with this, with a most generous heart and most ardent thirst, He *offered Himself to suffer much more* if His Father wished it, and it might be needful

(30) Joan x. 18. xiv. 31.   (31) Heb. xii. 2.
(32) Marc. x. 39.

for our good; for if St. Paul, when the prophet Agabus told Him that he was to be bound prisoner in Jerusalem, answered that he was "ready, not only to be bound, but also to die for the name of the Lord Jesus," (33) how much more would our sweet Lord Jesus, when His Father proposed to Him the afflictions of His life and death, immediately answer that He was prepared, not only to suffer those afflictions, but much greater for His love.

3. And, that I may perceive how much I am indebted to this our Lord, I must consider how, in that instant, *He presented to His imagination all mankind,* and myself among them, and offered Himself to suffer all this for every one in particular, and for myself, as if I alone had stood in need of this remedy. So that then was fulfilled that saying of St. Paul, "He that loved me, and delivered Himself for me" (34) to death, offering Himself to it for my love.

Colloquy.—O tender babe, and valourous giant, with what shall I repay the affection with which Thou this day offerest Thyself "to run Thy course," (35) accepting all those afflictions which, in the course of it Thou art to endure? Let the angels praise Thee for the singular favour that Thou hast done to men, and let my soul glorify Thee for the love that Thou didst bear me; for which I offer myself to suffer whatsoever shall happen to me in the course of my life, if Thou favour me with Thy grace, that I may not fail. Amen.

(33) Acts xxi. 13.   (34) Gal. ii. 20.
(35) Ps. xviii. 6.

MEDITATION XI.

OF THE JOURNEY WHICH THE ETERNAL WORD INCARNATE MADE IN HIS MOTHER'S WOMB, TO THE HOUSE OF ZACHARIAS, TO SANCTIFY HIS FORE-RUNNER ST. JOHN THE BAPTIST.

POINT I.

First, I will consider how the Word, made flesh, being yet in the womb of His blessed Mother, with the exceeding great desire He had to save men, presently fixed His eyes upon John, who was in the womb of St. Elizabeth, and was to be His fore-runner. And seeing him to be in original sin, He was grieved at it, and determined with Himself to *free him from that misery*, and *to sanctify him*, taking possession of His office of Redeemer, which was given Him in charge. And for this end He inspired His mother to go visit her cousin, that He might effect this great work. Here I am to consider,—

1. The great desire that our Lord has of our salvation, thanking Him for it, and confounding myself for the little desire that I have of mine.

2. How careful He is of the good of His elected, and how vigilant in exercising His office of Redeemer, since He began it from the womb of His mother, not willing to be idle any moment.

3. I will likewise consider what a grievous evil sin is, and how much our Lord is displeased that His elect should be in sin but for one moment ; since, for this, He inspired His mother so hastily to undertake that journey, to free from sin His chosen John Baptist.

Colloquy.—O divine Word, that madest Thyself man to deliver us from sin, and desiredst to execute this office with such speed, that Thou tookest for Thy surname: " Take away the spoils with speed, quickly take the prey :" (1) as Thy names are not empty, but full, come, Lord, "with speed," to free me from my sins: make haste to sanctify me with Thy grace; robe my heart for Thy service, and take it for the spoil of Thy victory, that from henceforth I may begin fervently to serve Thee.   Amen.

POINT II.

1. I am to consider how our Lord, having power to sanctify the Baptist from the place where He was, would, notwithstanding, *inspire His mother to carry Him to the house of St. Elizabeth*, and there to work this miraculous sanctification, for *causes very wonderful* and profitable for our instruction.

i. To give new demonstrations of His *humility and charity*; for, as these virtues moved Him to come down from heaven, and to come into the world to draw it out of "the darkness and shadow of death," (2) wherein it stood ; so likewise they moved Him to come from Nazareth to visit John, and to draw him out of sin ; the greater coming to visit the lesser, to honour him, and the physician the sick, to cure him.

ii. The second cause was, *that His most blessed mother might have a share in this action*, taking her for the instrument of the first sanctification that He wrought in this world, justifying by her means the child John that was in sin, and replenishing with the Holy Ghost His mother, who was just, that we sinners might understand that, to obtain pardon of our sins, the Blessed Virgin was to be our mediatrix ; and that the righteous might understand that, by her means, they were to obtain the fulness of the Holy Ghost and of His grace, with the virtues and gifts that descend from heaven ; and that, therefore, all

(1) Is. viii. 1.   (2) Luc. i. 79. Beda, ibid.

might endeavour to love and serve her, and to be devout to her.

Colloquy.—O sovereign Virgin, since to-day, together with thy Son, thou takest possession of the office given thee for our benefit, prosecute it this day with me, obtaining for me pardon of my sins, and abundance of spiritual graces.   Amen.

iii. The third cause was, because it is the property of our Saviour Christ, on entering into a soul, *to inspire it to make acts of virtue*, and to move it zealously to aspire to the height of perfection.   Sometimes He inspires it to exercise prayer and contemplation, and the other actions of a contemplative life ; at other times to come out of that retirement, and to exercise the works of the active life with their neighbours.   And so, in the instant that He entered into the womb of the Blessed Virgin, He moved her to go up to the mountainous country of Judea, to exercise noble acts of charity, mercy, and obedience.   He might speak to her heart that of the "Canticles," "Arise, make haste, my beloved, my dove, my beautiful one, and come." (3)   " O fruitful dove, that hast thy nest in the holes of the stone, and in the chink of the wall, contemplating the secrets of my divinity and humanity, and living always under my protection, arise in haste out of this secret place, and get up to the mountains of Judea, that there thou mayest confess, and glorify me with deeds of charity to the good of those souls that I have created."

2. From hence I will collect, how it is likewise the property of our Lord Christ, when He *enters into the righteous by the communion* of the most Blessed Sacrament of the Altar, *to inspire them with the like exercises of virtue*, that they may climb to the perfection, both of the con-

(3) Cant. ii. 10.

templative and active life, inspiring every one with what is most suitable to him. And if I feel not in myself these inspirations when I communicate, it is through my wicked disposition, and through my over much tepidity, by which I make myself unworthy of this favour. For which I ought to humble myself, and beseech Him to shew me His mercy, inspiring me effectually with what may be agreeable to His holy will.

POINT III.

1. Thirdly, I am to consider the *perfect obedience of this sacred Virgin* to *this inspiration*, which the Evangelist takes notice of, saying, " Mary, rising up, went with speed to the mountainous country of Judea."

i. For she *waited for no precept*, nor express order ; but, as soon as she perceived that it was the good pleasure of God that she should visit her cousin, this inspiration was sufficient to make her accede to it. For the obedient Christian fulfils whatsoever he understands to be most conformable to the will of God, and of his superior.

ii. Secondly, she was very *prompt* and punctual, for she deferred not for many days her visitation ; but, with what promptitude she could, she effected it, and went with great haste, through the efficacy of the Spirit, that moved her suddenly to fulfil her obedience ; for divine grace is an enemy of slowness and delay.

iii. Thirdly, she was very *pure* in her intention, proposing to herself only the glory of Almighty God, and the accomplishment of His holy will, without any inferior motives such as are usual in similar visitations ; and she went not, as St. Ambrose says, to the house of Elizabeth through any curiosity or doubt, to ascertain if what the angel had said were true ; (4) but because she was assured

(4) Ex. D. Amb. l. 2. in Lucam.

of it, and would glorify God in beholding the work that He had done.

iv. Fourthly, it was *mixed with much charity*, patience, and humility ; for, without standing upon the dignity that was given her of being the Mother of God, she was pleased to visit one inferior to herself, and to congratulate her for the favour that God had done her. And although the way was long and rough, and she was tender, and unaccustomed to such travel, yet she hesitated not to abandon her retirement, and to go out in public, because such was the good pleasure of our Lord.

v. Lastly, I will meditate on the manner how this, *our Blessed Lady made her journey ;* for she possessed rare and singular *modesty*, not curiously diverting herself to gaze on those that passed by the way; so that if any happened to fix their eyes upon her, they were immediately moved to sanctity and purity. She carried her heart nailed to her Son, whom she bore in her womb, with whom, by the way, she framed sweet colloquies; and with Him went so contented, that she felt not the travelling, nor the poverty, nor the want of that which was necessary.

Colloquy.—O sovereign Virgin, how full art thou of Almighty God, and how delighted to accomplish His will! Oh, how well it befits thee in this way to be the "litter" of the true Solomon, formed with admirable art to carry Him from one part to another. The "silver pillars" are thy virtues, "the seat of gold" thy contemplation, the "going up of purple" thy humility and patience, and that in "the midst," which is thy heart, is adorned with "charity ;" (5) for within thee is God Himself, who is all charity. And, seeing all this was given thee, because of the daughters of Jerusalem, which are weak souls, I beseech thee, O most com-

(5) Cant. iii. 9.

passionate mother, obtain for me another such ornament, that, imitating thy virtues, by soul may be the litter of thy Son, in which He may repose, and by which He may be made known to the whole world. Amen.

MEDITATION XII.

ON THE OCCURRENCES WHICH HAPPENED IN THE BLESSED VIRGIN'S VISITATION OF ST. ELIZABETH.

POINT I.

First, I will consider the *entrance of the Virgin into the house of Elizabeth*, and the great *benefits* that entered in with her.

1. For the Blessed Virgin, as being the most humble, saluted her first; and the Word Incarnate, which was in her womb, took the words of His mother, for an instrument by which to effect wonderful works in the babe that was in the womb of Elizabeth. He cleansed him from original sin, justified him with His grace, filled him with the Holy Ghost, hastened into him the use of reason, made him His prophet; He gave him light and knowledge of the mystery of the Incarnation, and communicated to him such great joy, that he leaped with delight in his mother's womb; manifesting, as well as he could, the content that he took in the coming and visitation of his Lord; and all this was in a moment.

2. In this I must meditate on two things of great consolation :—

i. The first is the omnipotency and liberality of our Saviour, who so suddenly does such great works of His *mere grace*, without any merit of him that receives them, accomplishing in this the saying of the Wise man : " The king that sitteth on the throne of judgment, scattereth away all evil with His look;" (1) for this King of kings, seated on the throne of the Virgin's womb, beheld with the eyes of mercy His forerunner, and with this one view only in a moment, He dissipated all the evil of sin that was in him. Upon which I may build an assured confidence, that He will use mercy towards me, remembering that saying of Ecclesiasticus : " Trust in God, and stay in thy place, for it is easy in the eyes of God to make the poor man rich." (2)

Colloquy.—O omnipotent King, shew towards me Thy omnipotence, delivering me from my evil, and filling me with Thy good, that the greatness of Thy mercies may be discovered in one so unworthy of them. Give to me, as to Thy precursor, remission of my sins, light and knowledge of Thy Incarnation, and spiritual alacrity in Thy service. Amen.

ii. The second thing to be considered is the *efficacy of the word of the Blessed Virgin*, by being the Mother of Almighty God; and how much she may be able to obtain of her son in a moment, since by her means so many benefits together were suddenly heaped upon the Baptist, who was the first fruits of our Saviour Christ, and of His redemption; and He by the mediation of His mother, was willing to ripen this first fruit before his due time, in order to give us confidence that by her intercession we shall be prevented and aided by the mercy of Almighty God. And therefore I must humbly beseech this Sovereign Queen, to use in my behalf her great power, obtaining for me somewhat of that abundance which by her mediation was given to this happy forerunner.

POINT II.

Secondly, I am to consider how *St. Elizabeth* likewise

(1) Prov. xx. 8. (2) Ecclus. xi. 22. 23.

was replenished with the Holy Ghost, Almighty God communicating to her, by means of this salutation, the light and knowledge of this mystery, and the gift of prophecy, by which He wonderfully discovered four effects which these gifts caused in her, in which are resplendent *four properties* of the *interior visitation of our Saviour Christ,* and of the presence of the Holy Ghost, when He replenishes souls with His sacred gifts.

1. First, St. Elizabeth with great affection moved by the Holy Ghost, *broke forth into praises* of Almighty God, and of His blessed Mother, saying with a loud voice : " Blessed art thou among women, and blessed is the fruit of thy womb." As if she had said, " True was that which the angels said to thee, that thou art blessed among women; to which I add, that blessed is also the Son of thy womb : for He being blessed, thou also art blessed, because from Him, as from a fountain, proceed all heavenly benedictions." Hence we may see that it is the property of the Holy Ghost to move us to glorify Christ, and His Mother, with great fervour of spirit, for such praises are very acceptable to Him.

2. Secondly, she greatly *humbled herself* with a profound knowledge of her own *baseness,* and on the other hand with a high sense of the greatness of that blessed one who visited her, saying: "Whence is this to me, that the Mother of my Lord should come to me ?"(3) And then with acts of thanksgiving she confessed the greatness of Almighty God, and published it to one who knew that she was to praise and glorify Him for them, saying to the Virgin : " As soon as the voice of thy salutation sounded in my ears, the infant in my womb leaped for joy." (4) Wherefore I will consider how it is also the property of the Holy Spirit to cause humility, and thanksgiving, in the midst of the

(3) Luc. i. 43.   (4) Luc. i. 44.

favours which He does us, that they may be profitable to us, and that His gifts may be secure, holding ourselves as unworthy of them, and giving thanks to the giver for them. And therefore in imitation of this saint, when our Lord God shall interiorly visit me, or when I am going to receive Him in the most Blessed Sacrament, I will revive in myself these two sentiments of my own baseness, and of His greatness, and beholding whence so great a good comes to me, which is the mere bounty of God Himself, with great astonishment I will say :—

Colloquy.—Whence is this to me that my Lord should come to me ;—to me, so vile a slave, so ungrateful and wretched a sinner? To me does my Lord come, who is a Lord of infinite greatness and majesty, to visit me, and to enter into my poor and contemptible cottage? Whence to me so great a favour? Is it, peradventure, for my services, or merits, or by my nature, or own industry? Oh! blessed be the immense charity of Almighty God, who, merely of His own infinite mercy, vouchsafes to visit so base a creature.

3. Thirdly, St. Elizabeth *confirmed the Blessed Virgin in her faith* and resolution, saying to her : " Blessed art thou that hast believed, because those things shall be accomplished that were spoken unto thee by our Lord." (5) In which words she discovered the sovereign gift of prophecy that she had received, knowing all that appertained to the Virgin, as well the past,—what the angel had said, as the present—of being the Mother of Almighty God, and the accomplishment of that which was to come. By which we see that it is the property of the Holy Spirit to inspire the righteous to make use of His gifts to the benefit of their neighbours, confirming them in faith,

(5) Luc. i. 45.

and in the love of Almighty God. In these four marvellous affections I will endeavour to imitate St. Elizabeth, beseeching her to obtain for me of our Lord grace to the end.

4. And lastly, I will ponder how this day was published the most glorious name of the Virgin, which is "the Mother of God," which she heard with great humility and joy, and with it I am to salute her, and to congratulate her concerning this name, praising Him who gave it her.

POINT III.

In which is meditated the Canticle of the Magnificat.

The third point shall be to consider *what the Virgin answered*, having heard the words of St. Elizabeth, for she likewise was forthwith replenished with a most lofty spirit of prophecy, and composed the sovereign Canticle of Magnificat, concerning which we are to consider :—

1. How the Blessed Virgin having heard such great things in her own praise, directed not her answer to St. Elizabeth, who praised her, as persons are accustomed to do to express their gratitude; but she directed all her words to *God our Lord*, teaching us the manner how we are to converse with men when they praise us, for the best and securest way is to change the conversation, and to speak to God, from whom proceed those gifts, for which we are praised.

2. Secondly, I am to meditate how the Blessed Virgin, who was so brief and so measured in her words, when she spoke with angels and with men, *dilated* herself much more when she spoke to *Almighty God*, recounting His greatness. For the first is prudence and respect, but the second is excess of love and thankfulness, according to that of the Wise man : "Blessing the Lord, exalt Him as much as you can, for He is above all praise." (6)

(6) Ecclus. xliii. 33.

3. And as he who is replenished with God only speaks of God, and excites his affections to magnify and glorify Him in all things that he is able, for "of the abundance of the heart the mouth speaketh;" (7) so our Blessed Lady the Virgin, as she was replenished with God, uttered with her mouth this sovereign canticle, full of affections of Almighty God; which canticle has ten verses, and is as it were an instrument or harp "of ten strings," (8) like to those which David commands us to touch to glorify Almighty God: and therefore it will not be amiss to meditate all her words, that we may know how spiritually to rehearse them to the honour of the Virgin, joining to every word or verse some holy affection, or joy, for the virtues of this our Lady, with the petition and colloquy belonging to it.

"MY SOUL DOTH MAGNIFY THE LORD."

In this first verse the sacred Virgin teaches us the *spirit of* praising Almighty God, consisting in thinking most highly of Him, and magnifying that which is His, in all that is possible, that is, His bounty and mercy, His wisdom and charity, and the excellency of His government; and this not only with our mouths, but with the soul, and all her interior faculties, inviting them with David to "bless the Lord." (9) And she said not, "my soul" *did* "magnify," or *will* "magnify," but "*doth* magnify," to signify that her principal office, and perpetual occupation was, to magnify Almighty God, doing on earth that which the angels do in heaven.

Colloquy.—O that my soul might always "magnify" our Lord! O Lord of infinite greatness, little can I "magnify" Thee with my praises; but, as I

(7) Matt. xii 14.

(8) Ps. xlii. 5.; xci. 4.; cxliii. 9.　　(9) Ps. cii. 1.; ciii. 1, 33.

may, I praise and "magnify" Thee, and confess that Thou art "above all praise." (10) O sovereign Virgin, whose soul always "magnified" our Lord, and, like another David, (11) invited all others to "magnify" Him, obtain for me, that my soul may likewise "magnify" Him, employing herself continually in singing His greatness, world without end.   Amen.

"AND MY SPIRIT HATH REJOICED IN GOD MY SAVIOUR."

In these words the Blessed Virgin discovers the manner of our rejoicing in Almighty God, noting five conditions of this joy to make it pure and perfect.

i. For we are not to place our principal joy and desire in carnal things, but in things *spiritual.*

ii. Nor so much in gifts received, as in the *giver* of the gifts, who is God Himself.

iii. And although we are to rejoice in God, as He is our Creator, yet principally as He is our *Saviour* and sanctifier, for in this sense He is the fountain of spiritual cheerfulness, which is founded upon the salvation of the soul sanctified by God's grace.

iv. And this joy is principally to consist in the *spirit* or superior part of the soul, that it may be the more pure from all that savours and tastes of flesh, as the sensual joy of the body generally does, although sometimes the joy of the spirit redounds likewise to the flesh, according to that of David, "My heart and my flesh rejoiced in the living God." (12)

v. Finally, our spirit is not to rejoice in itself, as if it had those gifts for which it rejoices, through its own merits, but our joy is to be *in God* our Saviour, who gave them to us, and upon whom our joy is to rest, as says the prophet David : " My soul shall rejoice in the Lord, and

(10) Ecclus. xliii. 33.   (11) Ps. xxxiii. 4.
(12) Ps. lxxxiii. 3.; xv. 9.

shall be delighted in His salvation." (13)   Such was the joy of the Blessed Virgin, who at this instant beheld our Saviour, whom she bore in her womb, and wrapt with His exceeding love, she said, " My spirit hath rejoiced in God my Saviour."

Colloquy..—O my soul, exalt Thyself above thy-self in spirit, like the Virgin, and rejoice purely in Christ thy " Saviour," placing in Him thy whole desire.   If thou desirest joy, " Delight in the Lord, and He will give thee the request of thy heart," (14) that " thy joy may be full," (15) and that " your joy no man shall take from you," until at last thou mayest " enter into " the eternal " joy of thy Lord." (16) Amen.

" BECAUSE HE HATH REGARDED THE HUMILITY OF HIS HANDMAID."

In this verse, and in those following, the Blessed Virgin declares ten sovereign benefits; three *special*, and seven *general*, which are the principal causes and motives which she has to magnify God, to rejoice in Him, and to show herself so thankful to Him.

1. The first is because He regarded the " *humility* " and *lowliness* of His handmaid; in which words the Virgin points at *two roots* of the divine benefits.

i. The principal one on the part of God, and the other on our own.   It is on the part of Almighty God that He deigns to regard us with a gracious eye, and to be mind-ful of us, to do us good.   For although it is true that He sees all things, yet He is not said to regard nor make account of those which He leaves in the abyss of nothing, or in the depth of their misery, but of those which He regards, to use His great mercy towards them.

(13) Ps. xxxiv. 9.   (14) Ps. xxxvi. 4.
(15) Joan. xvi. 22, 24.   (16) Matt. xxv. 21, 23.

ii. The root on our part is, the acknowledgment of our lowliness, by which we may dispose ourselves to receive the gifts of His divine liberality.

And so the Blessed Virgin as illuminated by God, joined both these together, magnifying God, because He deigned to regard the humility· of His handmaid. By which words she does not so much confess that she has the virtue of humility, as exercise it; for as one truly humble, she either esteems not herself, or she would have concealed it; but with humility she confesses that she is lowly, base, and contemptible as a slave, or a "handmaid," and that, notwithstanding all this, Almighty God disdained not to regard her, by which she teaches us that the foundation of the praises of God, and of thanksgiving for the benefits He does us, is the acknowledgement of our own baseness and unworthiness, for in this manner there will be no danger of vain self-complacency, as it happened to the proud Pharisee. (17) Rather this lowliness is to be the motive why I should beseech Almighty God to regard me with a merciful eye, and to do me great favours, for He is wont, as David says, "to look down on the low things in heaven and in earth," (18) and to do them great mercies. And this David had experience of, saying to himself : "For Thou hast regarded my humility; Thou hast saved my soul out of distresses." (19)

Colloquy.—O most high God, whose habitation is in the highest heavens, behold the lowliness of this Thy vile slave, and use towards him Thy accustomed mercy, "raising up the needy from the earth, and lifting up the poor out of the dunghill," that "He may place him with princes," (20) and to sanctify him as well as them. Amen.

(17) Luc. xviii. 14.　　(18) Ps. cxii. 6.　　(19) Ps. xxx. 8.
(20) Ps. cxii. 5.

" FOR BEHOLD FROM HENCEFORTH ALL GENERATIONS SHALL CALL ME BLESSED."

2. And this is the *second* motive which the Blessed Virgin had to magnify Almighty God, because from that moment that He beheld her humility, and that He regarded her, *all nations of men* that believed in Christ, as well the present as those to come throughout all ages, *should " call her blessed."* In which the Virgin takes not for the motive of her joy her own praises, but the excellencies which God had given her, upon which they were founded, and the good that should arise from them to all those who should serve and praise her.

O sovereign Virgin, I for my part am willing to fulfil this prophecy of thine, and to be one of those who call thee " blessed." Thou art " blessed," as thy cousin said, because thou didst believe, (21) and thou art " blessed " for bearing our Saviour in thy womb, but much more " blessed" for hearing *His word*, and *keeping* it. (22) Thou art blessed, likewise, with those eight beatitudes preached by thy Son, our Saviour, upon the mountain. Thou art " poor in spirit," and thine " is the kingdom of heaven." Thou art " meek," and dost " possess the land" of the living. Thou didst " mourn" for the sins of the world, and therefore art " comforted." Thou didst " hunger and thirst after justice," and therefore thou art " filled." Thou art " merciful," and hast obtained " mercy." Thou art a " peace maker," and therefore for thy excellency, thou art the *daughter* " of God." Thou art " clean of heart," and now thou art clearly beholding " God." Thou didst " suffer persecution for justice," and now " the Kingdom of heaven" (23) is thine, and thou art the supreme queen of all the inhabitants thereof.

(21) Luc. i. 45.   (22) Luc. xi. 28.   (23) Matt. v. 3.

Colloquy.—O sovereign queen, I rejoice that thou art " blessed," for many reasons. Oh! that all the nations of the world were converted to Thy Son, and might all, with great faith, call thee blessed, that by thy mediation they might all come to be blessed, imitating here on earth thy life, and enjoying afterwards thy glory in heaven. Amen.

Hence I will likewise gather what a great motive it is to rejoice in God, to have an assured hope of being blessed, for which our Saviour Christ said to His disciples, " Rejoice not in this, that spirits, namely, the devils, are subject to you, but rejoice in this, that your names are written in heaven." (24) And St. Paul says that we should " rejoice in hope," (25) to obtain the blessedness which is promised us.

" FOR HE WHO IS MIGHTY HATH DONE GREAT THINGS TO ME, AND HOLY IS HIS NAME."

3. This is the third motive the Blessed Virgin gives us to glorify God, for at this instant she revolved in her memory the *wonderful things* which God had wrought in her, and the great benefits He had done her, from the instant of her conception until then, especially the great miracle of being a virgin and a mother, and that not an ordinary mother, but the Mother of God Himself; wondering at all these things, she praised God for them, attributing them to His omnipotency, and to the holiness of His name, for He wrought them by His omnipotence, and with His holiness He would enact them, that throughout all ages His name might be sanctified and glorified.

And in saying that God " hath done great things to" her, she gives likewise to understand, that He magnified her in those things which magnify men before God, which are

(24) Luc. x. 20.   (25) Rom. xii. 12.

sanctity and celestial gifts; for the Son being great, the Mother was likewise to be magnified, from which it appears, that it is not contrary to humility to acknowledge the gifts of God in ourselves; rather as St. Paul says, "God reveals them by His spirit," (26) that we may be thankful for them, attributing them not to our own merits, but to the power and sanctity of Almighty God, connecting these two attributes, as the four living creatures did which gave glory to God, saying : " Holy, holy, holy, Lord God Almighty, who was, and who is, and who is to come." (27)

"AND HIS MERCY IS FROM GENERATION TO GENERATION, TO THOSE WHO FEAR HIM."

4. This is the fourth motive why the Blessed Virgin magnifies Almighty God, not only for the benefits *received*, but for many others which she *hopes to receive*, and not only for her own benefit, but also for those which all the nations of the world receive, rejoicing that the mercy of Almighty God is continual, infinite, and eternal, and extends itself to all those who serve and fear Him, of whatever nation they may be, for it is peculiar to holy men, when they acknowledge the favours which God has done them, to expect of His mercy that He will do them many others, as St. Paul said : " God hath delivered, and doth deliver, us out of so great dangers, in whom we trust that He will also deliver us." (28) It is also the property of holy persons to think that the Sun of justice rises not upon their houses only, but to conceive highly of His mercy, and that He extends Himself to many others, and throughout all ages, for which they are thankful to Almighty God, and taking the general benefit of all as their own in particular, and rejoicing to have a God so merci-

<hr>

(26) 1 Cor. ii. 10.   (27) Apoc. iv. 8.   (28) 2 Cor. i. 10.

ful, that He denies His mercy to none that fear Him, as David confesses in the 102nd Psalm, (29) in which he does nothing else but glorify God for these two reasons,—namely, of mercy towards himself, and towards the rest of the just.

"HE HATH SHOWED MIGHT IN HIS ARM."

5. The fifth motive to glorify God, is the work of His omnipotence, which He has done by *His own virtue*, and might, without the aid of any other, which the Virgin reviewed in her memory, calling to her remembrance the creation of the world, its preservation, and government, with such great and such admirable providence, the prodigious things that He did, delivering His people out of Egypt, and leading them through the desert into the land of promise, with all the other things that the Scripture reports; and principally she called to mind this work of the Incarnation, in which Almighty God showed His power and the might of His arm. For all these reasons she magnified God, declaring in one word that which David did at large, recounting all these wonderful works of Almighty God very particularly. (30)

Besides, in this verse and the one following, the Virgin not only recounts what God has done, but what He is wont and accustomed to do conformably to His goodness: and therefore she glorifies Him, because with "His arm" He is wont to work powerful deeds, when, and how He will, and with whom He will; and as He did them in times past, He does them at this present, and will do them in time to come. All which may be of great motive to make me rejoice in Almighty God, trusting that He will also do powerful things in me by the might of "His arm."

(29) Ps. cii.   (30) Ps. cxxxv.

" HE HATH SCATTERED THE PROUD IN THE CONCEIT
OF THEIR HEART."

6. The sixth reason to glorify God is, not only the omnipotency which He shews in the works of His *mercy*, but also what He has shewed in the works of His *justice*, chastising the proud, defeating their inventions, and the imaginations of their hearts. This the Virgin revolved in her memory, recording how our Lord God had defeated the plottings of proud Lucifer, who had said: "I will ascend into heaven, I will exalt my throne above the stars of God, and I will be like unto the most High," (31)—as also the plots of those proud ones that would have built the tower of Babel: (32) and the punishments that He inflicted upon Pharaoh, (33) upon Nabuchodonosor (34) and other such proud ones. And for all these reasons she likewise magnified Almighty God, seeing that He is worthy to be praised for them, as did our Saviour Christ, when He said: " I give thanks to Thee, O Father, Lord of heaven, and earth, because Thou hast hid these things from the wise and prudent, and hast revealed them to little ones." (35)

" HE HATH PUT DOWN THE MIGHTY FROM THEIR SEAT, AND HATH
EXALTED THE HUMBLE. HE HATH FILLED THE HUNGRY WITH
GOOD THINGS, AND THE RICH HE HATH SENT AWAY EMPTY."

7. These two verses contain two other motives for praising God, for the *conjunction* He makes of His *mercy* with His *justice*, demonstrating His power in deposing the mighty of this world from their thrones and seats, depriving them of the kingdoms, dignities, and greatness which they held; and in their place exalting and enthroning the lowly and humble. As He threw from the celestial throne the

(31) Is. xiv. 13.   (32) Gen. xi. 5.   (33) Exod. x. and xi.
(34) Dan. iv. 28.   (35) Matt. xi. 25.

proud and arrogant angels, and in their place exalted humble men: and from the throne of this world He cast the proud prince Satan who had tyranized over it, and in his place exalted Christ the master of humility: who being little as a stone, descended from heaven without hands or work of man, overthrew the statue which signified the four monarchies of the world, and by His humility increased till He came to be a great mountain. (36) And this custom He has always observed, as it is said in the book of Job, fulfilling that which is written. That he "that exalteth himself shall be humbled; and he that humbleth himself shall be exalted." (37)

8. And, in like manner, the poor and hungry who are in necessity, "that hunger and thirst after justice," (38) He replenishes with spiritual benefits, fulfilling their desires; and contrariwise, "the rich" who think they have abundance, and that they have no need of others, He "sendeth away empty;" according to that of the prophet David: "The rich have wanted and have suffered hunger; but they that seek the Lord shall not be deprived of any good." (39)

Colloquy.—O my soul, magnify thy Lord for this most noble attribute which He shews in favouring so much the humble and hungry of the earth. O my spirit, rejoice in God thy Saviour, because He "crowneth thee with mercy," and "satisfieth thy desire with good things." (40) Prize thyself for being lowly, hungry, and full of need, that God may exalt thee, fill thee, and replenish thy desires : but tremble to be proud, rich, and disdainful, lest He cast thee out of thy seat, and leave thee empty of His grace.

<hr>

(36) Dan. ii. 34.
(37) Job v. 11.; xl. 6. et seq. Luc. xviii. 14.   (38) Matt. v. 6.
(39) Ps. xxxiii. 11.   (40) Ps. cii. 4, 5.

"HE HATH RECEIVED ISRAEL HIS SERVANT, BEING MINDFUL OF HIS MERCY, AS HE SPOKE TO OUR FATHERS, TO ABRAHAM, AND TO HIS SEED FOR EVER."

These two verses contain two other most powerful motives to move us to rejoice in Almighty God, and to praise His most holy name.

9. One is, the *care* and *providence* which He has to provide for those of whom He has taken charge, as for His children and domestics, coming personally to redeem them. And although it seems that for a time He forgets them; yet when He sees the right time He is mindful of His mercy, and remedies them, as He was mindful of Israel, and of the whole world, coming to remedy it when He made Himself man.

10. The other motive is, the great *fidelity* with which Almighty God accomplishes the promises He had made to our fathers, fulfilling them faithfully to all their seed for ever to the end of the world; as He fulfilled His word to Abraham, and to David which He gave them, that He would come to remedy them, and to give to their children life and salvation, world without end.

These two considerations inflamed the soul of the Virgin to magnify Almighty God, and her spirit to rejoice in God her Saviour; and with these, my soul and my spirit are to be kindled in the like affections, since every day, I behold the providence which God has for His children, and with what faithfulness He accomplished what He promised to the apostles our fathers, not forgetting the faithful, which are their seed to the end of the world.

And these are the ten causes and motives alleged in this canticle by the Blessed Virgin, to glorify God, to which she was inspired by the eternal Word Incarnate whom she bore in her womb: of which I may make another psalter, and harp of ten strings, to the same end praying, and glorifying Almighty God, sometimes for one reason, and sometimes for another, and because I cannot do this as I ought, I must humbly beseech the Word Incarnate to teach me, as He taught His blessed Mother; and she, to obtain it for me, to the glory of her Son. Amen.

POINT IV.

1. Finally, I am to consider how the Sacred Virgin remained with her cousin about "*three months*," considering the *great good she might do* to all who dwelled there, by her conversation and the example she gave of modesty, humility, and charity; for if she did so much at her first entrance, it is to be believed, that in those three months she would augment what she then did, especially towards St. Elizabeth, discoursing of these mysteries; and both of them exhorting one another to prayer, and conversation with Almighty God, and to other virtuous exercises. For if because the ark of the testament was three months "in the house of Obededom" "God blessed him," and all his household with such great benefits, (41) that David with a holy envy desired to draw the ark to his own house, that God might cast His benedictions on it; how much more are we to believe, that this divine ark of the New Testament, within which was Christ Himself, having remained "about three months," (42) in this house, would fill it with a thousand benedictions? And if I with a lively faith could understand them, I should presently be desirous to draw it to my house, and that the devotion to this sovereign Lady should dwell in my soul, not only three months, but all my life, that she might replenish me with all spiritual benedictions.

2. But it is not without mystery, that our Lord, by

(41) 2 Reg. vi. 11.   (42) Luc. i. 56.

9

means of the Blessed Virgin, having done such great mercies to St. John, and to his mother, yet would not heal his father Zacharias, nor dispense with the sentence pronounced by the angel, that he should be dumb *until the birth of the child:* for God is just, and this was convenient, to observe the order of His justice: and also reserved this His mercy, for another more convenient time. Whence I will learn to reverence the secret judgments of Almighty God, to humble myself, and to await His counsels, expecting the convenient time of His visitation, since there is no day that comes not at last, and that what He granted this day to St. Elizabeth, He afterwards gave more largely to Zacharias.

MEDITATION XIII.

ON THE BIRTH OF ST. JOHN, THE FORERUNNER OF OUR SAVIOUR CHRIST.

POINT I.

1. First, I will consider what happened before the conception of this saint, for God having elected him for His forerunner, (1) would honour him, to demonstrate in him the greatness of His mercy, and the height of the office which He gave him, all for the glory of Christ Jesus, whose forerunner he was.

1. He would that he should be miraculously conceived of *barren* parents, that he should be the son of *holy* parents, and the son of *prayers*, and holy desires; for prayer is the means which Almighty God uses to execute the designs of His eternal predestination; as St. Gregory says, speaking of the birth of the patriarch Isaac. (2) By this He moves us to have great affection, and confidence in prayer, though

(1) Luc. i. 11.　　　　　　(2) Lib. i. dial. c. 8.

it be concerning things which seem difficult, since it is available for all.

2. He would likewise that his conception should be announced by *the same St. Gabriel*, who announced that of *His Son*, and with the same spirit of prompt obedience, the angel came to declare both the one and the other, because it was God who commanded it. In the same manner that St. Raphael came to serve Tobias in very low things (3) with no less pleasure than if God had commanded him the most sublime things : for all the angels place their glory in accomplishing the will of Almighty God.

3. Then I will consider what great things St. Gabriel spoke of the child, that he might be esteemed by all, and to instruct his father in the manner of his education for so high an office.

i. The first was, that the angel himself, in God's behalf, gave him the *name* he was to have, saying that he should be called John, which means grace ; to signify that he should be an absolute expression of grace, in whom should be shewn the riches of God's graces; for he truly found grace before God, who without any merits of his, elected and called him, and was mindful of his name even from the womb of his mother. (4)

ii. The second that he should be *great* before God in those things which God esteems great, which are virtues, and gifts of sanctity. So that he should be great in humility, in patience, and obedience; great in prayer and contemplation, and great in the office which the great ones of the house of God have.

iii. The third, that he should be exceedingly *temperate*, without drinking wine or strong drink, as a Nazarene, wholly dedicated to the service of God. And because the

(3) Tob. v. 5.   (4) Is. xlix. 13.

divine promises are not empty, but full, giving a sufficient portion for all that is promised, He adds :—

iv. The fourth excellency, that he should be *replenished* from the womb of his mother *with the Holy Ghost*, with that fulness which was requisite for the dignity of the office for which he was elected, beginning from the womb of his mother, and going on forward to his death.

v. The fifth, that he should go before our Lord, as His precursor, with the zealous *spirit "of Elias,"* converting many Israelites to God, and preparing Him a people perfectly fashioned to receive the new law which He was to teach.

4. So that, according to the sentence of the angel, this child should be *perfect* in all manner of perfection, towards *God*, towards *himself*, and towards his *neighbours*. For towards God, he should be great in the gifts of His grace; towards himself rigorous in the works of mortification and penance; and towards his neighbours he should be zealous in seeking their salvation, not being contented to be perfect himself, but endeavouring that all might be perfect, and ordaining all this to the glory of our Lord Christ. This pattern of perfection, which is the same that is taught us by the prophet Micheas, (5) I am to set before my eyes for imitation. And of the great things which Almighty God so much esteems, I am to aspire after those which are convenient for my state, beseeching His Divine Majesty to give me them for the love He bore to His precursor, to whom He granted them so liberally.

POINT II.

Secondly are to be considered *the favours* which our Lord did to this holy babe when he was in his mother's womb, in the sixth month of his conception, the Word

(5) Mich. vi. 8. &c.

Incarnate Himself coming in the womb of His Mother to visit him, (6) and to sanctify him, as is declared in the preceding meditation, from which we may gather three excellencies of this saint.

i. That St. John was the *first fruits of all the saints* that our Saviour made after His Incarnation; and therefore He sanctified him with great excellency, giving him great sanctity, and many graces given after a very perfect manner, granting him the use of reason, and free will; illuminating his understanding to know His Incarnation, and inflaming his will with fervent affections of admiration and love, and with jubilees, and rejoicings in the Holy Ghost.

ii. The second excellency was, that whereas "the gifts of God," as St. Paul says, "are without repentance;" (7) it is to be believed, as St. Ambrose says, that he took *not from him the use of reason* which He had granted him, and consequently, that whereas the Blessed Virgin during those three months which she spent in the house of Zacharias (8) aided St. Elizabeth to grow in all virtue; so the child Jesus, who was in the womb of the Virgin, assisted the child John, who was in the womb of Elizabeth, to *grow up* in that holiness which He had granted him, increasing it by new acts of his free will, inflamed with divine grace by the Holy Ghost, of whom he was full.

iii. The third excellency was, as holy men say, that for the child John, God did so many favours to his mother, that *He filled her with the Holy Ghost*, and with the spirit of prophecy: (9) to give us to understand how much He esteems this child and what good He will do for his sake. For which I must excite myself to great love towards this forerunner, rejoicing at the favours which he received, and

(6) Luc. i. 39.   (7) Rom. xi. 29.   (8) Luc. i. 56.
(9) Ambr. et Bed. in Luc. i.

giving thanks to Almighty God who gave them him; beseeching him to be an intercessor for me; that I may have
some part in them.

POINT III.

Thirdly, I am to consider the *most special things* which
happened at the birth of St. John.

i. The first was, that when his parents came to circumcise
him, they by God's inspiration, against the will of their
kindred, said his name should be John, (10) which is as
much as to say, "grace;" to signify that as this child by circumcision, was laden with the heavy burthen of the old
law, Almighty God gave him most abundant grace to bear
it, and to be in a manner, the beginning of the new law, (11)
which was the law of grace, of which some part fell to his
lot, and in which this grace is granted to all.   And therefore I will beseech our Lord, that since He has imposed
upon me the burthen of His law, He will grant me
abundance of His grace to fulfil it.

ii. The second miracle was, to *restore to speech* (12) *his
father*, Zacharias, whom He filled forthwith with the
Holy Ghost; giving him the spirit of prophecy, with
which he composed the canticle of "Benedictus Dominus
Deus Israel," beginning with the praises of Almighty God,
who showed Himself so liberal in coming to visit us ; and
then with the praises of His precursor. For it is the property of the Divine Spirit, to inspire praises of God for
His benefits, and of His saints for the gifts which He has
given them.   But the excellency of this child, and how
much God loves him, is most resplen dent, as this was
granted to his father as soon as he had written on a table
the name of John, that we may perceive the grace and

(10) Luc. i. 59.   (11) Luc. i. 16. et xvi. 16.
(12) Luc. i. 64.

favour He will show on his account to those who shall worship his holy name with devotion.

Colloquy.—O glorious child, I rejoice that thou art so beloved of our Lord; and since thou, according to thy name, art so full of grace, obtain for me of our Lord, that I may be replenished with it, that I may perpetually serve Him, and in thy company enjoy Him, world without end.   Amen.

iii. The third which happened, was the great *joy*, reverence, and admiration, in all people who knew of these things, (13) fulfilling that which the angel had said, that many should rejoice in his birth; to signify that God our Lord gave him to His church as the advocate of spiritual joy, which is the effect of devotion, and the pledge of life everlasting.

iv. The last, and most glorious, is that which the Evangelist says in the beginning of his life, that "*the hand of the Lord was with him;*" (14) that is, that his Omnipotency favoured him, and wrought for him great things, moved and directed him in all his ways, and protected him in all his necessities; for which the Church applies to him that of the holy prophet Isaias: " The Lord hath called me from the womb; from the bowels of my mother He hath been mindful of my name.   In the shadow of His hand He hath protected me, and hath made me as a chosen arrow : in His quiver He hath hidden me." (15)

Colloquy—O happy arrow, which movedst not by thy own impulse, but by the impulse of the Almighty! O chosen arrow, directed by the Holy Ghost to great things, never letting thee out of His powerful hand! O hand of the Almighty, which moved Thy precursor, move me with Thy impulse to fulfil Thy holy will; and be ever a helper to me, for Thou knowest that, without Thee I am able to do nothing.   Amen.

(13) Luc. i. 14. et 65.   (14) Luc. i 66.   (15) Is. xlix. 12.

MEDITATION XIV.

ON THE EVENTS HAPPENING ON ST. JOSEPH'S PURPOSING TO FORSAKE THE VIRGIN WHEN SEEING HER WITH CHILD, AND ON THE REVELATION MADE TO HIM BY THE ANGEL CONCERNING THIS MYSTERY,

POINT I.

For the foundation of this meditation, I am to consider the great sanctity of St. Joseph, and the virtues and graces granted him by our Lord, that he might be the worthy spouse of His mother, and His foster-father, so that he should be held for His father ;(1) and was so indeed, with regard to the office of educating and supporting Him. For, as our Lord filled the Baptist and the apostles with the Holy Ghost, and with that abundance of grace which was requisite to exercise the offices committed to them, so also would He replenish St. Joseph with most excellent gifts and graces, with which he might fulfil those ministries which He commended to him. And he negociated so skilfully with the gifts he received, that he increased them every day; and he was therefore called Joseph, which is to say, "accrescens," growing, (2) or he that increases.

1. First, he increased his *sanctity* above all the saints who had preceded him; for he had greater faith and obedience than Abraham, more patience in afflictions than Jacob, more chastity than his son Joseph, more familiar conversation with Almighty God than Moses, more charity towards the people than Samuel, and more humility and meekness than David. In these, and other virtues, he was resplendent, and daily augmented them, that being fulfilled in him which was spoken by the prophet David, " Blessed is the man whose help is from Thee;" for, with

---

(1) Luc. ii. 48.   (2) Gen. xlix. 22.

Thy favour "in his heart, He hath disposed to ascend by steps," ascending from one virtue to another, until "shall be seen the God of gods in Sion." (3)

2. Especially this happy saint increased, by mounting that spiritual ladder, which, as we have said, *his spouse* ascended, by whose example he was assisted ; these two Seraphim inciting one another to fly with their wings, and to glorify the Holy of holies in their prayer. (4) And to do this with more liberty of spirit, by inspiration of the Holy Ghost, he chose to observe perpetual chastity, which, as St. Paul says, removes the "impediment" (5) to prayer. And he advanced so far in this, that, by a special favour, he felt no evil motion, though he conversed with a virgin exceedingly beautiful, but, at the same time, so admirably chaste, that merely to behold her inflamed one with a desire of chastity. And in this very action he discovered his great love to Almighty God ; for whose sake he renounced the pleasures of matrimony, accepting the burthen of that state without its delights. With these virtues he joined others, of which we shall by-and-by speak, in which I am to endeavour to imitate him, beseeching him to be my advocate with his spouse, and Christ Jesus our Saviour ; for doubtless he can prevail much with them both, for the great services which he did them.

Colloquy.—O glorious patriarch, whose beauty the hierarchies of heaven admire, beseech "the desire of the everlasting hills," (6) who poured forth His copious benediction upon thy head, that He will likewise pour it forth upon mine, that in imitation of thee, I may increase in good works, and augment in virtues, persevering with constancy to the gaining of the everlasting crown. Amen.

(3) Ps. lxxxiii. 6.　　(4) Is. vi. 3.　　(5) 1 Cor. vii. 35.
(6) Gen. xlix. 26.

POINT II.

After the Blessed Virgin came from the house of Zacharias, "*she was found*" by her spouse "*with child* by the Holy Ghost. Whereupon Joseph her husband," ignorant of the cause, and in great affliction, "being a just man, and not willing publicly to expose her, was minded to put her away privately."

i. Upon this, I am to consider the *secret judgments* of Almighty God in *not revealing* this important mystery to St. Joseph, as He revealed it to Zacharias and to St. Elizabeth, which He did with the intention to prove the Virgin and her spouse. For St. Joseph, perceiving his spouse to be with child, might, without any sin, as many saints say, have judged that she was an adulteress, or doubt of a thing that was to him so new and so strange. (7) And this afflicted him much, it being so much to his dishonour. But much greater was the affliction of his spouse from whom this could not be hidden, it being a great infamy for a virgin so pure to be held by her own husband for an adulteress, and to see herself, therefore, at the point of being abandoned. All this our Lord ordained for the great good which arises from affliction and humiliation; by which He intended to perfect these two notable saints, and to dispose them to greater things. For as the Blessed Virgin had received great favour in the annunciation of the angel St. Gabriel, and in the house of Elizabeth, our Lord God was willing that she should suffer this infamy and humiliation, to exercise her in greater humility, and to dispose her for those favours which she was to receive soon after in the city of Bethlehem; for humiliation is the forerunner of exaltation, and affliction of a great feast of consolation. (8) And, haply for this cause, the holy Church sings the gospel of this mystery on the vigil of

(7) S. August. S. Chrys. et alii.   (8) S. Ber. serm. 34. in Cant.

the Nativity : and, for the same reason, God proved St. Joseph to receive the revelation of so high a mystery, and that he might be His sufficient witness.

ii. Hence I will gather, that although one may be very holy, and always converse with holy persons, and employ himself in holy works ; yet, in this life, he will not be without humiliations and afflictions, caused sometimes *even by those holy things* in which he is engaged.   For " the life of man upon earth is a warfare," (9) and the righteous man ought to be prepared "for temptation." (10) I am rather to hold afflictions from God as a favour, especially when they happen without any fault of mine, and much more when they happen in a case deserving of honour, as the Blessed Virgin ; who, for that which was most excellent in her, suffered this humiliation, which also her son did afterwards.   Encouraged by these examples, I will say to our Lord with the prophet David: " Prove me, O Lord, and try me ; burn my reins and my heart, for Thy mercy is before my eyes, and I am well pleased with Thy truth." (11) Which is to say : Exercise me in divers temptations, and afflictions of body and soul, for I am assured of Thy mercy and of Thy faithfulness, that Thou wilt measure them according to my strength, and wilt convert them into the augmentation of new gifts.

POINT III.

Then will I consider the excellent virtues which, upon this new occasion and proof, were discovered and exercised by these two excellent saints for our imitation; seeing that our Saviour, for this end, also permitted those afflictions which they suffered.

1. First, St. Joseph shewed great *patience* and *prudence.*— Patience in suffering this injury in silence, without seek-

(9) Job vii. 1.   (10) Ecclus. ii. 1.   (11) Ps. xxv. 2, 3.

ing to be revenged on his spouse by justice, or complaining of her to her parents and kindred, and without murmuring at her, or giving injurious words to her; rather as a just man, who contented not himself with fulfilling the commandments, he sought what was most perfect, resolving to be silent, and to suffer this pain within himself.—He shewed prudence in seeking and finding a means how, on the one side, to preserve the honour of his spouse, and, on the other side, not to bring her to his house whom he suspected to be an adulteress; nor giving her a secret bill of divorce, which was lawful in the old law; nor, on some good occasion, absenting himself from her. And he also shewed prudence in not doing this rashly, or on a sudden, without first meditating and considering it well, as may be gathered from these words, "Hæc autem eo cogitante," —"but whilst he thought on these things;"(12) for he had a great scruple to dwell with her who seemed an adulteress, and he had likewise as great a scruple to abandon her who seemed a saint. With this consideration, I am to confound myself for the little patience I have in bearing affronts, for my great indignation against those who injure me, when I see how easily I murmur at, and defame my neighbours, and discover their secret faults, and how furiously and suddenly, and without deliberation, I cast myself into all this. And thus confounded, I will beseech our Lord, through the merits of this saint, to assist me to imitate his notable example.

2. But the Blessed Virgin, as she was more holy, discovered more excellent virtues, exercising four very excellent ones proper to those who are most perfect; viz.— rare *humility* and *silence*, great *confidence* in God's providence, and continual prayer. Through humility, she was silent, not desiring to manifest the secret mystery of

(12) Matt. i. 20.

Almighty God, although great honour might ensue to her from it, nor consenting that St. Elizabeth or Zacharias should discover them.   And although it is very ordinary among good married people, to communicate their secrets one to another, yet she communicated not this to St. Joseph, although she conjectured what might happen, if her husband were ignorant of it.   Through humility likewise she was silent, when she saw herself disgraced in the estimation of her spouse, not seeking to excuse herself, nor to stand upon her honour, nor to allege a sufficient witness; but absolutely with great confidence, casting herself upon the divine Providence, and putting her honour into the hands of God, she made continual prayer to His Majesty, that He would be pleased to remedy that ignominy, in whatever way should seem to Him best.   With this example I will likewise confound myself for that pride and vain boasting of mine, with which I publish whatever may be to my honour; and for that perverseness with which I excuse my fault, standing vainly on punctilios of honour; and for my little confidence in Almighty God, and my still less recourse to prayer.   For this purpose I am to imagine that God says to me that of Ezechiel:—"Son of man, shew to the house of Israel the temple, and let them be ashamed of their iniquities, and let them measure the building : and be ashamed of all that they have done." (13)   O my soul behold this living temple of Almighty God, the Blessed Virgin, contemplating the marvellous virtues with which she is adorned, that thou mayest be confounded at those vices into which thou hast fallen : measure her marvellous building, considering the excellent order and harmony of her works, that thou mayest be ashamed of the baseness and disorder of thine. (14)

Colloquy.—O temple of the Word Incarnate, be-

(13) Ezech. xliii. 10.   (14) Greg. lib. xxiv. Moral c. 6.

seech this great God, whom thou carriest in thy womb, to adorn me with such virtues, that I may be a worthy temple which He may inhabit by His grace.

O my soul, consider that the just ought to be "like a grain of mustard seed," (15) which, when it is ground, discovers the heat and force which it has; therefore, if God be pleased to grind thee with afflictions, animate thyself fervently to exercise these virtues.

POINT IV.

While St. Joseph was thus thinking, "behold the angel of the Lord appeared to him in his sleep, saying: Joseph son of David, fear not to take unto thee Mary thy wife, for that which is conceived in her is" not the work of man, but "of the Holy Ghost. And she shall bring forth a son, and thou shalt call His name Jesus: for He shall save His people from their sins." (16)

1. In this is to be considered the *fidelity of the divine Providence*, in coming to remedy the afflictions of those that are His, when they are arrived at the last and sharpest point, using divine means when human means fail. For whereas our Lord saw that St. Joseph could not conceive the cause of her being with child, He sent an angel in a very sweet manner to reveal it to him; for calling him by his proper name "Joseph," he adds, "son of David," to recall to his memory, that the promise of the Messiah was made to David, that He should descend from him. He says to him, "fear not," to take from him both scruple and anguish; which is the office of good angels. He says that the Virgin had conceived "of the Holy Ghost," to take from him all suspicion, and to clear the honour of our Lady, and wholly to convert his mourning into joy. He adds that "she shall bring forth a son," of whom he must

(15) Matt. xiii. 31.   (16) Matt. i. 20, 21.)

have as tender a care, as if He were his own : and that to him it should belong to give Him His name, which should be "Jesus," which is to say, Saviour, for that He was to be the Saviour of the world.   And all this was revealed to him with such clearness, that forthwith he gave entire credit to it.

2. Hence I will ascend to ponder the *joyfulness of St. Joseph* at the hearing of this news, that being fulfilled in him which is written in Job : "When thou shalt think thyself consumed, thou shalt rise like the day star." (17) O how full of content was he to see himself freed from his suspicions!   How ashamed that he had admitted it, though ignorantly and without any fault of his! How wary afterwards not to judge evil of any body!   How thankful to Almighty God, for having given him a spouse so holy, and of so great dignity, and for committing to his charge the care of His Only-begotten Son; and how joyful to see that now the time of the redemption of the world was come.

3. I will likewise ponder the great joy of the Blessed Virgin to see her husband so full of quiet and content; how much she was confirmed in her hope in God's providence; and how thankful to our Lord for undertaking her cause, our Lord fulfilling in her what He spoke by the prophet Osee: "I will give her the valley of Achor," that is of affliction, "for an opening of hope : and she shall sing there according to the days of her youth." (18)

Colloquy.—I give Thee thanks, O eternal God, for the great care Thou hadst of these two glorious saints, turning from them, as Thou art wont, " the valley of Achor," (19) into the food and augmentation of their spirit.   By their merits, I beseech Thee to make me worthy to enjoy the fruit of Thy fatherly providence,

17) Job xi. 17.   (18) Osee ii. 15.
                    (19) Osee ii. 15.

relying thereupon with great security in the midst of my afflictions, since it is most certain that Thou, in Thy good time, wilt come to remedy them.

POINT V.

"And Joseph rising up from sleep, did as the angel of the Lord had commanded him, and took" (20) the Virgin to his house, and lived with her most chastely, until the birth of her son; and much more afterwards.

1. In which I am to consider, not so much the obedience of St. Joseph, for it was not much to take to his house so excellent a woman, as the *manner in which he did it:* that is, with what *reverence* he took her, speaking to her some words like to those of St. Elizabeth : "Whence is this to me, that the Mother of my Lord" (21) enters into my house! O how great was his love and affection to our Blessed Lady! how careful was he of her! what holy discourses did they hold between them! what more than angelical purity of life, and what conformity of wills! how subject and obedient was the Virgin to St. Joseph, as to her head! how did she reveal to him the particulars of what the angel had declared to her in the annunciation, and what had passed in the house of Zacharias! for now the time was come that she might speak, to inform him of the mystery, to the honour and glory of Him who wrought it.

Colloquy.—O happy saint, to whose lot it fell to have such good company! Oh! happy is the soul that serves them, and learns of them their obedience and charity! O Seraphim of the earth, as pure as those of heaven, who with your wings (22) fly lightly to accomplish the will of Almighty God, inflame my heart with the love of this our Lord, that I also may

(20) Matt. i. 24.   (21) Luc. i. 43.
(22) Is. vi. 2.

serve Him with obedience like to yours, and that I may love all my brethren with that pure charity with which you loved one another.   Amen.

MEDITATION XV.

ON THE EXPECTATION OF OUR BLESSED LADY'S DELIVERY ; AND ON THE PREPARATION FOR THE BIRTH OF OUR SAVIOUR CHRIST.

As in Spain, eight days before the birth of our Saviour Christ, we celebrate the feast of the Expectation of our Blessed Lady's delivery, I insert here this meditation for that day, and the days ensuing till the Nativity; in which we are to consider the lively *desires* which three persons had of this sovereign delivery, and birth:—that is to say;—the Child, the Virgin, and St. Joseph, in whom are represented the faithful.who firmly believe this mystery, and in imitation of them, desire to prepare themselves worthily to celebrate it.

POINT I.

First, I am to consider the most fervent *desire that our Lord* Jesus Christ had, being in the womb of His mother, to *perfect*, and bring to an end the *business of our redemption*, and consequently to be born in the world, to frame all things according to the will of His Father.

For even from His mother's womb that sentence was true, which He uttered afterwards :—"I have a baptism wherewith I am to be baptised : and how am I straitened until it be accomplished." (1)   For however His body was pressed, and straitened in that strait womb of His mother, His *heart was much more pressed* and straitened with the force of this vehement desire ; for which I ought to give Him infinite thanks, and to correspond with Him in such

(1) Luc. xii. 50.

another hearty desire truly to serve Him. But notwith-standing this desire, He would not be born before the nine months, which is the time when commonly all other children are born, in order,

i. To conform Himself to all and to suffer that imprison-ment entirely, without omitting as much as a single day; for in that which concerned suffering, He would admit of no dispensation, exception, or privilege for Himself; and therefore He would not be born at the seven months, nor at the eight, but at the nine months complete.

ii. To take all this retirement before His entrance into the world, spending it in perpetual prayer and contempla-tion; as He retired forty days in the desert before He manifested Himself to the world by His preaching ; ad-monishing us thereby how we ought to recollect ourselves, dedicating some time to retired prayer, and to treat with God only, before we appear in public, or begin any great enterprise, and also how we should recollect ourselves to celebrate His holy Nativity with devotion.

POINT II.

1. Secondly, I will consider the fervent *desires* of the most *Sacred Virgin* to see her son born, and that the happy hour of His nativity was now arrived.

i. First, that she might *know* Him *face to face* who was not only her son, but the Son also of the everliving God; to behold that sacred humanity which He had taken from her flesh, and to enjoy His excellent beauty.

ii. Secondly, to adore, to serve and to nourish Him and to fulfil towards Him the office of a mother, in gratitude for the great favour which He had done her in electing her to that end. And therefore with great tenderness of heart she might apply to Him that of the Canticles : "Who shall give Thee to me," O my son, "ut inveniam te foris, deosculer te :" "that I may find Thee without, and kiss Thee," (2) and cherish and serve Thee as Thou dost merit?

iii. Thirdly, that the world might enjoy that good which was inclosed in her; for although she loved Him exceedingly, yet she would have Him not for herself alone, but for all, because He was Incarnate for all universally. And as "hope that is deferred afflicteth the soul," (3) every day seemed to her a whole year : though on the other side she was most contented to contain Him within her, understanding that such was His pleasure.

2. With these considerations I am to move my heart, and to awake fervent desires in it, that this Son of Almighty God may be born spiritually within my soul, and within the souls of all men, that He may be adored, served and loved by all, repeating to this end certain verses of the psalms and of the prophets, which Holy Church uses in the time of Advent : such as these :—

Colloquy.—" Stir up Thy might, and come to save us." (4) " O that Thou wouldst rend the heavens, and wouldst come down," (5) that in Thy presence all my vices might be melted. " Drop down dew, ye heavens, from above, and let the clouds rain the just ; let the earth be opened, and bud forth a Saviour." (6) " Show us, O Lord, Thy mercy, and grant us Thy salvation." (7)

3. To this purpose I may frame certain ejaculatory prayers, like those which the holy Church uses in these days in those seven antiphons which are sung at evensong, calling our Saviour Christ by those names which He holds as He is God, or as He is man, by reason of the offices He does in those souls, whom He visits : and therefore I may say to Him :—

(2) Cant. viii. 1.

(3) Prov. xiii. 12.   (4) Ps. lxxix. 3.   (5) Is. lxiv. 1.

(6) Is. xlv. 8.   (7) Ps. lxxxiv. 8.

Colloquy.—O infinite " Wisdom," come to govern me in the way of heaven !   O "Splendour of the glory of the Father," come to illuminate me with the splendour of Thy virtues !   O "Son of Justice," come to give light and heat of life to him who is seated in the shadow of death !   O "King of kings," descend to govern me !   O "Master of nations," come to instruct me   O "Saviour of the world," make haste to save me !

And in this form may be framed other such like petitions, according to the time, conforming myself in them to the spirit of the Catholic Church.

4. Finally, I may *spiritualize* the desires of the Blessed Virgin, and of her son whom she bore in her womb, quickening my *desire*, that those good *purposes*, which by the inspiration of the Holy Ghost I have conceived, may come to light, and be effected in such time, place, and season, as God shall require, absolutely conforming myself to His most holy will. For as the infant conceived, naturally desires to come into the light of this world at its due time, and if it comes not, it torments its mother and dies, endangering likewise her life; so the good purpose which the Holy Ghost inspires me with, of altering or bettering my life, is, as it were, crying and desiring to come to light in its due time. And if by negligence or contempt, it be not effected, it torments the conscience with remorse, and is wont to be an occasion of great falls, Almighty God permitting them as a chastisement for having extinguished "the spirit," (8) and the good purposes which proceeded from His inspiration. And upon this the Holy Spirit says, that "desires kill the slothful :" (9) that is, desires conceived by the virtue of Almighty God, and not accomplished through our own sloth.

(8) 1 Thess. v. 19.   (9) Prov. xxi. 25.

POINT III.

1. Thirdly, I am to consider the *assured hope* that our Blessed Lady had, that her virginity should *suffer no loss* by this birth, firmly believing that she was a virgin in conceiving the Son of. Almighty God, without the work of man; so likewise should she be in bringing Him forth, *without* any *prejudice* of *her virginal integrity;* for the experience of what was passed, assured her of what was to come, remembering that both these things were jointly prophesied by the prophet Isaias, saying : "Behold a virgin shall conceive, and bear a son, and His name shall be called Emmanuel," which being interpreted is, "God with us." (10)   These words she might revolve within herself, and with great astonishment might say : "Whence so great good to me, that I should be this miraculous virgin? What is it possible that I have conceived within me that very Son whom the Eternal Father contains within Himself ? And that this Emmanuel is with me, whom so many have desired to be with them; and that without loss of my virginity, He should issue out of me, to be and remain with all universally ?"

Colloquy.—I give Thee thanks, O most blessed Emmanuel, for having chosen this humble virgin for Thy Mother.   O that the hour of Thy birth was now come ; for although as Thou art man Thou issuest out of me, yet, as Thou art God, Thou wilt always remain with me.

With such affections as these might the Blessed Virgin be inwardly touched at this time, this hope filling her with great joy, for the great love she bore to virginity.

2. Hence it proceeded that she was *free from those fears* that other pregnant women have, and from those cares about their delivery, which are wont to afflict them with

(10) Is. vii. 14. Matt. i. 23.

great pain; for she was only careful to prepare her soul with heroic acts of virtue, to serve her son the better, and likewise to provide, as far as her poverty would permit her, for all things needful for His birth. In imitation of her, I am to prepare myself for the Nativity, which I am looking forward to, of the Son of Almighty God, removing those impediments which I may find in my soul, and adorning it with excellent acts of virtue, according to that which we have declared in the preceding points, and to that which holy Church commands on those days, with the very words of St. John Baptist : "Prepare ye the way of the Lord, make straight His paths. Every valley shall be filled; and every mountain and hill shall be brought low : and the crooked shall be made straight, and the rough ways plain : and all flesh shall see the salvation of God." (11) As if to say :—Remove from vices, which are contrary to the Saviour who is born : and adorn you with virtues, like His—remove the baseness of pusillanimity, the loftiness of pride, crooked intentions and rough manners, endeavouring as much as you possibly can, to exalt your spirit to the highest with confidence, and to abase it to the lowest with humility; directing your intentions to that which is heavenly, without any mixture of what is earthly; being meek and gentle to all, without giving occasion of stumbling to any; for such is the Saviour who is to be born, and with such dispositions you are to receive Him.

These four virtues opposed to the four contrary vices, I am to procure for the end aforesaid, by the mediation of our Blessed Lady the Virgin, saying to her :—

Colloquy.—O most sacred Virgin, who with fervent desires, expectedst the nativity of thy Son, and with excellent works disposedst thyself to behold, and to embrace Him, intercede for me, that I may remove

<hr>

(11) Luc. iii. 4, 5, 6. Is. xl. 3, 4.

myself the impediments to His coming, and may prepare myself for it with great diligence.   Amen.

MEDITATION XVI.

ON THE JOURNEY OF OUR BLESSED LADY THE VIRGIN FROM NAZARETH
TO BETHLEHEM.

POINT I.

First, for the foundation of the meditations ensuing, I will consider, how the Word Incarnate, being in the womb of His mother, would make the *newest*, most *admirable*, and *holiest* entrance into the world, that ever was, or shall be,—painful to Himself, and profitable to us, (1) in order to settle the foundation of that Evangelical perfection, which He was to preach.   So that His first entrance into the world was, as St. Cyprian saith, a pattern of our first entrance into Christian religion, (2) that His disciples might enter by the way He entered, exercising those virtues which He exercised.   And to this end He left all that the world most loves, and seeks : and sought after all that which the world abhors and flies.   And therefore, for the day of His birth, He disposed things so as to get out of Nazareth, to leave those conveniences that He might have had if He had been born in the house of His mother, and among His kindred and friends, where He could not have wanted the shelter of some warm lodging and covering, besides some delicacies for His nourishment, which John the Baptist failed not to have, having been born in his father's house.   But He abandoned it all, thus demonstrating how much He abhorred the pampering of the flesh, and what a lover He is of poverty, since He forsook that little which His poor mother had, and like a stranger

(1) S. Th. 3. p. q. xxxv. art. 7 et 8.   (2) Serm. de Nativit.

would be born in Bethlehem, and in such a season, when all things would be wanting to Him. With this example I will confound myself, for being so great a lover of my own conveniences and delicacies, that not only I do not fly from them, but I carefully seek for them, and if I find them not, I am afflicted.

Colloquy—O Jesus of Nazareth, flourishing with the flowers of celestial virtues, who comest out of Nazareth to abandon the flowers of earthly delights, I humbly beseech Thee by this, Thy coming from thence, that Thou wilt be pleased to favour my weakness, that I may renounce the flowers and flatteries of my flesh, desiring only the flowers of Thy virtues, with which Thou mayest so adorn my soul, that Thou mayest vouchsafe to be born in it. Amen.

POINT II.

Secondly, I will consider the *occasion* that our Saviour Christ took to make this journey, and the *end* He had in view : for, "In those days there *went out a decree* from Cesar Augustus, *that the whole world should be enrolled.* And all went to be enrolled, every one into his own city. And *Joseph also* went up from Galilee out of the city of Nazareth into Judea, to *the city of David* which is called *Bethlehem,* because he was of the house and family of David, to be enrolled with Mary his espoused wife, who was with child."

i. In this action, I will ponder how *different* are the thoughts of *Almighty God,* from those of *men,* those of the *King of heaven* from those of a *king of earth.* For this his edict was founded upon pride, ambition, arrogance, and avarice, commanding more 'than he had a right to do; that is, that the whole world should be enrolled, as if all the world had been his; and desiring that all should profess themselves to be his vassals, and should pay him tribute, were they never so poor and needy. But contrariwise the King of heaven, Christ Jesus, had all His thoughts placed in humility, poverty, and subjection, and in treading down pomps, riches and vanities. He comes not to command, nor to be served, but to *obey*, and serve the whole world. And in confirmation of this, He wills that His mother, and Himself should be enrolled, and profess themselves to be the vassals of Augustus Cæsar, and pay him tribute; to confound by this His example, the pride, and covetousness of the world. For if the "King of kings," and Monarch of all that is created, (3) enters into the world humbling Himself, and protesting vassalage to an earthly, and wicked king; what is it for me to humble myself, and to be subject to every human creature for His love? And what a pride will it be, not to humble myself before God, acknowledging myself His vassal, and paying Him, with obedience, the tribute that I owe Him?

Colloquy.—O King of heaven, permit not in me such pride, since Thou, to remedy it, didst so much humble Thyself.

2. Secondly, I will ponder, that though this edict was founded upon *pride and avarice*, yet Almighty God wills that thou who art His should obey it : for He is pleased that we should obey our superiors in all that they shall command us lawfully, (4) although they command it for their own interests and wicked ends, acknowledging God in them whose vicegerents they are. And this obedience our Saviour Christ Himself raised to the height, making this journey to accomplish the will of the eternal Father, who had ordained that His Son should be born in Bethlehem of Juda; (5) although His providence took this edict of the

(3) 1 Tim. vi. 15.   (4) Matt. xxiii. 3.   (5) Mich. v. 2.

Emperor Augustus, as a means to compass His end. (6) And as our Lord Christ came into the world not to do His will, but the will of Him that sent Him, (7) He would be born in that place which His Father had ordained, and be born obeying, as He died obeying, that all of us might learn to obey.

Colloquy.—O my beloved, since my life consists in doing Thy will, "keep my coming in and going out," and all whatsoever I shall do, conformable to Thy will, "now and for ever." (8)　Amen.

POINT III.

Thirdly, I am to consider the *journey* of the Virgin; the *manner* how she travelled, and the *virtues* which she exercised, with desire to imitate her in them.

She, being poor,—the way long,—and in the rigorous time of winter, experienced many trials; and yet she bore all with admirable patience and alacrity. She carried great modesty in her eyes, her heart being placed on Almighty God, and on the son whom she bare in her womb, with whom she entered into those colloquies, and discourses, which before have been spoken of. If some other time she talked with her husband, it was wholly of God, and with very great sweetness; and she was not weary, though she was far gone with child, for her son was not burdensome to her; and the hope to see Him speedily brought forth, gave her great alacrity, and pleasure in departing from Nazareth, that she might the more quietly enjoy her son, being born far off from all acquaintances.

Colloquy.—O Blessed Virgin, there is no need to say to thee, as there was to the spouse: "Arise, make haste"…"for winter is now past, the rain is over and gone, the flowers have appeared in our land;" (9)

(6) Matt. ii. 6.　　(7) Joan. vi. 38.　　(8) Ps. cxx. 8.
(9) Cant. ii. 10.

for the desire of suffering and obeying, makes thee travel in the rigour of winter, that the flower of Jesse may be brought forth, in whom centres our repose. O that I might imitate the virtues thou didst exercise in this journey, accompanying thy steps in spirit, though it were not granted me to do it in body.

POINT IV.

Fourthly, I will consider the *entrance* of the Blessed Virgin into Bethlehem, which was on an occasion of so great a concourse of people, that she found nobody that would lodge her, neither was there any room in the inn where she was; so that she was forced to have recourse to a poor *stable* intended for beasts; the divine providence so disposing it, that the Son of Almighty God might enter into the world begging, and suffering, without any one to compassionate His afflictions.

1. On this passage, I am to ponder the excellency of this our Lord, who seeketh a lodging to be born in, and *finds none;* the blindness of men, that know Him not, nor provide Him one; the benefits of which they deprive themselves, for not giving Him one, and how He chooses for Himself the worst of the world; gathering out of all this, tender affections, and hearty feelings.

2. I will ponder how the men of the world have *palaces,* and *houses well accommodated:* and the rich of Bethlehem were under good shelter, and warmly lodged at their ease; but the Son of the eternal Father, Lord of all that is created, coming to seek a lodging in His own city, to the appointed place of His birth, and among those of His own tribe and family, finds none there that would harbour Him. (10)

Colloquy.—O eternal Word Incarnate, how soon the world begins to reject Thee, Thou having come

(10) Joan. i. 11.

to redeem it. Now mayest Thou well sa y, thattl.e "foxes have holes, and the birds of the air nests," wherein to hatch their eggs, and to bring up their little ones, "but the Son of man," and IIis poor mother, find not "where to lay" their "head." The foxes chase Thee from their caves; for the crafty and rich of the earth abhor Thy simplicity and poverty. The birds admit Thee not into their nests, (11) for the noble and proud of the world despise Thy humility and lowliness, and therefore Thou goest to a poor and humble stable, where the ox "knoweth" his owner, "and the ass" (12) will leave his manger, to resign it to his master. O Lord of lords, and owner of all that is created, cast out of my soul all fox-like subtleties, and high-soaring pride that possess it, that Thou mayest find therein a fit lodging for Thyself. Amen.

3. Hence I will ascend to consider, that the cause why our Saviour Christ found no harbour in Bethlehem, was the *ignorance* of that *people;* for God coming to their gates, they acknowledged IIim not, neither did they know what good might come to them by admitting IIim, although they admitted other guests from whom they could receive little or no profit. O how happy had *he* been who had harboured this our Lord, that He might have been born in his house ! What spiritual riches would IIe have given him ! How well would He have recompensed his hospitality, as He recompensed that of Martha and of Zacheus! O how happy were my soul, if it should happen to harbour this our Lord, and to give IIim place to be born spiritually in it.

Colloquy.—O infinite God, who goest round "knocking at the gate" of my heart, calling on me by inspirations to open to Thee, who desirest to enter in, to enrich it with the gifts of Thy grace ; (13) permit me

(11) Luc. ix. 58.   (12) Is. i. 3.   (13) Apoc. iii. 20.

not to disown Thee, by shutting the door against Thee, nor to dishonour Thee by sending Thee away: come, O Lord, come, and call, for I will hear Thee; knock at my door, and I will open unto Thee, and I will give unto Thee the best part of my house, which is my heart, that Thou mayest repose in it at Thy pleasure.

4. Finally, I am to ponder the *patience* with which the Blessed Virgin and St. Joseph bore this affliction, and abandonment; with what joy they suffered the reproaches of those who rejected them because they were poor, and with what content they retired to the stable, taking for themselves the most contemptible place of the earth; by which, in a wonderful union, they joined humility and poverty, with patience and joy. In imitation of them, I will endeavour to desire for myself, that which is worst, and most contemptible in the world, bearing it with alacrity, when it falls to my lot; for there is no better lot than to imitate these glorious saints as they imitated our Saviour Christ, in such manner as we shall see hereafter.

MEDITATION XVII.

OF THE BIRTH OF OUR SAVIOUR CHRIST IN A STABLE AT BETHLEHEM.

POINT I.

First, I am to consider what the Word Incarnate *did in the womb* of His mother, when the hour was come of His deliverance from thence.

1. I will consider first, that as He would not anticipate the time of His birth, so also He *would not defer it*, but would punctually be born at nine months end, to manifest Himself to the world, with an hearty desire to begin His course with great fervour, and alacrity of heart; fulfilling that of David:—"*He hath rejoiced as a giant to run the*

way: His going out is from the end of heaven," (1) not staying till He come to the other extreme. For although He knew what a sharp course He was to have from His nativity to His death, yet He rejoiced with fortitude to begin it, issuing from the womb of the Virgin, which was His heaven, and presently setting His feet upon the vilest and basest place on the earth. For which I ought humbly to thank Him, beseeching Him to give me light to know and understand what passed in this His entrance.

Colloquy.—O child more strong and valiant than a giant, seeing that, resplendent like a new sun, Thou wilt issue from the east, to run Thy course to the west, that is, to the cross, illuminate my understanding, and inflame my will, that I may behold and contemplate Thy coming forth, and may love with fervent zeal the virtues Thou discoverest in it. Amen.

2. Next I will ponder *how liberal* He then *shewed Himself* to *His mother*, and like a great and rich man, who has been lodged, and has received good entertainment in the house of a poor labouring man, not through self-interest, (2) but only to serve him, is accustomed at his departure to recompense him well, and to give him some precious gift, either in gratitude, or for alms; so likewise as the Blessed Virgin had so well harboured her Son for nine months, when the time came for Him to depart from His lodging, He gave her the richest gifts of grace—a most high contemplation of that mystery, and certain extraordinary ecstasies of gladness, instead of those pains which others are wont to feel when they are in child-birth. For it was not reasonable, that she who had no sensual pleasure in conceiving, should have any pain in bringing forth. And although as regards the suffering of pain He dispensed not with Himself, yet He would not that His mother in

(1) Ps. xviii. 7.   (2) S. Th. 3. p. q. xxxv. art 6.

this case should suffer any. In like manner I may con-sider, that when our Saviour Christ enters sacramentally into us, at His first entrance He gives us sacramental grace, and if we give Him good hospitality, before His departure He gives us rich jewels of affections of devotion, and contemplation; and emotions of joy, with which He recompenses the good entertainment we give Him.

Colloquy.—Therefore, O my soul, take care how thou harbourest this Sovereign guest, that He may leave thee rich and abundantly stored with the gifts of heaven.

3. Thirdly, I will ponder how our Saviour Christ would, for the same cause, *issue out* of His mother's *womb* after a *miraculous* manner, she not suffering any loss of her virginity, for it was not reasonable that He should depart out of a house, where He had been so well entertained, with any injury to its integrity;—thus honouring His mother, and admonishing us all, that in entertaining and serving Him, we shall receive no detriment; rather if need be, He will do some miracle to prevent it. For though He did none to preserve Himself from suffering, yet He is wont to do it, to preserve His elect when it is expedient for them.

Colloquy.—O Sovereign master, how well Thou teachest me by this example the nature of true love, which is rigorous to itself, and gentle to others; for itself it will have severities to afflict it, but for its neighbour it will have favours to delight him. Aid me with Thy abundant grace, that in both things I may imitate Thy fervent and admirable charity. Amen.

POINT II.

1. Secondly, I am to consider *what the Blessed Virgin did,* when by those transports of joy she knew that the

hour of her delivery was come, pondering her *affections,* her *actions,* and her *words.* Retiring to a corner of the stable, and settled in very high contemplation, *she brought forth her only begotten Son,* and forthwith she took Him in her arms. O what content and joy she received at that first view, not staying upon the outward beauty of the body, but passing to the beauty of the soul and of the Godhead! On the one side she embraced Him and kissed Him lovingly as her son; and on the other side she shrunk back and humbly retired, considering that He was Almighty God; for with these two arms God desires to be embraced; with charity and humility; with love and reverence; and so am I to do spiritually, taking Him as it were in my arms, loving and reverencing Him; approaching to Him with love, and withdrawing myself with humility.

2. This done the Virgin *swathed* her Son in such *swaddling clothes* and mantles as she had prepared, and with an affection of humility laid Him in a manger, esteeming herself unworthy to hold Him in her arms; and falling on her knees she adored Him as her God and her Lord, and also very lovingly spoke to Him, for she was assured that He understood her. She humbly thanked Him for the great favours He had done to mankind, coming to redeem them. She likewise gave Him thanks for having taken her for His mother, without any merit of hers: and there she offered to serve Him with body and soul, and with all her powers, employing them all in His holy service; and all this she uttered with such loving words and tender affections, as are rather to be imagined than explained. The like doubtless did St. Joseph,—adoring the Child,— humbly thanking Him for taking him for His foster-father, also acknowledging it for a great favour, and offering himself truly and really to serve Him. The like am I also to do,

accompanying these saints in hearty thankfulness, offering to Him my body and soul, and all my faculties.

Colloquy.—O most sweet and most Sovereign Lord, what thanks can I give Thee, for this great favour Thou hast done me, in coming as a Child to redeem me, *and in extreme poverty?* O that I might have been present at the time to serve Thee in Thine infancy! I here present myself in spirit before Thy divine Majesty, and I offer to Thee all that I am, or may be able to be, to employ it wholly in Thy service; accept, O Lord, this my good will, and give me Thy grace to effect it. Amen.

POINT III.

The third, and principal point is, to consider the *wonderful excellencies* of that divine child, laid in the manger; considering the dignity of His *Person*—the *words* that He spake in His heart—the *works* that He did; and the *things* that He suffered;—and for whom;—and how;—and the heroic virtues that He there exercised. All this I am to ponder, as the most sacred Virgin pondered it, in this form.

1. I will behold the *Person* of that child, making a comparison between what He is, as Almighty God, and what He is there as man, with the greatest affection of admiration and love that I am able. I will consider on one side this child is that God of majesty, whose seat is heaven, whose throne are the Cherubim, and whose servants are the hierarchies of angels; (3) being in the midst of them as an Emperor, whom all adore, and to whom all acknowledge subjection; (4) and on the other, that He is there laid in a manger, between two stupid and simple beasts; that He who is the Word of the eternal Father, by whom He created all things, and who sustains them with

(3) Is. lxvi. 1.　　　　　(4) Ps. lxxix. 2.

11

His power, (5) is become a child (6) not yet able to speak, His hands and feet being swathed, and He not able to stir; that He, whose vesture is the infinite light of the Godhead, being the brightness of the glory of His Father, (7)—He who clothes His creatures with beauty, (8) and with a liberal hand gives them sustenance for the conservation of their life; (9) that He, even He is wrapped up in poor clothes and rags, and has need to be sustained with the milk of His mother.

Colloquy.—O most excellent and most humbled babe, (10) in all things to be adored, in all things loved; yet, *quanto pro me vilior, tanto mihi carior,* the more Thou art despised for me, the more worthy Thou art to be loved, and the more Thou art humbled, the more to be exalted; for in Thy humiliations Thou demonstratest the greatness of Thy incomprehensible charity. O that I could love Thee as Thou deservest. O that I could debase and humble myself as I deserve to be, for to debase me in myself were to exalt myself in Thee. How is it, O my soul, that thou art not confounded to see this Person so great, and yet so humbled, and to see thy own person so vile, and yet so proud? Learn of this child to humble thyself; for he that with Him shall humble himself on earth, shall by Him be magnified and exalted in heaven. (11)

2. Secondly, I will ponder the *words* this child might speak, not with the tongue, but with the *spirit;*—not with voice, but with *example.* To His eternal Father He might speak, giving Him thanks, that the hour was come, in

(5) Abac. iii. 2. juxta Septuag.   (6) Joan. i. 13.   (7) Heb. i. 2, 3.
(8) Ps. ciii. 2.   (9) Heb. i. 3.   (10) S. Ber. serm. 1. in Epiph.
(11) Matt. xviii. 3.

which it was His pleasure (12) that He should be laid in that manger; offering to Him, with great love, all the afflictions that He was to suffer in the world, and again saying to Him that which the apostle considers He might say to Him on entering into the world: "*Behold I come to do thy will, O God.*" (13) To mankind He likewise spake, and cried out to them by His examples, speaking that from the manger, which He afterwards spake when He preached: "Learn of me, because I am meek, and humble of heart;"—and "unless you be converted, and become as little children, you shall not enter into the Kingdom of heaven;" and "whosoever shall humble himself as this little child, he is the greater in the kingdom of heaven." (14) These, and other like words He is there preaching by His example; which I am to hearken to with great devotion, beseeching Him to open the ears of my heart, that I may understand this language and put it in practice.

Colloquy.—O Sovereign child, who even from this manger art inviting me to become a child, and wast always so great a lover of little children, (15) that Thou didst lovingly embrace them; make me like Thee, a child in innocency, a little one in humility, an infant in silence, and a tender one in charity. In these four things consists the making ourselves children, to become great in the eyes of Almighty God. (16)

3. Then will I contemplate the *works* that He does; in which there is one marvellous thing to consider;—that being a man, as perfect in judgment as when He was thirty years old, He did all the actions, gestures, and signs of a child, not counterfeited or feigned, but really and

---

(12) Heb. x. 9.   (13) Ps. xxxix. 8.
(14) Matt. xi. 29. et xviii. 3, 4.   (15) Mar. x. 16.   (16) Matt. xviii. 4.

truly as other children do, with an admirable harmony, which he understands who knows how to ponder the connexion of these two things together. In particular I will now ponder that *weeping* of the child, and the causes of His tears: He weeps not so much for grief of what He suffers (as other children do) as for that which we suffer by our sins, lovingly bewailing them; and with those tears joining interiorly most zealous prayers to the eternal Father, doing that which St. Paul said of Him : "Who in the days of His flesh, with a strong cry and tears, offering up prayers and supplications to Him." (17) And it is to be believed, that the Blessed Virgin wept, seeing her son weep, and considering the causes wherefore He wept.

Colloquy.—O sweet Jesus, why lamentest Thou so bitterly my miseries, forgetful of Thine own? O my soul why weepest thou not, seeing this child weep, that so weepeth for thee? Weep thou for compassion to see him weep, weep because thou art the cause of His weeping, and weep for thy sins that afflict His heart; and if this make me not weep, then weep because thou art so hard-hearted that thou canst not weep, having so much reason to shed abundance of tears. O most Sacred Virgin, obtain for me the gift of tears, if it be but to accompany thee with them, to comfort thy Son, who is comforted to see us weep, and said :—" Blessed are they that mourn, for they shall be comforted." (18)

4. Lastly, I will contemplate *what things* this child *suffers;* which are, poverty, contempt, cold and pain, with other inconveniences, all which He suffers not by compulsion, nor of necessity, but willingly and cheerfully; for as He is God and Man perfect in judgment, He makes

(17) Heb. v. 7.   (18) Matt. v. 5.

choice of all that He suffers. (19)   He chose to be born in the most rigorous time of the winter,—in the coldest hour of midnight;—in the most vile and contemptible stable of all the city;—in the greatest possible poverty, contempt, and forgetfulness from men;—and all under the veil of such humility, that though voluntary, it seemed forced, and consequently most vile and contemptible.

5. Finally, as He Himself says in one of the Psalms, *He was "poor and in labours from" His "youth,"* (20) from the manger taking for His inseparable companions even until death, poverty, contempt, pains and afflictions, and in all these things He suffered a thousand kinds of afflictions, selecting a manner of life so contrary to that of the world, that He might discover by His example the deceits and errors of worldlings who follow the same.   For as St. Bernard says: "It is a matter very evident that the world errs, in choosing for its companions, riches, honours, and delicacies, whilst Christ, the infinite Wisdom, who can neither deceive Himself, nor beguile us, chooses the contrary." (21)   With this consideration, I am to confound myself in the presence of this most blessed babe, seeing how contrarily I have lived to that which He teaches, purposing to imitate Him henceforward, choosing to suffer what He suffers, and beseeching Him to make me worthy to suffer with Him, and like Him, not of necessity, but gladly, and willingly for His love.

Colloquy.—O Sovereign child, who like another David, art the " wisest" prince " among three," (22) for of the three divine Persons Thou art the second, to whom wisdom is attributed ; what art Thou doing " sitting in the chair" of the manger, silent, without

<hr>

(19) S. Th. 3. p. q. **xxxv**. art. 3.
(20) Ps. **lxxxvii**. 16.   (21) S. Ber. serm. 3. de Nativit.
(22) 2 Reg. **xxiii**. 8.

speaking to us? Thou art "the most tender little worm of the wood, who killed eight hundred at once," for with the contempt and humiliation that Thou hast in the worm-eaten wood of Thy poor harbour, Thou killest by the violence of Thy divine love, the innumerable violences of the love of the world. O most wise and most valiant Prince who silently instructest, and silently killest, teach me to follow with silence Thy ignominies, and to kill in my heart worldly affections, that making myself a worm in imitation of Thee, I may deserve to ascend to behold Thee in the throne of Thy glory. Amen.

MEDITATION XVIII.

ON THE JOY OF THE ANGELS AT THE NATIVITY OF THE SON OF GOD; AND ON THE TIDINGS WHICH THEY RELATED TO THE SHEPHERDS.

POINT I.

First, I will consider what passed in *heaven*, at such time as our Saviour Christ was born on earth. For the hierarchies of the angels, as on the one side they clearly beheld the infinite majesty and greatness of God : (1) and, on the other, saw Him so humbled, so thrust aside, and so unknown among men, they extremely admired such great humility, and, being very solicitous that He should be honoured and reverenced by all, desired, if Almighty God would give them leave, to come down into the world, to manifest and make Him known. Then did the eternal Father give that commandment to all, which the apostle St. Paul mentions, "Et cum iterum introducit primogenitum in orbem terræ; dicit, et adorent cum omnes Angeli ejus ;" and again when He bringeth in the first-begotten into the world, He saith, "*And let all the Angels of God adore*

(1) S. Th. 3. p. q. xxxvi.

Him;" (2) He says "all," not excepting any one.　And all of them from heaven adored with high reverence this blessed babe, when on earth they beheld what they did. The Seraphim inflamed with love, on beholding Him held themselves as cold, and with profound humility acknowledged Him for their Almighty God.　The Cherubim full of knowledge, in presence of this child, esteemed themselves as ignorant, and with great trembling adored and reverenced Him as their Lord : and the like did all the other choirs of the angels.

Colloquy.—I rejoice, O all my good, to see Thee so adored by Thy angels: and it grieves me greatly to see Thee so forgotten, and unknown among men, I, O Lord, adore Thee, together with these blessed spirits, and heartily desire that all men might know, and adore Thee : and if it lay in my power to give them tidings of it, Ecce ego, mitte me; (3) "Behold me here, send me," for if Thou sendest me, I will fly with those wings which Thou shalt give me; and like the Seraphim I will cry out through the world, saying : "Holy, Holy, Holy art Thou, Lord God of hosts, the earth is full of Thy glory," although by the cloud of humiliation, under which Thou art in the poor stable, it seems to be obscured.

POINT II.

Secondly, I am to consider how the eternal Father would *manifest* the *birth* of His Son to the *shepherds*, who were near about Bethlehem watching, and keeping their flock; sending to this end an angel (which, as it is thought, was St. Gabriel) invested with a resplendent body, who environing them with a celestial light, said to them :—"*Behold I bring you good tidings of great joy that shall be to all the people; for this day is born to you a Saviour, who is*

(2) Heb. i. 6.　　　　(3) Is. vi. 2.

Christ the Lord, in the city of David; and this shall be a sign to you, you shall find the infant wrapped in swaddling clothes, and laid in a manger." (4)

1. On this passage, I will consider first, how Almighty God would not manifest this mystery, nor send this angel to the sages of Bethlehem,—for they were proud; nor to the rich,—for they were covetous; nor to the noble,—for they were pampered; but to *the shepherds*, because they were poor, humble, labouring men, who were watching, and attending their duty, for such dispositions Almighty God requires in those to whom He imparts His mysteries; and if He imparts them not with me, it is because I want such a disposition, since it was for this He said:—"That He hideth these things from the wise and prudent, and revealeth them to little ones," (5) that are humble and lowly.

2. Secondly, I will consider, that it is a matter of very great joy that a Saviour is born to *us*. He is not born to Himself, for He comes not to save Himself; nor is He born to the angels, for He comes not to save them; but to *men*, and to *me*, for He comes to save me. For me He is born and circumcised, and all whatever He did and suffered, it is all for me; and that which passes in the manger, is all to pardon my sins, to inflame me with the love of virtues, and to enrich me with merits.

Colloquy.—O sweet Jesus, that which to Thee is matter of suffering, is to me matter of joy. I rejoice that Thou art so good, as to embrace my sufferings, to give me Thy joys: let not me, O Lord, be so unhappy, as that seeing Thou art born for the good of all men, I should live, as if Thou hadst not been born for the good of me, hunting proudly after greatness, and forgetting Thy lowliness and humility.

(4) Luc. ii. 10.   (5) Matt. xi. 25,

3. Thirdly, I will ponder how the *signs* to find out the Saviour that is born, are *infancy, swaddling clothes*, and a *manger*.

Colloquy.—O infinite greatness of Almighty God, who would ever have imagined, that things so base should be the signs to find out, and to know the God of majesty! But I now know, O Lord, that Thou art delighted with these humiliations, and that Thou art in the midst of them, to move me to procure them; teaching me at the same time, that the signs to know that Thou art born spiritually within me, (6) are innocency of an infant in life, silence in tongue, poverty in apparel, and humility in choosing for myself that which is most vile, and contemptible on earth. Imprint them, O my Saviour, in my soul, that it may be like to Thee, that Thou mayest be pleased to be born, and to dwell therein.   Amen.

POINT III.

And while the angel was telling this to the shepherds, "suddenly there was with" him "a *multitude of the heavenly army, praising God*, and saying :—Glory to God in the highest, and on earth peace to men of good will." (7)

On this point, I am to consider, *who* sent these angels, and *for what end;* and the *hymn*, or *canticle* which they repeat.

He who sends them, is *the eternal Father*, to honour His Son, who was so humbled for His love; for He had always a care to exalt Him, when He humbled Himself: and in order that the angels likewise might instruct mankind by their example, what they are to do on this occasion.

Colloquy.—I humbly thank Thee, O eternal Father, for this care that Thou hast to honour Him, who

(6) S. Ber. serm. 4. de Resurr.   (7) Luc. ii. 13.

humbleth Himself. Well hath He merited that Thou shouldest honour Him, since He hath humbled Himself to honour Thee. And as it is just that I should honour and praise Him, teach me to sing this hymn of the angels, with the same spirit with which they sang it. Amen.

"GLORY TO GOD IN THE HIGHEST." (8)

In these words the angels teach us, that all this work of the Incarnation, is the glory of Almighty God in a supreme excellency; so that no one of His works is so glorious to Him as this, for which He deserves to be praised by all such as profess holiness of life: and in heaven, on this account, He is especially glorified: and it is reasonable He should be so here on earth; since for this cause it is "full of" the "glory" of this our Lord, (9) as the Seraphim said, when the prophet Isaias saw His glory.

Colloquy.—O King of glory, lift up my heart to the highest, that I may glorify thy name on earth, as the angels glorify it in heaven. (10) Whatever I shall do, or say, let it be to Thy glory, without seeking mine own, and from my mouth may this word never depart; Glory be to God three, and one. Glory to the Father, and to the Son, and to the Holy Ghost. Glory to the Father, for having given me His Son. Glory to the Son, for having become man for my redemption. And Glory to the Holy Ghost, from whose love this work did proceed. Amen.

"AND PEACE ON EARTH;" (11)

Which is as much as to say,—By this most excellent work comes peace to the inhabitants of the earth, a peace not partial or stinted, but very complete;—peace with

(8) Luc. ii. 14.   (9) Is. vi. 3.   (10) Joan xii. 41.
(11) Luc. ii. 14.

God and with angels;—peace to each one with himself and with all others; for this Saviour brings reconciliation of the world to His Father, the remission of sins, victory over the devils, subjection of the flesh to the spirit, union and concord of wills one with another and with God, whence proceeds cheerfulness of conscience, and that peace which "surpasseth all understanding." (12)

Colloquy.—O prince of peace, seeing it is written that in Thy "days justice shall spring up, and abundance of peace till the moon be taken away:" I humbly beseech Thee, to take from me all worldly mutability, and to fortify me with divine sanctity, and peace. (13) Amen.

"TO MEN OF GOOD WILL." (14)

In this third word we are to ponder, that all peace originally springs from the *good will* that Almighty God bears to us, with which He offers it to all men :—yet in effect *they* only enjoy it who *have* good will, well intentioned, conformable to the will of Almighty God, and subject to His divine law. So that peace is not promised to man for being of good understanding, or sharp wit, or great abilities, or notable talents and natural parts; for with all these things there may be much strife, discord, and enmity with Almighty God; whereas if all these should fail me, yet *peace* shall not fail me, if I have *good will.* And therefore I am to make more account of it, than of all the rest; for as St. Gregory says, Nihil ditius bona voluntate. (15) "There is nothing more rich, more amiable, or more peaceable than good will." As, contrariwise there is nothing more miserable, more full of disturbance, and of horror, than evil will. And therefore with great fer-

---

(12) Phil. iv. 7.   (13) Ps. lxxi. 7.
(14) Luc. ii. 14.   (15) Hom. 5. in Evang.

vency I am to beg of the Saviour that is born, that He will deliver me from the evil, and give me the good, since it lies in His gift. On this another version reads:—*Hominibus bona voluntas* : "good will to men."

Colloquy.—O most sweet Saviour, give me this good will which Thou offerest us, that I may deny my own will, and may follow Thine, good, pleasing, and most perfect; (16) for thine is the beginning of all good; and mine, left to its own free will, the root of all evil. Amen.

POINT III.

The angels having been awhile with the shepherds, *returned to heaven;* and we may piously believe, that they went by the stable at Bethlehem without any sensible noise, and that there they renewed their song, so that the Blessed Virgin and St. Joseph might hear it, and adore the new-born child with greater reverence, as their God, and their King. O what joy the Blessed Virgin received on hearing this music! and how thankful was she to the eternal Father for the honour He did to His Son! and how joyful to behold so great an host of angels, and how confirmed in faith, calling to mind that which is written, "*Let all the angels of God adore Him.*" (17)

Colloquy.—O my God, I adore Thee with them, and with them I sing: "*Gloria*" in this poor manger of Thine; and I desire that all the world may sing it to Thee in Thy church, that by all Thou mayest be glorified, world without end. Amen.

(16) Rom. xii. 1.   (17) Heb. i. 6.

MEDITATION XIX.

ON THE GOING OF THE SHEPHERDS TO BETHLEHEM; AND WHAT HAPPENED TO THEM THERE, WITH OTHER INCIDENTS UNTIL THE CIRCUMCISION.

POINT I.

The angels being departed, the shepherds exhorted one another, saying,—"Let us go over to Bethlehem, and let us see this word that is come to pass, which the Lord hath showed to us. And they *came with haste;* and *they found Mary,* and Joseph, and *the infant* lying in the manger."(1)

1. Here I am to ponder, first, how the shepherds forgot not this revelation, but *charitably animated one another* to this journey; for the inspirations and commandments of Almighty God, are not to be forgotten, but executed; exhorting ourselves with words and examples to the accomplishment of them; in such manner, as the "four living creatures" (2) followed the impulse of the Holy Spirit, "striking one against another" with their wings, and provoking as it were one another to follow their Lord more fervently. (3)

2. Secondly, they shewed great *obedience:* for although the angel did not expressly command them to go to Bethlehem; yet it was sufficient for them, that he showed that it was the good pleasure of Almighty God, for to this end He revealed and inspired it. And to one perfectly obedient, it suffices to have *any* signification whatsoever of the divine will, to put it presently in practice, although it were needful to leave for it, as the shepherds did, both his flock and all that he has.

3. Thirdly, they executed the will of Almighty God

, (1) Luc. ii. 15.   (2) Ezech. iii. 13.   (3) Greg. l. 24. mor. c. 6

with great *zeal.* Upon which it is said, that they went "*with haste,*" moved by the divine Spirit, with a desire to see the word that the angel had said to them, which was the eternal Word of God made flesh for our sakes. And their zeal made them worthy to find what they sought, the angel guiding them to the manger where He was.

Colloquy.—O that I might imitate the zealous obedience, and diligence of these holy shepherds, in seeking, and finding out the Saviour. O sovereign Shepherd, whose sheep all other shepherds are, discover to me with Thy divine illumination the place where Thou liest and feedest in Thy holy nativity, that I may so seek Thee, and find Thee, that I may know and love Thee, world without end. Amen.

POINT II.

Here is to be considered *what these* devout *shepherds did,* when they *found* what they sought.

1. The first is, to believe that on entering into the stable, there did shine from the face of the most blessed babe such a light and splendour, as penetrated their un derstandings, and discovered to them by a lively faith, that He who was there was God and man, the Saviour of the world, and the Messiah promised in the law; and with this light inflamed in His love, with great reverence prostrating themselves on the ground, *they adored Him,* and were thankful for His coming into the world, beseeching Him to go forward with this work, and to be compassionate to His people of Israel: and they likewise offered with words very full of devotion to serve Him.

2. It is likewise credible that *they offered Him* something of what they had, according to their poverty; for our Lord recalled to their memory that of Deuteronomy which says: "No one shall appear with his hands empty before

the Lord." (4) O with what affection would they offer, and with what love would the child accept, returning to them such abundant gifts of His grace, that they should not depart empty from His presence !

3. It is also credible, that the Blessed Virgin was thankful with humility, and that *they spake to her with great respect*, admiring her resplendent sanctity, and recounting to her all that had passed with the angels; at which she received exceeding great joy on account of the glory of her Son.

Colloquy.—O sweet Jesus, I adore Thee with these holy shepherds, and I desire to adore Thee with that devotion with which they adored Thee: and, not to appear empty in Thy presence, I offer Thee my heart, and liberty, and all that I have. And I beseech Thee, O my God, suffer me not to depart empty from Thy presence, but fill me with Thy grace, that by its aid I may serve Thee, and obtain life everlasting. Amen.

POINT III.

"And the shepherds returned, *glorifying, and praising God* for all the things they had heard and seen," (5) and they published it to all that they met, causing great admiration in all: "but Mary *kept* all these words, pondering them in *her heart.*"

Concerning this truth, it will not be amiss to consider for our own profit, *four sorts of persons* that were in Bethlehem, and its neighbourhood; and the manner how they behaved themselves about this nativity of the Son of God, applying it to myself for my own profit.

1. Some came *not at all* to the stable at Bethlehem; for although they heard what the shepherds said, and won-

(4) Deut. xvi. 16.   (5) Luc. ii. 20, 19.

dered at hearing it ; yet notwithstanding we read not, that they went to see it, being steeped in their own affairs and business. So there are many now who do not come to contemplate these mysteries on account of sloth, and of busying themselves in other affairs of their own pleasure.

2. Others *by chance entered* into the stable, as they were passing by, but they neither knew the infant nor the mother, nor rested on any thing more than what they saw before their eyes. Such are they who assist at these mysteries with a dead faith, without staying upon them, or sounding the depth of them; and so they gather no profit.

3. Others, like the shepherds entered, *being moved* to it by *Almighty God*, and with *a lively faith adored the child* and reaped great profit; but they *remained not* there, but returned to their office, praising God, and publishing His wonderful works. Such are the just who at times give themselves to prayer, and contemplation of these mysteries, and thence go to fulfil their obligations, and to preach what they have known of Almighty God; moving others to seek and to know Him.

4. Others, finally, as St. Joseph and the Blessed Virgin, *remained* in the stable, assisting the child, and serving Him with love, *keeping in their memory* all that they saw and heard, and pondering it in their heart. O how divine a contemplation had the Blessed Virgin of all this ! She compared what God was in heaven, with what that child was upon earth;—what the prophets said, with what she beheld with her eyes;—what the angel and shepherds had spoken, with what was present in that manger; and this conference was not dry but tender, full of great admiration, and of fervent affections of devotion. And in this she spent the eight days until the circumcision. So they who imitate this our Lady, dedicate some days entirely to the

contemplation of these mysteries, making these spiritual conferences in their hearts.   Happy those in this manner, can, and know how to attend on this infant in the manger.

Colloquy.—O sovereign Virgin, teach me to ponder within myself, what faith teaches me of thy son, and what thou didst ponder of Him in thy heart; that imprinting it in my spirit, I may never depart from His presence, but employ myself, in knowing, loving, and serving Him for ever, and ever.   Amen.

In the twenty-sixth meditation, another manner of meditating this mystery will be proposed.

MEDITATION XX.

ON THE CIRCUMCISION OF OUR SAVIOUR ON THE EIGHTH DAY. (1)

POINT I.

First, is to be considered how, on the eighth day after the nativity, the Blessed Virgin and St. Joseph determined *to circumcise the child in accomplishment of the law*, which imposed on the parents a precept of it : (2) on which I am to ponder :—

1. First, the *obedience* of the Virgin, and of St. Joseph, which was very punctual, and prompt to fulfil this precept, though they knew that its execution would be very sharp and painful to the child, whom they so much loved; yet the will of Almighty God was to be preferred before all; and this the Blessed Virgin esteemed so much, that if need had been, she herself like another Sephora, (3) would have taken the knife, and would have circumcised the child; (some say that she herself circumcised Him :— some others that St. Joseph did it); howsoever, certain it

(1) S. Th. 3. p. q. xxxvii. art. 1.   Luc. ii. 21.   (2) Levit. xii. 3.
(3) Exod. iv. 25.

is, they were prepared to put in execution whatever they might deem most agreeable to the will of Almighty God.

2. Secondly, I will ponder the *charity*, and *devotion* of the Blessed Virgin, who doubtless would be present at this spectacle, both to nurse her son, and to cure Him of His wound, as one whom she so much loved; as also to gather up the most precious blood which He there shed, and to keep it : for she knew it to be the blood of God, and to be of infinite value, and how did she beseech the eternal Father, that in consideration of it He would vouchsafe to pardon the world, beseeching Him, if it were possible to be satisfied with this alone, it being so infinitely worth!   She likewise directed her words to the Holy Ghost, whose spouse she was; saying to Him, as Sephora said to Moses, being at an inn with her son :— (4)

Colloquy.—O most Holy Ghost, though a "bloody Spouse" Thou art to me, desiring that the blood of my son should be shed, bathing with it His sacred feet, yet for all this, I will not leave Thee, as Sephora left Moses; for I esteem more Thy will, than my own, though it were needful to shed my own blood to fulfil it.

3. On the other side the Blessed Virgin was transpierced with *compassion* and *sorrow* for the suffering of her son. She wept with Him to see Him weep, and for the cause for which He wept, saying :—"O original sin, how dear dost thou cost my Son!   O sin of the terrestrial Adam, how bitter art thou to this celestial Adam!"

Colloquy.—O most Blessed Virgin, that I might accompany thee in this lamentation, bewailing my sins, to obtain the remedy of them, by the virtue of the precious blood of thy son.

(4) Exod. iv. 26.

POINT II.

Secondly, I will consider the *heroic acts of virtue*, which our Saviour Christ *exercised* in His circumcision; which in Him was not only an exercise of suffering as in other children, who want the use of reason; but it was an exercise of most excellent virtue.

1. First, it was *obedience to the law:* for as He was God, and the supreme lawgiver, He might have dispensed Him-self in this thing, and had sufficient cause for it, being not obliged by the rigour of the law, since He was not con-ceived by the work of man, nor with the debt of contract-ing original sin; yet for all this, He would of His own will obey this painful, and rigorous precept, protesting thereby that He would observe all the old law; for, as St. Paul says, "every man circumcising himself is a debtor, to do the whole law," (5) how burdensome soever it be; and therefore this blessed child offered Him-self at that time to undergo this heavy burden, setting this whole law, as Himself saith by the prophet David, "in the midst of" His "heart," (6) in order to give us a perfect pattern of obedience.

Colloquy..—O my soul, why dost not thou offer thyself to bear the burden, and sweet yoke of the new law, when thy Saviour offers Himself to bear for thee the most heavy burden, and insupportable yoke of the old law? If He for thy example obeys in these hard things, to which He is not obliged, why dost thou refuse to obey Him in those easy things that He has commanded thee? Pardon, O Lord, my disobedience, and assist me to follow the example Thou gavest me, observing Thy law in such a manner, as Thou didst always observe it.   Amen.

2. The second virtue was *humility:* for although our

(5) Gal. v. 3.   (6) Ps. xxxix 9.

Lord could not account Himself a sinner, since He neither was, nor could be so; yet He would be held as such, subjecting Himself to circumcision, which was the sign of sinful children; so that such as saw Him circumcised might have said that He was a sinner; and this He ordained for our confusion; who being sinners would not seem so to be, but would put on the mask of being righteous. Therefore, O my soul, seeing that thou art humbled by truth itself, be humbled also by charity; and seeing thou knowest thyself to be worthy of humiliation for thy sins, desire, with thy Lord, to be humbled even although thou wert without sin. (7)

3. The third virtue was *patience;* for other children wanting the use of reason, fear neither circumcision, nor the knife, nor the wound, and until the blow light upon them, they feel it not; but this blessed child knew, as a perfect man, what was in hand, and naturally feared the blow and the wound, yet for all this, He was as quiet and motionless as if He had not known it. And though when He felt the wound, He wept like a child, and cried much through the delicacy of His complexion, yet in His heart He was glad, for shedding His blood with such pain, delighting, in this affliction, to accomplish the will of His Father for our good.

4. The fourth virtue, was most *fervent charity*, shedding those drops of blood with so great love, that if need had been to shed all instantly, He would have effected it : and had it been expedient to have received many other, and much greater wounds, He would have offered Himself for the love of His Father, and for our good.

Colloquy.—O immense charity! O invincible patience! O profound humility, and perfect obedience of

***

(7) S. Ber. serm. xlii. in Cant.

my Redeemer! O sovereign virtues with which is weaved the priestly garment of our high priest Jesus, much more precious than "purple and scarlet twice dyed, and fine twisted linen!" (8)   O High Priest, who on this day didst clothe Thyself with this garment to offer this "morning sacrifice," and didst afterwards again put it upon the cross, to offer the "evening sacrifice," (9) invest me with such another, that I may offer up my body and soul, "a living sacrifice, holy, pleasing," to Thy sovereign majesty.(10)   I am ashamed, O Lord, to see myself so naked of these four virtues; let Thy grace aid me, to invest myself with them, and to cover my nakedness.(11) Amen.

POINT III.

1. Thirdly, I am to consider the *spiritual* circumcision which our Lord Christ *exacts of me*, by the example of this corporal circumcision, with which He moves, and teaches me to circumcise, and cut off all my superfluities in pampering, esteeming and indulging my flesh, (12) to mortify my inordinate vices and affections, to accomplish the law of Almighty God, even if need be, to shed my blood for it; (13) for in this manner is the true spirit obtained.   And in this sense, said an holy man, as St. Dorotheus reports, Da sanguinem et accipe spiritum; (14) " Give blood, and thou shalt receive spirit :" for the perfection of the spirit is not obtained but by the price of blood, mortifying and circumcising all the affections of flesh and blood.

2. Besides this I am willingly to *suffer others to* circumcise me, and to aid me to take away these superfluities, whether they do it with a good or with an evil intention:

(8) Exod. xxxvi. 8, 9 ; xxxix. 2.   (9) Num. xxviii. 8.
(10) Rom. xii. 1.   (11) Apoc. iii. 18.   (12) Rom. ii. 28.
(13) Col. ii. 11.   (14) Serm. x.

suffering them with patience to circumcise, and cut off from me some of my delicacy, my honour and comforts, although it be with the shedding of my blood : for, as St. Paul says, it is not much to "*strive against sin*," if one do not "*resist unto blood*," (15) as our Saviour Christ did : to whom I am to say, "Sponsus sanguinis tu mihi es," "A bloody spouse thou art to me," (16) since for Thy sake I will suffer with a good will, any circumcision, or mortification that may happen, though it be to the shedding of my blood for Thee.

3. To this end, it will help me to consider, that our Saviour Christ shed His precious blood in *three places*, and by the hands of *three sorts of persons.*—i. In *circumcision* by the *minister* of Almighty God, who did it to a holy end. ii. In the *garden* by *Himself* through the consideration of the afflictions of His passion, which made Him sweat blood. iii. In the *house of Pilate*, and on *Mount Calvary* by the hands of the *tormentors*, and ministers of Satan. And all this that I may persuade myself, that I am likewise to be prepared to shed my blood, and to suffer in these three ways.—i. By subjecting myself to what the ministers of Almighty God shall ordain, although it be to the cutting off and circumcising what I most love. ii. By being the punisher of myself, moving myself by such consideration to works of penance and mortification, chastising my flesh, and depriving myself of whatsoever hinders me in the service of God, though it may grieve me never so much.—iii. By suffering those pains and afflictions which happen to me by the hands of my enemies, though they do it with an evil intent.

Colloquy.—O good Jesus, by that blood which Thou didst shed upon these three occasions, I beseech

(15) Heb. xii. 4.   (16) Exod. iv. 25.

Thee encourage my heart, that if need be, it may offer itself to shed its blood upon the like occasions. And seeing it has so much to circumcise, which self-love detains it from doing, circumcise it, O Lord, by Thine own hands, and contrive that others may circumcise it, that there may remain in it no superfluous thing that may be displeasing to Thy divine majesty.

(Of this shedding of blood which happened in the circumcision, there may be made another very devout meditation, in the form that shall be set down in the fourth part, concerning the blood which our Saviour Christ shed in His passion.)

MEDITATION XXI.

ON THE IMPOSITION OF THE NAME OF JESUS TO OUR SAVIOUR (1)

POINT I.

First, I am to consider *who imposes* this name upon the child and *for what cause*, and *how he accepts* it.

1. The principal giver of this name, was not the Virgin, nor St. Joseph, nor the angel, but the *eternal Father;* for the excellency of this child is so great, that no creature either of earth, or of heaven was able of himself, to give Him a name befitting Him, but only His eternal Father, who knew Him, and knew the end for which He was incarnate, and what office He was to execute, as man.

2. And for this cause, among many names that He might have given Him, He would have Him called JESUS, which is to say, "Saviour." For His coming into the world was principally to save us, and this was His office.

(1) Luc. ii. 21. S. Th. 3. p. q. xxxvii. art. 2.

And although others had this name, yet they were but figures, and shadows of this sovereign child, who with an exalted voice, and by excellency deserves to be called Jesus, Saviour, and deliverer,—not only of bodies, but also of souls. This He performs in three admirable ways.

i. First, because He delivers us from *all kind of evils,* of ignorances and errors, of sins and punishments, as well temporal as eternal; so that there is no evil so great, from which this Saviour is not able to deliver us.

ii. Secondly, because He not only delivers us from evil, but also *grants us most excellent good ;* that our health, and salvation might be most abundant and perfect : and therefore He communicates to us celestial grace and wisdom, the virtues, and gifts of the Holy Ghost, with abundance of merits to gain the crown of eternal glory, until we enter even into the land of promise;—not as Jesus the son of Nun, into the land that flows with the "milk and honey" (2) of temporal delicacies, which gratify the body,—but into the land that flows with the milk and honey of eternal delicacies, which gratify and fill the soul without end.

iii. The third is, in *the manner* of saving us, by reason of which this name of Jesus could not agree with Him who was only God, or only man, or to any of all the angels that are created, but only with Christ, to whom it properly belongs by reason of His being true God and true man : for if He were man alone He could not save us;—if He were God alone He might have saved us merely by His mercy : but as God and man, He saves us also by the rigour of justice, gaining by conquest and by His own merits, the salvation signified by His name. And therefore this our Lo d being asked who He was, answered : Ego qui loquor justitiam, et qui propugnator sum ad sal-

(2) Deut. xxxi. 7—20.

vandum. (3) "I that speak justice, and am a defender to save."

Colloquy.—O most sweet Jesus, happy be to Thee this name so glorious which is given to Thee this day. I rejoice that it is not an empty name, or the shadow of a name, as others have had it; but a name full of truth and of all perfection. Rejoice, O my soul at the excellencies of this so sovereign a Saviour, and say with the prophet:—"I will rejoice in the Lord, and will joy in God my Jesus," (4) and my Saviour; for He the Lord God is my strength, and He will make my feet like the feet of harts, to fly from sins, and as a conqueror will lead me above the heavens with His saints, with whom I may praise Him with hymns, and with psalms, world without end. Amen.

3. I may likewise ponder, how our Blessed Lady the Virgin, declared in the circumcision the name of her Son, whose excellencies she most perfectly knew, since the time that the angel revealed them to her, and "in her heart" ruminated and pondered them; and therefore on this day she with great reverence and devotion, pronounced His name with her lips, and said : "His name shall be JESUS." O what great joy the most sacred Virgin felt, when this first time she pronounced this most sweet name of JESUS; and not she only, but glorious St. Joseph, and the rest who were present, and heard this name, felt a celestial fragrance and sweetness. For then began to be fulfilled that which is written in the Canticles: "Thy name is as oil poured out: therefore young maidens have loved thee." (5) Until this hour, this sweetest name made no odour of itself because it was locked up, and enclosed ; now that it manifested itself, it poured out a most sweet, and

(3) Is. lxiii. 1.　　　(4) Abac. iii. 18, 19.　　　(5) Cant. i. 2.

odoriferous fragrancy, cheering, comforting, and affecting those pure and chaste souls who either pronounce it or hear it pronounced, which are inflamed with the love of this our Lord, through the sweetness of His holy name,—but above all our most Blessed Lady the Virgin being most pure and undefiled, and knowing best the sovereign mysteries of His name. O with what pleasure did this Blessed Lady repeat those words of her Canticle; "My soul doth magnify the Lord, and my spirit rejoiceth in God my 'JESUS,' and 'Saviour;' because He hath regarded the humility of His handmaid, for behold from henceforth all generations shall call me blessed :—because He that is mighty, hath done great things to me, and holy is His name."

Colloquy.—O sovereign Virgin, beseech thy son to imprint in my heart that esteem, and love of this holy name, that He imprinted in thine. O most sweet name, pour down upon me thy celestial fragrancy, that my weak, sick and miserable soul may be comforted, and healed by it, and may be free from those miseries in which it is plunged, enjoying the fruit of her abundant salvation.

4. Lastly, I may ponder, how this blessed babe, accepted the name, and office of our Saviour, and rejoiced in it, offering with great delight to His eternal Father to stand for the honour of His sweetest name, and entirely to fulfil all whatever it signified for the good of men.

Colloquy.—I thank Thee, O good Jesus, for the will which Thou hadst to save us, accepting the office with the name of our Saviour: fulfil it, O Lord, effectually in me, and seeing Thou art Jesus, "Esto mihi Jesus," "Be to me Jesus, be my Saviour." Amen.

POINT II.

Secondly, I will consider the *causes*, why this name was given Him on the eighth day, at His *Circumcision:* for although the angel declared it before the Incarnation to the Blessed Virgin, and afterwards to St. Joseph, yet in the Circumcision it was manifested for two principal causes.

1. First, *for the honour of the child:* for His Father seeing Him so humbled, that He bare the likeness of a sinner, would that He then should be exalted, giving Him a name above all names, which is the name of JESUS, that we might understand, that He has not only no sin, but that He is the Saviour of sinners, and the pardoner of sins. This is, to move me to give infinite thanks to the eternal Father, for thus honouring His Son, when for His love He humbles Himself: by which He gives me an assured pledge, that if I humble myself, He will also exalt me, and will give me a new name, so glorious, that none will know how to esteem it as it ought to be esteemed, "but he that receiveth it," (6) and that God communicates His greatness in glory.

2. Secondly, to *make it manifest that the name* and *office of Saviour* was to cost Him the *shedding of His blood:* for "without the shedding of blood," says the Apostle, "there is no remission" (7) of sins. And therefore our sweet Jesus, taking now the office of a Redeemer, gives in earnest of the price that He is to pay for our ransom, a little of that blood which He shed in His Circumcision, with a determination to pay the whole price entirely in His passion, shedding for us all the blood that He has. True it is, that this little was a sufficient price for all the sins of the world, even if there had been a thousand other

(6) Apoc. ii. 17.　　(7) Heb. ix. 22.

worlds, because it was the blood of Almighty God : but His charity, and liberality would, that the price should be all His blood : to which end He gave license to all the instruments that are on earth for the shedding of blood, to draw out His blood with grievous pain, and contempt: to wit; the knife, whips, thorns, nails, and spear. The knife on this day opened the first fountain of blood, but that was presently closed. The other instuments afterwards opened others, which closed not till all His blood was drawn forth to the last drop.

Colloquy.—O sweetest Saviour, whose "fountains," although they are of blood, shed with so great pain, are yet also fountains of the "living waters"(8) of infinite graces, which are to be gathered with great rejoicing and love. Let my soul praise Thee for this infinite charity, with which Thou openest these fountains, commanding me to approach with alacrity, to enjoy the price that Thou didst give with such pain. O my soul what hast thou not reason to do for thy own salvation, when thy Saviour does so much for the same? If it cost Him His blood, is it much that it should cost thee thine? Behold me here, O Lord, ready to shed my blood for Thy love, so that Thou wilt make me partaker of Thine. Amen.

POINT III.

Thirdly, I will consider the *greatness of this sweet name;* the great *profit* that *we reap by it;* and the *manner* how we are to *derive advantage from it:* but before we ent into this consideration, I am to beseech the eternal Fath that for the glory of this most holy name, He wil pleased to enlighten me, that I may know its great s, for if, as St. Paul says, "no man can say the Jesus, but by the Holy Ghost:" (9)—then can no L

(8) Is. xii. 3.   (9) 1 Cor. xii. 3.

worthily ponder, and understand what is contained in the name of Jesus, if he be not previously aided by the same Holy Ghost.

1. This presupposed, I will consider how the name of Jesus is a *summary* and memorial of all the *greatness* that is in *Christ* our Lord, considering it under three heads:—i. For that it is the *sum* of all the *perfections* that belong to Him as He is God, and of all the graces and virtues that He has, as He is man, and of all the offices that He does to men, as He is God and man. So that I may well infer, if He be Jesus,—then is He infinitely good, holy, wise, omnipotent, and full of mercy, and the very goodness, sanctity, and wisdom of Almithis necessarily belongs to the name of Jesus, who, as St. Paul says, "is made unto us, wisdom, justice, sanctification, and redemption." (10)—ii. Likewise if He be Jesus, then He is exceedingly mild, humble, patient, strong, modest, obedient, and charitable: for He is to be the pattern of all these virtues; and "of His fulness" (11) all men are to receive the graces, and virtues wherewith they are to be saved.—iii. Again, if He be Jesus, then He is our master, our physician, our father, our judge, our pastor, our protector, and our advocate. So that in Jesus only we have all things : and therefore I may say to Him, *Jesus meus et omnia.*

Colloquy.—O my Jesus, and my all,—if I be sick, Thou art my health; if hungry, Thou art my fulness; if I be poor, Thou art my riches; if weak, Thou art my strength; if I be ignorant, Thou art my wisdom; and if I be a sinner, Thou art my justice, my sanctification, and redemption. (12) O my Jesus, and my all, grant that I may love Thee above all

(10) 1 Cor. i. 30.

(11) Joan. i. 16.   (12) S. Amb. l. de Virg. ad finem.

things, and that in Thee only I may seek my repose, and perfect satiety: for in Thee only is altogether all that which can satiate me: for Thou only art my sole *summum bonum*, to whom be honour and glory, world without end.   Amen.

2. Upon this, I may also discourse, how in this sweetest name are included all the *glorious names* that the prophets give the *Messiah*,—such as are those related by the prophet Isaias, saying: *That He "shall be called Wonderful, Counsellor, God the mighty, the Father of the world to come, the Prince of peace,"* (13)—pondering how the name of God is adapted to Jesus; for if He had not been God, He could not have redeemed us; and He has the name of "mighty," for He is to fight against, and to vanquish the devils; the name of "wonderful," for all that is in Him, His Incarnation, life and death is all new, and wonderful. Jesus likewise is a "Counsellor," and the "Angel of the great Council," for His doctrine is replete with admirable counsels. Jesus is also "the Father of the world to come," engendering us in grace, and giving us the inheritance of glory. He is "the Prince of peace," pacifying us with God and with men, with abundance of all peace.

Colloquy.—O great Jesus, how well the greatness of these names suits Thee: and since they are not empty, but full names, work in me that which all of them signify, that I may glorify Thee for the glory that Thou hast from them.   Amen.

3. Hence I may ascend, to consider the *benefits that I have* in this sweet *name of* JESUS :—which is the only means to obtain pardon of all my sins : it is the reason why I should be heard in my prayers : it is the medicine for all my spiritual infirmities : it is my offensive and de-

(13) Is. ix. 6.

fensive armour against the devils in all my temptations : it is my protection in all dangers : it is my light and my guide in all my ignorances : it is to me a pattern, and example of all virtues : and finally, it is the fire and spur that inflames, and incites me to procure them. From these considerations, I am to excite in myself a great desire that this most holy name may be always fixed in my memory to be mindful of it,—in my understanding to meditate on it,—and in my will to love and to rejoice in it. I am to imprint it in my heart, that it may be always united with me, and to keep it in my tongue, to praise and to bless it, delighting to publish its greatness, taking it for the beginning and ending of all my words, and using it with great reverence both interior and exterior : since, as the apostle says, "In the name of JESUS every knee shall bow, of those that are in heaven, on earth," (14) and purgatory; yea, and those of hell, who in despite of themselves, shall be forced to respect it.

Colloquy.—O sweet Jesus, be Jesus to me in all my faculties, exercising in them the office of Jesus, that they may likewise be exercised in all that appertains to Thy honour, for ever, and ever. Amen.

MEDITATION XXII.

ON THE COMING OF THE THREE KINGS OF THE EAST, TO ADORE THE CHILD: AND ON THEIR ENTRANCE INTO JERUSALEM.

POINT I.

First, is to be considered the *apparition of the star* in the east : *when it appeared:* for *what end:* and *what effects* it wrought in those three kings, or sages. (1)

(14) Phil. ii 10.   (1) S. Th. 3. p. q. xxxvi. art. 7, et 8.

1. First, I will ponder how the eternal Father, desiring that His Son newly born (2) in Bethlehem should be known and adored, not only by some Jews, but also by some Gentiles, having sent an Angel to declare the news of this birth to the shepherds, the same day *created* in the east a most beautiful and bright shining *star*, to be a *sign* that the Messiah, and King of Israel was born, of whom Balaam had prophesied, (3) desiring that they also should come to acknowledge, and to adore Him, since He was born for the good of all mankind.

Colloquy.—I give Thee thanks, O sovereign Father, for the care Thou hast, that Thy Son should be known and adored by the Gentiles, as well for His glory and honour, as for the profit of those that are to know and to adore Him. O that all only knew and adored Him, that all might partake of the fruit of His coming. Amen.

2. Secondly, I will consider how that there were many in the east that saw this star, that wondered at the beauty of it, and that understood what it signified ; but there were none that moved, except the *three kings*, who resolved to go to seek this King, whose star they had seen : the rest would not stir, for they were loth to leave their houses, their wealth, their wives, and their friends, and to go out of their own country to undertake such a long and laborious journey, into a strange land, and an uncertain place : and the flesh and the Devil augmented all these difficulties, to hinder them from this journey ; that being fulfilled in them which is written :—" The slothful man saith, There is a lion in the way, and a lioness in the roads, I shall be killed in the midst of the street, (4) to avoid this danger, I will not go from home." But these

<hr>

(2) Matt. ii. 1.   (3) Num. xxiv. 17.
(4) Prov. xxii. 13, et xxvi. 13.

wretches flying from the lion, encountered with the bear, (5) and flying from a temporal, fell into an eternal death : for it is to be believed that this was the cause of their eternal condemnation, because they remained in the darkness of their infidelity. And this I am to apply to myself, pondering how often the star of divine inspiration appears within my soul soliciting me to seek Christ, and to embrace His poverty, humility, and other virtues : and although I understand what this Star means, yet I will not move, nor stir a foot to seek Him, because I will not lose my case and convenience, nor abandon those things that I love, and because I will not suffer a little affliction, feigning difficulties when there are none at all : and so flying the "hoary frost," which is the afflictions of the earth; "the snow shall fall upon me," (6) which is the chastisement of heaven, our Lord God leaving me frozen and abandoned : and the Star which appeared for my salvation, will be a witness against me to my condemnation.

3. Thirdly, I will consider the *great favour* of Almighty God to these three kings, in *inspiring them so effectually*, and enlightening them with such an interior light, to form the resolution of leaving their own country, and their homes, to come to seek Christ, letting others alone in their blindness and misery. And by this I shall know the efficacy of God's divine inspiration, and I will humbly beseech our Lord to assist me by His preventing grace, and to say to me, as He said to Abraham,—" Go forth out of thy country, and from thy kindred, and out of thy father's house, and come into the land which I shall shew thee." (7) But if Almighty God has already done me this favour, that with the light of another Star He has effectually called me out of the world to seek Him in Religion, leaving others in the midst of those turmoils aud traffics,

(5) Amos. v. 19.　　(6) Job. vi. 16.　　(7) Gen. xii. 1.

13

I am to give Him many thanks, and humbly beseech Him, that He will be pleased to send often into my soul such like stars and illuminations, that they may move me to abandon all that hinders me from loving Him, and from following Him with perfection.

4. Lastly, I will consider how in this was fulfilled the truth of that dreadful sentence, that "*many are called, but few chosen*," (8) for among so many men of the east, three only were chosen for this enterprise, the Holy Trinity selecting them for the first fruits of the elect among the Gentiles.

Colloquy.—O blessed Trinity, make me of the number of these three, that, following Thy divine vocation, I may confess, adore, and glorify Thee, world without end. Amen.

POINT II.

Secondly, I am to consider the *departure of these kings* from the east, and their *voyage*, till they arrived at Jerusalem.

1· Consider first, how these kings, with that lively faith which they had, cast themselves into the hands of Al-mighty God, and began their voyage, carrying with them gifts to offer to the child : and setting themselves upon their way, they suddenly *perceived the Star to move*, as if it would be their guide in that journey, wherewith they rejoiced with exceeding great joy, praising and glorifying Almighty God for the great providence and care He had of them : whence I will draw the conclusion, that if trusting in God, and building upon faith, I begin to seek Him, His providence will not be failing to provide me a guide and a helper, to prosecute my journey : and the divine Spirit, and the grace of my vocation, will go

(8) Matt. xx. 16.

always before me like a star guiding and directing my paths, as He guided the Israelites through the desert, going "before them, to shew the way by day in a pillar of a cloud," to defend them from the sun; "and by night in a pillar of fire," (9) that might give them light, to be at both times their guide. So likewise our Lord will guide me, protecting me in the day of prosperity, and in the night of adversity, defending me from the heats of sensual and worldly temptations, and likewise from coldness, lukewarmness and pusillanimity.

2. Secondly, I will consider, how, having beheld this, the *kings went forward on their way;* always following the star, without turning one way or other, staying where it stayed, and going when it moved, endeavouring to do nothing unworthy of our Lord, whom they acknowledged in the star. And in imitation of them, I am to take for the star and guide of my life, the light of reason, and the light of faith, the inspiration, or illumination of the divine Spirit, and the direction of my prelates, or confessors. These four stars, are reduced to one which is Almighty God, who guides us by them. (10) And to me it belongs directly to follow whatever this Star dictates unto me without turning to the right hand or to the left, endeavouring not to do anything that may be offensive in His eyes.

3. Thirdly, I will consider, how these kings going forward on their way, and approaching near to Jerusalem, suddenly by God's command *the star disappeared*, and they remained therefore very sad and afflicted. This the divine providence ordained to make proof of their faith and loyalty, and to give them occasion to exercise great virtues at their entrance into Jerusalem, and that wanting the guide of heaven, they might seek such guidance as Al-

(9) Exod. xiii. 21.   (10) Apoc. ii. 28.

mighty God has left on earth, which is, the doctors and teachers of His law, and the prelates and superiors in His Church: and therefore these sages were not dismayed, neither accounted they themselves deluded, nor did they therefore leave their enterprise and return to their own country; but determined to enter into Jerusalem to seek what they desired; instructing me by their example, what I ought to do, when Almighty God hides Himself from me, and when sensible devotion fails me, and when I find myself in darkness, and in temptations:—for in such cases, I must not be distrustful, nor turn back from what I have begun, but must use such means as are in my power, to seek, and to find God, having recourse to His ministers, as it is said in the book of Canticles, of the spouse (that is the just soul) ; who being through the absence of her husband in darkness, and in the obscurity of night, rises up to seek Him "in the streets" and corners of the city, (11) exercising herself in holy works, and imitating the example of other just ones : and then she asks those who watch and guard the city, (who are the prelates,) whether they have seen him whom her soul desires, that they may inform her, and teach her where and how she may find him, and in this manner she found him ; and so the Sages found Him.

Colloquy.—O Eternal God, give me the faith and constancy of these men, that I may seek Thee with that loyalty and perseverance with which they sought Thee, having recourse with humility to human means, when divine means are hidden from me.   Amen.

POINT III.

Thirdly, I am to consider the *entrance of these kings into Jerusalem,* and the demand they made saying : " *Where*

(11) Cant iii. 2.

is He that is born king of the Jews?"—in which are re-splendent the great virtues of these men.

i. For first, they shewed *great faith*, believing what they had not seen, confessing that there was born a child, who was the King, and Messiah, promised to the Jews, and they doubted not of it, but only of the place where He was to be born; for that He who revealed to them the first, revealed not the second to them.

ii. Secondly, they shewed *great magnanimity* and fortitude : for foreseeing what peril they might put themselves in, of being put to death by Herod, for asking in his country and court, for another king,—yet for all this, they entered not secretly, nor demanded in corners, but publicly, and in his own palace. O heroical confidence, O courageous fortitude, inspired by this new born King, who though yet hid from these sages the light of the visible Star, yet hid not from them the invisible light of faith, by whose power the Saints "conquered kingdoms, wrought justice, and obtained the promises !" (12)

Colloquy.—O my soul, have a lively faith in thy God, for by Ais power thou shalt go over "the wall," (13) animate thyself to break through difficulties, fear not to encounter dangers: for He will protect thee, and set thee at liberty from them.

iii. From this faith, and fortitude of these Sages it came to pass, that although at the hearing of this demand Herod was troubled, and all Jerusalem with him, yet *they themselves were not* troubled. In this I will ponder how Herod was troubled because he was a tyrant and ambitious, and therefore feared lest He that was born, might deprive him of his kingdom. But what is most to be wondered at is, that the Jews also were troubled at that, for which they should rather have rejoiced, choosing

(12) Heb. xi. 33.   (13) Ps. xvii. 30.

rather to flatter, and to give pleasure to a tyrant king than to the King of Heaven that was promised to them. By which I may learn how dangerous a thing it is to entertain close intimacy with powerful and vicious persons, who are easily troubled with passions of hatred, anger, revenge and ambition; for when they are troubled, I may also be troubled with them. But if I trust in Almighty God, as did the Sages, I shall not be troubled, though all others be troubled : rather I shall say with the prophet David :—" The Lord is my light and my salvation; whom shall I fear? The Lord is the protector of my life; of whom shall I be afraid? If armies in camp should stand together against me, my heart shall not fear; if a battle should rise up against me, in this will I be confident." (14)

POINT IV.

Fourthly, I must consider, how Herod having heard this demand, *consulted* thereupon with the *high priests*, and the scribes of the people; who answering him that this King should be born "*in Bethlehem of Juda*," (15) for that it was so foretold by Micheas the prophet, he said to the Sages : "that they should there enquire and seek for the child, and having found Him, they should bring him word again." In this the providence of Almighty God shines forth in many ways.

i. First, because He makes use of the wicked, to favour the intentions of those that are good : as He made use of Herod, to discover to these sages the place of the birth of our Saviour : fulfilling that which is written, that "*the fool shall serve the wise;*" (16) and "*to them that love God, all things work together unto good.*" (17)

ii. Secondly, it is resplendent in this, that by means of His ministers, although they are wicked, He discovers

<hr>

(14) Ps. xxvi. 1, etc.   (15) Mich. iii. 2.   (16) Prov. xi. 29.
(17) Rom. viii. 28.

the truth of holy Scripture, to those that desire to know it for their profit; as in this case He did not permit the high priests and teachers of the law, to conceal this truth from the sages. And if I with a good zeal desire to know the will of Almighty God, He will discover it also to me by the means of His ministers ; of whom He says by a prophet—"*that their lips keep knowledge,*" (18) which they hold as it were in a chest of trust, to teach the doubtful things of the law to those who demand them, for they are the Angels and messengers of our Lord, and the expounders of His will.

iii. The providence of Almighty God is likewise resplendent, in having given us the divine Scriptures, in which there is abundant light to know Christ, to seek, and to find Him, without having need of any miraculous Star, or new revelation, but only fervent prayer and profound meditation : according to that which our Saviour Christ said unto the Jews :—"Search the Scriptures; for you think in them to have life everlasting, and the same are they that give testimony of me." (19)

Colloquy.—O sweet Jesus that saidst:—"Ask, and you shall receive, seek, and you shall find :" enlighten me that I may seek Thee in Thy sacred Scriptures, so that I may find Thee, and that I may search out the eternal life contained in them, in such a manner that I may obtain it. Amen.

iv. Finally, the secret judgments of Almighty God manifested in this case may affright me, and make my hair stand on end ; considering that the Gentiles came from countries so far distant, and with such great labour and fatigue to seek Christ, and that the Jews, who so many years had expected Him, and were so near Him, yet moved not to seek Him. And though they informed the Sages

(18) Malac. ii. 7.   (19) Joan. iv. 39.

where they might find Him, yet they took not this intelligence to themselves; that the truth of that might be manifested, which was afterwards spoken by our Lord : "No man can come to me, except the Father that sent me, draw him." (20)   But these wretches were not drawn by the Father, for they delighted more in pleasing a tyrant : and deferring their going till the Sages returned, they never went.   Wherefore taking warning by other men's misfortune, I will remove all impediments, that may in anywise hinder the eternal Father from calling me by His inspirations, and uniting me with Christ, not deferring to another time to obey those which He shall give me : for delay may be the cause of my perdition.

Colloquy.—O eternal Father, whose "counsels over the sons of men," are "terrible," (21) but yet just; by that love which Thou bearest to Thy Son I beseech Thee, that since Thou hast so great a desire that He should be known and adored by all men, cast me not off through my own sin and remissness, leaving me overwhelmed therein, but with an efficacious grace draw me to Thee, that I may seek and find Him, know and adore Him, world without end, to Thy glory.   Amen.

MEDITATION XXIII.

ON THE DEPARTURE OF THE SAGES FROM JERUSALEM, AND THEIR ENTRANCE INTO THE STABLE AT BETHLEHEM, AND THE OCCURRENCES THERE.

POINT I.

"Having heard the king," they "went their way; and behold the star which they had seen in the East, went before them.   And seeing the star, of which they rejoiced

(20) Joan. vi. 44.   (21) Ps. lxv. 5.   (1) Matt. ii. 9.

with exceeding great joy." (1) "*Gavisi sunt gaudio magno valde.*"

1. Here I am to ponder, first, the *care of these kings*, in prosecuting their intention : for as soon as they had knowledge of what they desired, they departed from Jerusalem, and from the court of king Herod, flying from the noise and tumult of the city : by which they teach us how punctually we ought to apply ourselves to the business of our salvation, departing from the noise of the world, and flying to the place where we are to find Almighty God, saying with David :—"Who will give me wings like a dove, and I will fly, and be at rest?" and having them given him, he says : "Lo, I have gone far off flying away, and I abode in the wilderness." (2)   And if king David desired to fly the noise of his own court, and these Sages the noise of Herod's court ; how much more reasonable is it, that if I either be a religious man, or desire to be a spiritual man, I should fly from the courts of kings and princes, except it be, when some precise necessity, and the will of Almighty God oblige me to remain in them.

2. Secondly, I will ponder the loving *providence of our God*, and His fidelity in rewarding the labours of those that seek Him. For although these kings when they knew the place where the child was born might have gone to Bethlehem without the Star ; yet our Lord would that it should again appear to them, and cause joy in them, and that no ordinary joy, but an exceeding great joy, thus rewarding the afflictions they suffered in Jerusalem, the dangers they exposed themselves to, their diligence to know where they should find the king they enquired after; thus turning their sorrows into exceeding great joy, and fulfilling that of the prophet David, who said :—"Accord-

(2) Ps. liv. 7.

ing to the multitude of my sorrows in my heart, Thy comforts have given joy to my soul." (3)

Colloquy.—O great God and loving Father! who will not carefully seek Thee? who will not suffer Thy absence with patience? who will not do his utmost to find Thee, when Thou treatest with such love, those who seek Thee with perseverance?

POINT II.

On the Sages arriving at Bethlehem, the Star "came and stood over the place where the child was," "and entering into the house, they found the child with Mary His mother." (4)

1. In this point, I will first consider the great novelty, and *wonder* it caused in the Sages, to see the star stay over a *place so poor* and mean, as that stable was : for being such eminent princes as they were, they might rather have thought that this King should have been born in some palace, or in the best house of the city, where other kings are accustomed to reside : but being favoured with an interior light, they acknowledged that the greatness of that King did not demonstrate itself in the pomps of this world, but in the true contempt of them : and therefore they subjected their judgment to the testimony of the miraculous Star.

Colloquy.—O blessed King, since already Thou beginnest to triumph over the world, captivating the understandings of the wise for the triumph of divine faith, captivate also mine very strongly, that I may triumph over the world, contemning for Thy love, all that is therein.   Amen.

2. Secondly, I will consider the mystery of these words, "*they found the child with Mary* His mother." (5)   Which

(3) Ps. xciii. 19.   (4) Matt. ii. 9.   (5) Matt. ii. 11.

were likewise spoken to the shepherds; to signify, that generally Jesus is not found without His mother, nor the mother without Jesus : for whosoever is a true lover of Jesus, is immediately devoted to His mother; and whosoever is devoted to His mother, obtains the love and friendship of Jesus : and since both are so united together, I am to advance myself in the love and service of them both ; for the love of the one, confirms and perfects me in the love of the other.

3. Thirdly, I should consider, how, in the very instant that the Sages beheld the child, there *issued* from His divine countenance *a ray of celestial light,* which penetrated their hearts, and discovered to them, that He was God and man, the King and Messiah promised to the Jews, and the Saviour of the world, and caused in them such an exceeding interior joy, that it replenished their whole soul : for if the sight of the material star caused in them so great joy, what joy would arise in them on beholding Jesus the star of the morning, (6) and Lord of all the stars?   O how full of content were they to behold this divine star ! that being proportionally fulfilled in them, which was spoken by the prophet David : "I shall be satisfied when Thy glory shall appear." (7)

Colloquy.—O glory of the Father, bright shining star of the morning, illuminate me with Thy light: fill me with beholding Thee: recreate me with Thy splendour, and replenish me with good things by Thy celestial influence.   Happy are they that find Thee, though it be in a manger; for the baseness of the place, obscures not the greatness of Thy glory: it rather tempers the immensity of Thy splendour, that men may contemplate Thee with more delight.

(6) Apoc. ii. 28, et xxii. 16.   (7) Ps. xvi. 15.

POINT III.

Immediately "falling down," they "adored Him, and opening their treasures, they offered Him gifts; gold, frankincense, and myrrh." (8)

1. Three especial things the Sages observed here in their conduct towards the child; all which were foretold by the royal prophet David.

i. The first was, to *prostrate themselves* on the ground in token of the great, both exterior and interior reverence, which they shewed towards this child : for as the body was humbled as much as might be, even to prostrating and fastening itself to the earth ; so the soul was humbled before this King, acknowledging itself in His presence as dust and as nothing. The prophecy of David (9) beginning here to be fulfilled, which says : The Ethiopians shall fall down "before Him," and His enemies shall "lick the ground," (10) in token of subjection.

ii. The second was to *adore Him*, not only as the kings of the earth are adored, but with that *supreme adoration* which is given only to Almighty God, and is called *Latria*, acknowledging with a lively faith, that that child was their true God and Creator, who was born for the redemption of the whole world. And in this faith they spake unto Him, and gave Him thanks for the favour He had done them, in coming to redeem them, and especially in having drawn them by His Star to acknowledge Him. And there they offered themselves to be His perpetual vassals, with a determination to serve Him for ever, fulfilling that of the prophet : "All the kings of the earth shall adore Him, all nations shall serve Him." (11)

(8) Matt. ii. 11.   (9) Ps. lxxi. 9.   (10) Ps. lxxi. 9.
(11) Ps. lxxi. 11.

Colloquy.—O King of kings, and Lord of lords, I rejoice to see Thee so reverenced and adored by these kings and Sages of the earth: O that all others would reverence and adore Thee, as they did! (12) Cause, O Lord, that that may be presently fulfilled, which Thou spakest by Thy Prophets, that all nations should bow their knees before Thee: let all people " whom Thou hast made, come and adore before Thee, O Lord, and glorify Thy name." (13)   Amen.

iii. The third thing that the Sages did, was to *open* the coffers *of their treasures*, which they had brought shut all the way, and to *offer gifts* to the child in token of their vassalage, and in protestation that they would serve Him with their persons, and with all that they had. And with the same gifts they made profession of the faith that they had: for they offered Him gold as to their king;—incense as to a God and high priest;—and myrrh as to a mortal man. But much greater were the interior gifts where- with they accompanied these exterior ones, offering them to Him with the gold of love, with the incense of devotion, and with the myrrh of the mortification offering them- selves, to serve their Lord, fulfilling that which was spoken by the prophets, that the kings of Arabia, and of Saba, should offer Him gifts, (14) and presents of incense, myrrh and gold with praises of our Lord. (15)

2. Then will I consider how *pleasing* to the *child* Jesus was the *offering* of these men, beholding the faith, de- votion and love with which they offered it : for if He was so much pleased with the widow who offered her two mites, (16) on account of the good will with which she offered them; how much more was He pleased with these kings, who with such great good will offered to Him, like

(12) Is. xlv. 14.   (13) Ps. lxxxv. 9.   (14) Ps. lxxi. 10.
(15) Is. lx. 6,   (16) Luc. xxi. 2.

Abel, (17) the most precious that they had? O what thankfulness did He show to them, not with exterior words, for He spake not: but with the interior words of inspirations, communicating to them great and celestial gifts! And here I may piously consider, that in return for these three gifts, He gave them three others, largely augmenting in them the gold of wisdom and charity;— and the incense of prayer and devotion; and granting unto them the myrrh of incorruption, preserving them from falling into grievous sins, with perseverance in love.

3. In imitation of these holy kings, I am to *prostrate myself* before the child Jesus, with all possible humility, and to adore Him, as He will be adored, *in spirit* and *in truth:* and to open the treasures of my *heart*, not in the presence of men to be pleasing to them :—but in the presence of Almighty God, only to give Him pleasure, and to offer to Him the burning and shining gold of charity, and love towards God, and towards my neighbours ; the most odoriferous incense of prayer, with high elevated affections of devotion ; and the most select myrrh of perfect mortification of myself ; exercising virtuous works, without opening my treasures in such manner, that the thieves of pride and vain-glory may rob me of them. And particularly every exterior work that I shall do, should carry these three gifts for companions, doing it for love, with prayer and devotion, and with necessary mortification, that it may be done well and perfectly, relying upon the liberality of this our Lord, who will also reward this my offering, returning me in exchange great augmentation of these gifts : (18) for the Holy Ghost says: that, he that is swift and diligent in his works, shall have no infirmity, (19) and shall obtain favour with kings. (20)

(17) Gen. iv. 4. (18) Joan. iv. 14. (19) Ecclus. xxxi. 27.

(20) Prov. xxii. 29.

4. Besides this, if I be a Religious man, I am to offer to Him anew the *three vows:*—that of *chastity*, with the myrrh of mortification of the flesh; that of *poverty*, with the gold of all the temporal things that are in the world, desiring to give Him them all, if they were mine ; and the vow of *obedience*, denying myself, and burning like incense, in the fire of divine love, to give myself wholly to Almighty God.

Colloquy.—Go then, O my soul, offer thy vows and presents to our Lord, beholding Him, not like David, as he is dreadful and terrible, as He takes away the spirit and life from the princes and kings of the earth, (21) but as He is an amiable child, giving to these kings a divine spirit, by taking away their worldly spirit. O King of Heaven, accept the vows and gifts that I have offered Thee, taking from me my own spirit, that beguiles me, and giving me Thy spirit, that revives me. Amen.

POINT IV.

1. Then I am to consider the sweet *conference between* the Blessed Virgin, and these *kings*, they making relation to her of the star, which they had seen in the east, and of what had passed in Jerusalem, pondering how they offered themselves to her service, how full of admiration they were of the resplendent sanctity of our Lady, and of the poverty of the place where she was. And although St. Joseph was not present at their first entrance (that the Sages might understand that the child had no father on earth;)—yet soon after he might come, and they might discourse with him upon the same things. O how full of content might the Virgin be to hear them! and how might she keep them in her memory, to meditate upon them by herself! How thankful might she be to the Sages for

(21) Ps. lxxv. 13.

the journey they had undertaken, in coming to adore her son! and what divine things might she recount unto them, to confirm them in their faith! O Queen of Saba, (22) that in the person of these kings thy children, comest anew with gifts to behold the true King Solomon, how full of admiration wast thou, contemplating the infinite wisdom that shone in His poor house, and in His poor company! O with what an affection mightest thou say, beholding the Blessed Virgin and St. Joseph : "Blessed, O Lord, are Thy servants, that stand ever before Thee, hearing and learning Thine infinite wisdom!"

Colloquy.—O Sovereign Virgin, more wise than the queen of Saba, who like a mistress didst on this day teach the Sages the wisdom of heaven, which the world attains not unto; teach me the way how to serve thy Son, as these new disciples of His and thine, served Him.

2. Then I will consider how the Sages, being doubtful whether they should return to Herod, or not, because of their word that they had given him, and desiring to know the will of Almighty God, in this perplexity they lay down to sleep (23) : And having received an answer in sleep that they should not return to Herod, *they went back another way* into their country. In this we see displayed the providence and care that Almighty God has over those that serve Him, advising these Sages what was proper for them to do, not only to deliver the child from the persecution of Herod, but also to free them from the vexations they would have had from that cruel tyrant, if they had returned to him. Whereby I may see how happy I shall be, if I rely upon Almighty God, since His providence will not fail me in afflictions, but will cut off perils, before I fall into them.

(22) 3 Reg. x. 1, etc.   (23) Matt. ii. 12.

3. The kings having heard this commandment, *immediately fulfilled it*, desiring rather to obey Almighty God than men, esteeming more to hear the word that God spake to them, than to keep that which they had given unto man; for there is no greater wisdom, nor security, and assuredness than to hear the voice of Almighty God, and to stand for His gove rnment, seeing as our Lord Himself said by the prophet Isaiah:—All is ordained for our righteousness and abundant peace. (24)   Oh, how full of content these kings returned on their way, and how well did they think of the labour and fatigue employed for the things of God, which, although they be painful in the beginning, they have always good endings !   And, therefore, it is great wisdom to begin by that labour, the end of which shall be temporal and eternal repose, rejoicing in God world without end.   Amen.

MEDITATION XXIV.

ON THE PURIFICATION OF THE BLESSED VIRGIN, AND OF THE PRESENTATION OF THE CHILD IN THE TEMPLE.

POINT I.

The Old Law commanded, that a woman, having conceived by a man, if she had brought forth a male child, should remain forty days retired in her house, as unclean; at the end of which she should go to the temple to be purified, offering for her sin a lamb and a turtle; and, if she were poor, a pair of turtles or pigeons, desiring the priest to pray to God for her. (1)

This law the Blessed Virgin accomplished (2) with the exercise of admirable virtues; especially she exercised six,

(24) Is. xxxii. 17.   (1) Levit. xii. 2.   (2) Luc. ii. 12.

14

like the six leaves of the whitest lily, for which the speech of the celestial spouse is very fitting to her:—" As the lily among thorns, so is my love among the daughters." (3)

i. The first virtue was great *love of retirement,* with such delight that, although the law had not commanded it, yet it would have pleased her to continue those forty days in her secret corner, solicitous only to contemplate the greatness of her son, and to nourish Him; in which exercise she remained so full of contentment, that, in regard of Him, she respected not the company of the whole world.

ii. The second virtue was great *love of purity* and cleanness of heart, giving good demonstrations thereof; because, although she was most pure, she sought to be more purified, observing the law of purification, that her beloved might say of her, "Thou art all fair, O my love! and there is not a spot in thee." (4)

iii. The third virtue was *heroic obedience,* for although she knew that she was not obliged to keep this law, for that she had not conceived by the work of man; yet, as her son fulfilled the law of circumcision, so she would entirely fulfil this law, to conform herself to other women, and to observe the common laws of all, without having exemption, privilege, or dispensation, and without using therein images or interpretations, even in that in which she might lawfully have used them. And so, the forty days being fully ended, with great punctuality and readiness she set forward on her way to Jerusalem, with rare modesty and alacrity, rejoicing with her son, whom she bore in her arms, by whose example she learned this manner of obedience.

iv. The fourth virtue was *rare humility,* in willing to be treated as one *unclean,* and as one that stood in *need* of being purified, as if she had not been a virgin, demonstra-

(3) Cant. ii. 2.   (4) Cant. iv. 7.

ting herein great love of purity and humility; by whose example I may be ashamed to see myself so proud, and so desirous to be reputed as pure and holy, being, contrariwise, a sinner, and that so wretched and abominable, that my righteousness, as says the prophet Isaiah, is like a cloth stained with blood. (5)

v. The fifth virtue was great *love of poverty*, the sister of humility; for though with the gold that these kings gave her, she was able probably to buy a lamb, and to offer it, as rich and noble women used to do, yet she would be treated as a poor woman, and offer the sacrifice that was assigned to the poor, which was a pair of turtles, or two young pigeons.

vi. The sixth was the *great devotion* and *reverence* with which she gave this offering to the priest, requesting him with great humility to pray unto Almighty God for her, she herself being one that might have prayed for all. For as the lily within her six leaves contains other six little sprigs, with their buttons like gold; so the Blessed Virgin to these six virtues, conjoined diverse affections of an intention, purely and directly for the glory of Almighty God, enkindled by the fire of charity, and resplendent with the gold of celestial wisdom.

Colloquy.—O most Sacred Virgin, I rejoice to behold thee so rich in virtues, and so careful and diligent in exercising them; now I perceive how exceedingly true it is, that thou art "as the lily among thorns," (6) for in comparison with thee, we are blacked, and besmeared with the thorns of our sins, and thou art a most white and pure lily with the six leaves of these sovereign virtues. Well may we see, O Sovereign Queen, that thou didst always contemplate this king laid in His manger, and in thy lap, seeing thy spirit like spikenard, gave its accustomed odour to imitate

(5) Is. lxiv. 6.   .(6) Cant. ii. 2.   Ex. S. Ber. serm. 42 in Cant.

Him, sending out the most sweet odour of purity, humility, and obedience, (7) warmed by the fire of charity; obtain for me, O Blessed Lady, that I may behold Him and thee with such a spirit as may send forth the like odour.　Amen.

POINT II.

The law likewise commanded, that all the first-born of the Hebrews should be offered to God as holy, in acknowledgement of the favour He did them, in bringing them out of Egypt, killing in a night all the first-born of the Egyptians. (8)　And for the accomplishment of this law, our Blessed Lady, the Virgin, carried her son to the Temple to offer Him to the eternal Father.

1. Here I should consider, first, the *spirit* and *devotion* with which the Blessed Virgin *made this offering* in her own name, and in the name of all mankind, to the eternal Father : "Behold here, O eternal Father, Thy Only-begotten Son as He is God, and my only first-born as He is man, He that was represented by all the first-born that hitherto have been offered unto Thee, and whose offering Thou hast so much desired.　I offer Him with all my heart in thanksgiving, for having given Him to me, for I have nothing more precious to offer to Thee : He is Thine, take Him to Thyself, where He will be better entertained than in me.　I likewise offer Him to Thee in the odour of sweetness for the salvation and redemption of the whole world.　Receive, O my God, this offering more precious than that of Abel, more sweet than that of Noe, more holy than that of Abraham, and more excellent than all those that Moses ordained; and by this I beseech Thee to pardon all mortal men, and to admit them into Thy grace and friendship."　O how well pleased might the eternal Father be with this oblation, as well for the devo-

(7) Cant. i. 11.　　　　　　　(8) Exod. xiii. 2.

tion of the person that offered it, as for the sanctity of the offering that was presented Him.

2. Secondly, I will consider the spirit with which this most blessed *child offered Himself* in the Temple to His eternal Father. "Behold here," might He say, "O eternal Father, Thy Only-begotten Son, who was made man to obey Thee, and comes into the temple to honour Thee, here I present myself before Thy Majesty, and I offer myself to Thy service, and to the accomplishment of Thy will. And because neither the death of so many first-born who perished in Egypt, (9) nor the offering of the first-born of Israel, has been acceptable to Thee for the salvation of men, I offer myself to-day for them, that my death, and the sacrifice of my blood, may appease Thy wrath, and deliver Thy people from the servitude of sin. In this manner was fulfilled that speech of St. Paul. Qui dilexit nos, et tradidit semetipsum hostiam, et oblationem Deo in odorem suavitatis.(10) "Who hath loved us, and hath delivered Himself for us, an oblation, and a sacrifice to God, for an odour of sweetness." And it is to be believed that this offering took place in the morning, when the sacrifice of the lamb, called the morning lamb, (11) in the temple was offered, that there might be a correspondence between the figure and the figured. O how sweet was this offering to the eternal Father, and how content remained He with it as one that He was desirous of, for the offerings of all the other first-born were of no value, but as they were representations of this.

3. Thirdly, I am to imagine, that although our Saviour Christ made this offering for all men, yet He made it likewise particularly *for me*, holding me present in His memory and heart. And with this consideration in the temple of my soul, I will present myself in spirit before

(9) Ps. xxxvi.   (10) Eph. v. 2.   (11) Exod. xxix.39; Num. xxviii. 4.

the eternal Father, and in the company of the Blessed Virgin, and of the child Himself, I will offer myself to Him in thanksgiving, for having given Him to me for my Redeemer and master, beseeching Him to accept this offering, that it may reconcile me to Himself, and make me partaker of His gifts.

Colloquy.—O Sovereign Father, with all the affection of my heart, I offer to Thee Thy Only-begotten Son, and though I offer Him, who deserve to be rejected, yet the offering being so excellent, I hope to be admitted. Receive it, O Lord, in an odour of sweetness and for it grant me remission of my sins, that with a pure heart I may appear in Thy presence in the Temple of Thy glory. Amen.

POINT III.

The same law likewise commanded that these first-born should be *redeemed for five sicles*, (12) and so the Blessed Virgin redeemed her son, paying them to the priest, who took them, and returned her son to her. Upon this passage I am to consider, *who make* this sale of the Child,—*who* it is that *buys* him,—with what *price*, —*for* whom,—and what *benefits* arise from it.

1. First, I will consider how the eternal Father, to whom this child offered Himself, will not keep to Himself that which was given Him, but would anew *give Him to the world*, and to men, and sell Him to them for their good, displaying by this His infinite liberality and bounty, which is so far from repenting of having given us, what He once gave us, that He ratified the donation, inventing new reasons to give what He has given us.

2. *She that buys* and redeems Him is *the Blessed Virgin*, to bring Him up as her son; and yet she also will not

(12) Exod. xiii. 13 ; Levit. xxvii. 6.

detain Him to herself, but will nourish him for us, and buy Him that He may be employed for our good.

3. The price is no more than *five sicles.*

Colloquy.—O eternal Father, how cheap dost Thou sell a thing that is so precious! Why dost Thou equal this first-born in price with the rest? If the rest were redeemed for five sicles, this was to be redeemed for many millions, for He is worth infinitely more than all the rest. But I now perceive, O Lord, that this is to admonish me, that although the name of this ransom has the terms "sale" and "price," yet He is given us freely, and of grace, that I may incessantly thank Thee for this new grace, for which mayest Thou be glorified and praised by all Thy creatures, world without end. Amen.

4. I may also consider the spirit that is included in the price of these five sicles, by which is signified the *price* with which is bought the *most precious gold of divine wisdom,* (13)—which is Christ,—in such a manner as it may be bought. (14) This price is the mortification of the five senses, and the acts of the five virtues, which dispose us to obtain grace, and the perfection of it ; that is to say, lively faith, fear of God, sorrow for sins, confidence in God's mercy, an effectual resolution to obey God, and wholly to accomplish His holy will.

Colloquy.—Therefore, O my soul, if thou desirest to possess Christ, consider that He is not bought with gold, nor silver, but with those "five sicles" of the spirit; offer them to the eternal Father, and He will give him Thee.

5. I will ponder *the end* for which He is redeemed and bought; which is to be the slave and servant of men, and to deliver Himself for them unto death.

(13) Apoc. iii. 18.   (14) Is. lv. 1.

Colloquy.—O sweet Jesus, how willingly dost Thou suffer Thyself to be sold and redeemed, to undo by the sale of Thyself what I by sinning did with my soul, and to redeem it with Thy ransom, that it might be perpetually Thine! And yet Thy love stays not here, for Thou art ready to be sold again by a false disciple, and bought by Thine enemies to take Thy life, accomplishing our redemption with Thy death. Blessed be Thy immense charity that is never satisfied, nor wearied in doing us good. O my soul, rejoice that the Blessed Virgin has bought her son for thee; be glad that Jesus is already thine, since His Father has given Him to thee for five sicles. O good Jesus, Thou art mine by this new purchase, but I yield myself to be Thine, and with great confidence will say, "my beloved to me, and I to Him :" (15) be it so, O Lord, that Thou leave not me, nor I leave Thee. Amen.

MEDITATION XXV.

ON THE OCCURRENCES AT THE PRESENTATION WITH SIMEON, AND ANNA THE PROPHETESS.

POINT I.

"Behold, there was a man in Jerusalem named Simeon, and this man was just and devout, waiting for the consolation of Israel and the Holy Ghost was in him; and he had received an answer from the Holy Ghost that he should not see death before he had seen the Christ of the Lord." (1)

1. Upon this point, I will consider, first, how the Holy Ghost, desiring to manifest Jesus Christ newly born,

(15) Cant. ii. 16.   (1) Luc. ii. 25.

raised up two prophets that might know Him, and manifest Him, as He made Zacharias and Elizabeth prophets to manifest Him before He was born. To this end He laid His hand upon Simeon, preparing him for his office with those admirable virtues recounted by the Evangelist; saying :—

i. That he was a just man, and religious, fearing God, and punctual in the observation of the whole law, without admitting any breach thereof ; for no man is said to fear but he that avoids the least sins of all, according to that saying of the wise man, " He that feareth God, nihil negligit, neglecteth nothing " (2) by making small account thereof.

ii. That he had great hope, and fervent desire of the coming of Christ for the salvation of this people.

iii. And he joined to this, fervent and continual prayers, earnestly requiring this coming, and that he might be worthy to enjoy it. In this manner he spent his life, and with these virtues he made himself worthy to be the habitation of the Holy Ghost. From whence I will collect that great purity and sanctity of life to give a man great confidence to ask, and desire great things at the hands of Almighty God; like Moses, when he said to God, " Shew me Thy glory," (3) and discover Thy face to me. And, like the spouse in the Canticles, " shew me, O Thou whom my soul loveth, where Thou feedest, and where Thou liest in the midday." (4) And, like this holy old man, who desired to behold the Messiah with his eyes, and obtained it; for, as St. Bernard says, (5) "Great faith merits great things, and the farther thou stretchest thy foot of confidence into the benefits of our Lord, the greater thou shalt obtain from His liberal hand.

(2) Eccl. vii. 19.   (3) Exod. xxxiii. 18.   (4) Cant. i. 6.
(5) Serm. xxxii. in Cant.

2. Secondly, I will consider how the Holy Spirit (who does the will of those that fear Him, and hear the desires of those that love Him) would *comfort and reward this old man*, answering his petitions, with an excellent promise that he should see Christ before his death; that we might understand what a happiness it is to know how to treat with the Holy Ghost, and to have Him within us with fulness of grace. For He Himself, as St. Paul says, requests in us and for us, with "unspeakable groanings," (6) giving us assurances, that the prayer which proceeds from Him shall be heard, and granted in proper time, although the accomplishment of it be somewhat delayed, (7) as it happened to holy Simeon; for Almighty God will have us to be unwearied with hoping, and in this manner to dispose ourselves to receive what we hope for.

3. Thirdly, I will consider how that which is promised to all the just after their death, is sometimes granted in part to such as are very devout *before their death;* that is to behold Christ in this life with the eye of contemplation; fulfilling in this, to them, that promise which says, "Blessed are the clean of heart, for they shall see God." (8)

Colloquy.—O eternal God, which saidst, "Man shall not see me and live," (9) Moriar ut te videam, videam ut hic moriar,—let me die to behold Thee, and let me behold Thee that I may die; let me behold Thee in this life by contemplation, that I may die to myself with perfect mortification, (10) and let me die this happy death, that I may afterwards behold Thee in Thy sovereign glory. Amen.

POINT II.

The same day that the Blessed Virgin carried her son

(6) Rom. viii. 26. (7) Dan. x 2. (8) Matt. v. 8.
(9) Exod. xxxiii. 20. (10) S. Aug. in Soliloq. c. i.

to the Temple, holy Simeon, inspired and moved by the Holy Ghost, went likewise thither, and seeing them enter, knew by the light of heaven that that child was Christ; and taking "Him in his arms, he blessed God, and said : Now Thou dost dismiss Thy servant, O Lord, according to Thy word, in peace, because my eyes have seen Thy salvation," &c. (11)

1. Here I will consider, firs t, the *fideli ty* and *liberality* of the *Spirit* in fulfilling His word, and consoling this just man, giving Him more than He promised him. He promised him that he should see Christ, and He gives him leave to take Him in his arms, to embrace and kiss Him, and very lovingly to invite him to Himself ; for, as the apostle said, God "is able to do all things more abundantly than we desire or understand;" (12) with which I am to animate myself earnestly to serve this our Lord, who is magnificent in promising, but much more liberal in accomplishing what He promises, if there be faith in him that receives it.   But applying this to what now passes, I will consider that, as when the Blessed Virgin entered into the Temple, there were present many persons of all states and conditions, as learned men, priests, noblemen, and plebeians; yet God opened the eyes only of Simeon with His celestial light, that he might know Him in rewar d of his good life, and of the spirit with which he came into the Temple; the rest making no difference between that child and others, because, exteriorly, He differed not from them:—so likewise now, among many that come to the church, there are but few that know with celestial light the presence of Jesus in the Blessed Sacrament, and adore Him with devotion, meriting to receive Him in their hearts, and to be partakers of His gifts with joy. For, although our Saviour Christ desires to give Himself to be known to all men, yet

<hr>

(11) Luc . ii. 27.   (12) Eph. iii. 20.

few dispose themselves like Simeon to accomplish His desire in themselves.

Colloquy.—O my soul, come in spirit to the Temple where Jesus is, that thou mayest enjoy His happy sight, and mayest embrace Him with the arms of His sweet love.

2. Secondly, I will ponder the great *cheerfulness* of this holy man, and the *abundance of joy* that he received on beholding and touching that holy babe, and the great satiety that his soul received, acknowledging himself well rewarded for all the afflictions passed in the long life that he had lived. And as it seemed to him that he had no more to desire and no more to see in this life, having seen the Saviour, he turned all that was in him to glorify God, and to praise Him for this favour, protesting that now he should die in peace whensoever it should be the pleasure of Almighty God.

Colloquy.—O my soul, seek the eminent knowledge of Jesus, with which Thou shalt esteem all that is created as dung, that thou mayest gain Christ, (13) in whom thou shalt have whatsoever thou canst desire. If thou beholdest Him with a lively faith, what more wilt thou behold ? If thou embracest Him with strict charity, what more wouldest thou possess ? And if He be thine, what can be wanting to thee ? Grant me, O most sweet Jesus, by the merits of this saint, some ray of that light which Thou gavest Him on this day, that I may know Thee, and love Thee, as He knew and loved Thee, for ever and ever. Amen.

3. From this example of holy Simeon, I must collect *two things* very *profitable* to obtain a *good death*.

i. That devout men experience in this life the accomplishment of the divine promises, which is a hundred

---

(13) Phil. iii. 8.

times as much as they left for Christ; namely, to be heard in their prayers, to be protected by the divine Providence in their necessities; and with this experience they recover great hope, that Almighty God will accomplish in them the promises of the life to come; and animated with this hope, they desire death to enjoy them, saying, with David, " In peace I will sleep and repose, for Thou, O Lord, hast singularly confirmed me in hope." (14.)

ii. The second is, that those holy men who have arrived by contemplation to see Christ and His greatness, and have tasted the sweetness of eternal things, are forthwith *weary of temporal*, as of things vile, and unworthy of their view; and so they hold life in torment and death, in desire saying, with St. Paul, (15) " I desire to be dissolved, and to be with Christ, to behold Him, and enjoy Him for ever.

Colloquy.—Therefore, O my soul, if the peace and quiet in which the saints and holy men die be pleasing to thee, imitate the fervour and spirit in which they live, for a fervent life, is the cause of a quiet death.

4. Finally, I will consider what *content the Blessed Virgin received* to see her son known and reverenced, and to hear the wonders that were spoken of Him; for, as Luke the Evangelist reports, she and St. Joseph were wondering to hear these things, (16) and glorified the eternal Father for the knowledge that He gave unto men.

POINT III.

The Blessed Virgin, being in the midst of this joy, Simeon, blessing her, said to her in a prophetic spirit,— " Behold this child is set for the fall and for the resurrection of many in Israel, and for a sign which shall be contradicted; and thy own soul a sword shall pierce, that out of many hearts thoughts may be revealed." (17)

(14) Ps. iv.   (15) Phil. i. 23.   (16) Luc. ii. 33.
(17) Luc. ii. 34.

1. Concerning this prophecy, I will consider, first, the *designs of Almighty God in allaying the transports* of the Virgin; for when she was most joyful for the honour that was done to her son, He would discover to her the afflictions that the child was to suffer, and the sword of sorrow that for His sake should pierce her soul, that forthwith she might begin to feel the piercing of that soul, and might taste the bitterness of His Passion.

Colloquy.—O most wise and most loving God, how much Thou likest to give to Thy elect these mixtures of consolations, and discouragements! Sometimes Thou exaltest them to heaven, and again Thou abasest them to the depths. (18) Sometimes Thou woundest their heart with the wounds of love, and sometimes with the word of sorrow; demonstrating in the one and in the other, the depth of Thy wisdom, and sweetness of Thy charity, and since Thou hast so designed, behold me here prepared for all; pierce my soul with this sword as Thou wilt, so that I may be accounted in the number of Thy elect. Amen.

2. Secondly, I will consider two memorable things that Simeon prophesied of the child, that He was *set for the resurrection* and *falling* of many; because many, through Him, would raise themselves from sin to a high degree of sanctity ; and others, because they would not make their profit of His coming, would come to fall into the depth of iniquity, of which they themselves have all the fault. For Christ our Lord, for His part, desires to be a resurrection unto all, and not a stone of offence unto any, (19) that He should be a new, prodigious, and admirable *sign*, but yet a sign which His enemies should *contradict*, resisting His doctrine, calumniating His miracles, and persecuting His life, even unto the nailing Him to a cross,

(18) Ps. cvi. 26.   (19) Is. viii. 14, 15.

where He should be to the elect a sign of life; but, to the reprobate, a sign of damnation, (20) by whose power should be discovered the fidelity and loyalty of the disciples, which was concealed in their hearts.

3. Meditating these two things, which continue even to this day, I should be astonished at the judgments of Almighty God in this case, and be compassionate for the perdition of such a multitude of infidels and wicked Christians, causing my soul to be pierced with the sword of sorrow, as that of the Blessed Virgin was pierced, and beseeching this our Lord, that His coming be not to my fall, but to my resurrection, and that it may be to me a sign of life, in whom I may believe and hope, and whom I may love and imitate in being one of His disciples, whom He calls, by the prophet Isaiah, a sign (21) and prodigy, endeavouring that my words and actions may be admirable like His. And if it shall happen that many contradict and persecute me, I will rejoice, taking it for an assurance that I am much favoured by Almighty God, since He makes me so like to His Son.

POINT IV.

At this time, also, the holy Spirit was pleased to manifest the child to *another* holy woman, as He manifested Him to a holy man, choosing to this end an ancient widow whose name was Anne, who spent her life in fasting and prayer, serving God in the "Temple night and day." "Now she at the same hour coming in" when the child entered, and knowing by the light of heaven that He was the Messiah, "confessed to the Lord, and spoke of Him to all that looked for the redemption of Israel." (22)

1. Here we may contemplate the *several ways* that Al-

(20) Is. xi. 10.   (21) Is. viii. 18.
(22) Luc. ii. 36—38.

mighty God has to *cherish* and comfort His *servants;* for to Simeon, before he saw the Saviour, He promised that he should see Him, to kindle the desire that he had to see Him, and to entertain him with the promise. But to Anne we know not that He made any such promise; but that He suddenly inspired her to go see Christ our Lord, with whose sight He comforted her, and rewarded the good and long services which, in fourscore and four years, she had done Him.

2. Secondly, I will consider *six virtues* of this holy widow, whereby she made herself worthy of this favour, that is, charity, continual prayer, fasting, observation of God's law, devotion to such things as belonged to the divine worship, with perseverance in all for many years. In these virtues I am to endeavour to imitate this holy woman, if I desire to obtain that which she obtained by them.

Colloquy.—O King of Glory, give me these six wings of the Seraphims that serve Thee in the Temple of Thy Church, that I may fly with them in Thy service, until I come to enjoy Thee in the Temple of Thy glory, world without end.   Amen.

MEDITATION XXVI.

CONTAINING A FORM OF PRAYER OF APPLYING THE INTERIOR FACULTIES OF THE SOUL, TO THE CONTEMPLATION OF THE MYSTERIES THAT HAVE BEEN MEDITATED.

In the eleventh section of the introduction of this book, I made mention of a form of prayer, by application of the senses on the mysteries of our faith ; and it is a form rather of contemplation than of meditation ; for as it is said in the tenth section, meditation runs from one thing to another, seeking out hidden truths, as has been done hitherto : but contemplation is a simple intuition of the truth without discursive reasoning, with great affections of admiration and love : and as these are regularly obtained after meditation, so, after we have meditated these mysteries of our Saviour Christ, it will not be amiss to run over each of them again with this manner of affectionate contemplation, which we call application of the senses ; for as the exterior senses perceive their objects directly, and without the searchings of the understanding, and are delighted and pleased in them ; so in this contemplation the interior senses of the soul, which are her own interior faculties with their various acts, without new reasonings, and presupposing those which have been done, at other times, perceive these truths, and collect from thence great affections of devotion ; our Lord preventing them with His special grace, without which we shall go astray, in entering into this method of contemplation, as has been said before. We may, however, on our part, assist ourselves in the following manner.

POINT I.

The first point shall be, to *behold* with the interior eye of the soul, either the imaginative, or the intellectual, all such *persons* as were in the stable at Bethlehem, or in the temple of Jerusalem, and *what they do*, with circumstances which are the objects of the *sight*, gathering from them affections of admiration, and love, of joy, or compassion, or imitation : and if there happen to proceed from these any new thoughts and meditations, as our Lord sometimes communicates in these cases, I must admit them, dwelling upon them so long as the light shall continue that was given me.

1. The following is the method :—on *beholding* the *God-man laid in a stable with beasts*, I will wonder, and in

15

astonishment, admire such profound *humility* resplendent in a Lord of such great majesty. Beholding Him made a tender babe to make Himself more amiable, because babes ordinarily are amiable, I will melt away through love of so precious and beautiful a babe, fondling Him as my elder brother, the heir of my Father, and so much mine, that He is born for me, and for my benefit. Beholding the heart of the child burning with love and desire for my salvation, shedding tears of sorrow for my sins, and offering Himself for them to the eternal Father, I will join my heart to His that He may fasten to it that love, and that sorrow, entreating of Him that He may join me to Himself.

2. In the same manner holding His virtues, His *poverty*, humility, meekness, and patience, I am to gather them for my own use, as one who gathers a nosegay of myrrh, to wear before his breast, and to join it to His heart, saying to Him with great tenderness :—"My beloved shall be to me as a bundle of myrrh."(1)   I will always have Him in my eye, that I may never lose the sight of Him, nor even forget Him.

3. The like may be done, contemplating our *Blessed Lady* the *Virgin* and *Mother*, with affections of admiration; contemplating with what *modesty, devotion, and reverence* she stands before the child; with a desire to imitate her; and beholding her compassion for the tears of the child, I will desire to accompany her, and compassionate with her.   Beholding likewise St. Joseph, and holy Simeon, and the fervour and spirit resplendent in them, I will admire the gifts which God has given them, with a desire to imitate them as far as I am able.

POINT II.

1. The second point is, to *hear* with the *ears of the soul*

(1) Cant. i. 12.

the *words that are there spoken*, listening to the interior words and inspirations that Almighty God shall speak to my heart. Here we may consider, that not only in this point, but for any other form of mental, or vocal prayer, that, as was pointed in the third chapter of the introduction of this book, being placed before Almighty God, and contemplating these mysteries, it is well for a time to stay with reverence, as one waiting to hear what is said, or to receive the alms that is usually given him, placing himself, as the woman of Canaan said, like a "whelp" (2) that stands at the table, fixing his eyes upon those that eat, hoping they will cast him some small morsel of bread: Or as the prophet David says, like the good servant that has "his eyes" fixed "on the hands" of his Lord, (3) awaiting his commands; as did the prophet Habacuc when he said : "I will stand upon my watch, and fix my step upon the tower; and I will watch, to see what will be said to me, and what I may answer to him that reproveth me." (4) The meaning of which is, that seated in contemplation, I will listen to the inspiration of Almighty God, and to what He may say to my heart; either reprehending and correcting me for the evil that I have committed, or encouraging and exhorting me to the good that I ought to do; or giving me some interior answer to what I desire, as the Holy Ghost did in prayer to holy Simeon. And if having continued awhile in this silence, I feel not some inspiration of our Lord, I am not to remain idle, but urge Him to speak to me, saying to Him, with Samuel : "Speak, Lord, for Thy servant heareth." (5) Or as He Himself said to the spouse : "Let thy voice sound in Mine ears, for thy voice is very sweet" (6) to me.

(2) Matt. xv. 27.   (3) Ps. cxxii. 2.   (4) Habac. ii. 1.
(5) 1 Reg. iii. 9.   (6) Cant. ii. 14.

Colloquy.—O eternal God, who hast said by the prophet, "I will lead her into the wilderness, and will speak to her heart," (7) create in my heart an interior solitude, free from wandering thoughts, that Thou alone mayest speak to me with Thy inspirations, and that I may hear and fulfil what Thou commandest me. Amen.

2. Then placing myself in the presence of the child Jesus, I will with the care of my soul, listen to the words which He speaks to His eternal Father, and to the affectionate colloquies He holds with Him concerning our salvation, rejoicing to hear them, and profiting by them, I will also listen to the exterior lamentations which He makes, and will learn to weep for my sins: I will hear what this child would say to me, if He were to speak to me there where He was; how lovingly He would reprehend my pride, and vanity, and preciseness in dress ; how He would exhort me to make myself a child, and to present and offer myself to the service of His eternal Father. All these words I should receive and hear, beseeching Him to inspire me with spirit and determination to fulfil them. I will likewise endeavour to hear what the Blessed Virgin said, and what the Holy Spirit said to Simeon, and what Simeon himself said when he saw his desire accomplished, learning from those words to address similar words to God.

POINT III.

The third point is, to smell with the interior smelling the most sweet *odour*, and celestial fragrancy that issues from this child Jesus, and from His virtues; meditating how fragrant they are to God, to the angels, and to the just : and how much honour and glory they yield to our Lord God, and edification to His Church. And with this

(7) Osee ii. 14.

odour I should encourage and animate myself to imitate those virtues.

1. To do this more effectually, I will consider how the sweet odour that issued from the works and virtues of that child, extremely delighted the eternal Father, who might say, as Isaac said of his son Jacob:—" The smell of my son is as the smell of a plentiful field which the Lord hath blessed." (8)

2. Then I will reflect how much this odour delights the just souls who smell it, as it did the spouse that said :—" We will run after Thee, to the odour of Thy ointments." (9) For the poverty, humility, aud meekness of Christ spread around them a fragrancy, which vanquishing the heart, carries it after Him to join it to Him.

3. Afterwards I will contemplate how sweet an odour both to God and to men is *obedience*, and modesty, humility, patience and charity in any person who has them in an excellent degree, and how much they edify the Church and his neighbours. For which reason St. Paul says of the just, that they "are the good odour of Christ," (10) and contrariwise, what an evil odour, both to God and to men, is pride and disobedience, immodesty, and every other vice : considering how far this evil odour was from that holy place, in which were the child and His mother, and how far it ought to be from my soul, not to cause any disgust, to those to whom I am so much indebted.

Colloquy.—O sweet child, whose garments, which are Thy works, are like a field of odoriferous flowers; clothe me with them, that I may yield fragrance to Thy eternal Father; that for Thee, He may give me the benediction which by them Thou didst merit: let my soul become redolent of Thy divine odours, that

(8) Gen. xxvii. 27   (9) Cant. i. 3.   (10) 2 Cor. ii. 15.

it may run after Thee, imitating Thy virtues, until it come to enjoy the reward of them. Amen.

POINT IV.

1. The fourth point is, to *taste* with the interior taste, the *sweetness* of that blessed child, and of His virtues; and how sweet they were to Almighty God, and to Himself, and are to all those that exercise them in imitation of Him: applying myself to prove what the prophet David says: "O taste and see that the Lord is sweet."(11) O how it pleased the eternal Father, to behold the virtues of His Son! and what pleasure had the Son in giving full content to the Father! O what a sweetness this blessed child felt, to see Himself poor, contemned, and laid in a manger among beasts ! How sweet to Him were the tears that He shed! And how pleasing it was to Him absolutely to fulfil the will of His Father, much more savory without comparison than the milk that He sucked from the breasts of His mother. And in imitation of Him I will endeavour deeply to feel this sweetness that God imparts to contempts and afflictions, to poverty and tears, sweetened by the example of this Blessed child. And with this affection, I will incite in my soul, a great hunger to taste of these things, and to relish the pleasing taste of the spirit, that the sweetness of the flesh may be made unsavory to me. With this affection I will contemplate the sweetness that holy Simeon felt at the presence of the child, which was so great that it disgusted him to see and taste anything of this life, and sweetened to him even death itself.

Colloquy.—O eternal God, "how great is the multitude of Thy sweetness which Thou hast hidden for them that fear Thee!"(12) But how much greater shall it be to those that love Thee! give me some part

(11) Ps. xxxiii. 9.   (12) Ps. xxx. 20.

thereof, O Lord, to prove, that I may with a good will, renounce the pleasures of the earth, and take pleasure only in those of heaven. Amen.

2. On the other hand, I may consider how much *bitterness* lies hidden in vice, and in the soul that follows her own will, and yields to her own passions : and reflecting upon what passes with myself when I sin, I will taste this bitterness that I feel in myself, and will immediately abhor it and spit it out, with a desire never more to taste of it, remembering that of the prophet Jeremias :—"Thy own wickedness shall reprove thee, and thy own apostacy shall rebuke thee.   Know thou and see that it is an evil and a bitter thing for thee to have left thy Lord God." (13)

POINT V.

1. The fifth point is with the interior *touching*, spiritually to *touch* the *clothes* of that child,—the hay of that manger,—the earth of that stable, kissing and embracing it with my heart,—engendering in myself a great estimation, price, and love of it all,—choosing it for myself as a thing of great value; and as if I were present, I am to come to the child, and to beg leave of Him to touch His *feet*, to kiss and embrace them, bewailing my sins, and like Mary Magdalen, humbly begging remission of them. And then with greater confidence to beg leave of Him to touch His *hands*, to kiss them, and to play with them, beseeching Him to give me His benediction; or like holy Simeon, I will take Him in my arms, and embrace Him with great love, beseeching Him to unite me to Himself, not permitting me to be separated from Him. And if I could attain to the perfection of the spouse, who said :— "Let Him kiss me, with the kiss of His mouth," (14) I might aspire to the desire to touch that divine face, and

(13) Jer. ii. 19.   (14) Cant. i. 1.

to unite myself to His Godhead with the union of perfect love, satiating myself with only seeing Him, and loving Him. O what sweetness is felt in this spiritual touching! with which as the same spouse said, all her "bowels were moved," (15) and mollified, desiring to admit therein her beloved.

2. I am likewise to feel the *hardness* of the child's *bed*, the *rigour* of the *cold* that He suffered, the *straitness* of those *clothes* wherein He was wrapped and swaddled, and to apply myself to desire, that, for our Lord's sake, my touching may feel always rough and hard things, avoiding soft and dainty things which He so much abhorred.

3. This meditation should be concluded with a colloquy to Christ Jesus our Lord, beseeching Him to purify and clear the senses of my soul, that I may understand Him, and love Him according to His will, desiring to reform and renew my senses, as St. Paul says, to prove and approve effectually " what is the good and the acceptable, and the perfect will of God," (16) to His honour and glory, world without end. Amen.

ANOTHER MANNER OF APPLYING IN PRAYER THE INTERIOR SENSES, WITH THE ACTS OF SEVERAL VIRTUES.

Among those virtues which perfect our understanding and will, which are the spiritual senses of the soul, those five are most excellent, which correspond to the five senses of the body, by whose acts is practised a very profitable form of prayer, exercising them in this form about the mysteries that have been spoken of. (17)

1. The *sight* is the light of *faith* with which we see, although through a mirror, and in obscurity, what

(15) Cant. v. 4.   (16) Rom. xii. 2.

(17) S. Bon. in Itinerario mentis ad Deum, cap. 4.

Almighty God has *revealed* in every mystery, actuating it by believing it with admiration, and pause, as has been declared in the thirty-fourth meditation of the first part, saying to the child Jesus: "Domine, adauge mihi fidem:" "O Lord, 'increase my faith,' (18) and so quicken it, that I may live before Thee, as if Thou were still present to my eyes."

2. The *hearing* is the virtue of *obedience*, with which I am to *hear* all that Almighty God *commands* or *counsels* in that mystery by word or by example, offering myself to accomplish it with great readiness and speed, saying to Him :—" 'My heart,' O Lord, 'is ready' (19) to obey Thee, command what Thou wilt, and give me what Thou commandest me, that I may obey Thee according to Thy will."

3. The *smelling* which by the *odour perceives* things *absent* and distant, is the virtue of *hope*, which comforts us with assurance of God's promises, before they be manifested and accomplished; hoping that He will hear my prayers,—that He will aid me with succours of His grace; —that He will have a care of all things belonging to me, and that I may be able to follow His example, and to obtain His rewards; and that all the rest that is presented in this mystery may be the object of this virtue, as h as been said in the place before-mentioned, saying to our Lord that of the apostle :—

Colloquy.—O "God of hope, fill" me "with all joy and peace in believing," that "I may abound in hope," (20) and in all virtues, with the fulness of the Holy Ghost.   Amen.

4. The *taste* is *devotion with love*, to which it appertains to *find* relish in things *belonging* to *God;* in rejoicing that

(18) Luc. xvii. 5.   (19) Ps. lvi. 8.   (20) Rom. xv. 13.

God is who He is, and at the wonders and virtues that are represented in that mystery; applying ourselves to take a pleasure in imitating Him, and in serving Him with all the devotion that we may, saying with the prophet :— "Ego autem in Domino gaudebo, et exultabo in Deo Jesu meo." "I will rejoice in our Lord, and will be glad in God my Jesus," and my Saviour. (21)

5. The *touching*, is perfect *charity*, which *joins* herself to her beloved, and embraces Him with her two arms, which are the love of God and of our neighbour, and of all things that may please Him; making it our pleasure, that our spirit may be united with His; (22) and that His heart may be as a seal imprinted in ours. (23)

Colloquy.—O Beloved of my soul, seeing Thou commandest me to put Thee as a seal upon my heart, and upon my arm, that my affections and actions may be like Thine;—unite Thyself to me, that I may be united to Thee, world without end.   Amen.

MEDITATION XXVII.

ON THE FLIGHT INTO EGYPT.

POINT I.

First, I am to consider what *great persecution* was raised against our Saviour Christ, being but new-born;(1)—the causes of it—and the means which He chose to defend Himself.

1. I will consider first, how our Lord God permitted king Herod, instigated by the Devil, and on his account, the Jews, to *persecute Christ* the new-born King, with a desire to deprive Him of life, although for different ends.

(21) Habac. iii. 18.   (22) 1 Cor. vi. 17.   (23) Cant. viii. 6.
(1) Matt. ii. 2.

—Herod, as a tyrant, fearing that He would have taken from him his temporal kingdom,—the Jews, as flatterers, in order to please their earthly king,—the Devil, as prince of this world, fearing lest this miraculous child should do him some great hurt. But the eternal Father ordained this to much higher ends, ordaining that His Son should from His infancy(2) walk in the way of persecutions and afflictions;—that beginning to be fulfilled which Simeon had prophesied,—that He " should be a sign which should be contradicted," (3) giving us thus to understand that His coming was contrary to the intentions of the world, which abhors not, nor persecutes those who are of its faction, but those who are contrary to it.

Thus we may also see imprinted in this example the state of the primitive Church, and of righteous souls; who, conceiving Christ within themselves, and desiring to manifest Him by their works, are to be persecuted by the dragon of hell, who, as St. John says in his Apocalypse, (4) desires in them to kill the spirit of Christ, that it may not grow up in their hearts, by the exercise of notable virtues. And this may serve me for an advice and consolation when I see myself persecuted for virtue's sake, remembering what our Saviour Christ said to His disciples:—" The servant is not greater than his master; if they have persecuted me, they will also persecute you." (5) Neither is it reasonable that I should be exempted from that universal rule mentioned by the apostle:—" All that will live godly in Christ Jesus shall suffer persecution," (6)—the Devil exciting it himself, and through his ministers the worldlings.

2. Secondly, I will consider how our Saviour Christ being

(2) Ps. lxxxvii. 16.　　　(3) Luc. ii. 34.　　　(4) Apoc. xii. 13.
(5) Joan. xv. 10.　　　(6) 2 Tim. iii. 12.

able to free Himself from this persecution by many very easy *means*, as either by killing Herod, or by making Himself invisible, yet would not,—*but took the means of flying*, an argument of weakness and misery; and this He did principally for two *reasons :—*

i. The first, because as in order to be born in the world, He left the conveniences which He might have had in the city of Nazareth; so also, He would *leave them throughout all His infancy*, going far off from His kindred and parentage. And for the same reason, now that He had to fly, though He might have gone into the country of the three Sages, where He would have been known and adored, He would not, but went into Egypt among strangers and enemies, in order to have occasion to suffer more : teaching me by this example, to fly from that which is pleasing to the flesh; and from being known and reverenced by men; delighting to conceal and hide myself until God be pleased to manifest me.

ii. The second reason of His flying into Egypt was, by the same means, *to do good to that idolatrous nation* abandoned by Almighty God :—that beginning to be fulfilled which was prophesied :—"behold the Lord will ascend upon a swift cloud, and will enter into Egypt, and the idols of Egypt shall be moved at His presence." (7) For our Lord Christ entering into Egypt, clothed with the cloud of His humanity, in the arms of the resplendent cloud His mother, began to tread under His feet those idols which the world adores ;—namely, riches, honours, and delicacies, embracing there poverty, contempt, and affliction. And with this example He laid the foundation of that perfection which afterwards shone brightly in Egypt, and that which He planted throughout the whole world, travelling through it in the swift cloud of His

(7) Is. xix. 1.

primitive Church, and of the congregation of His apostles and disciples, and to this day He ceases not to plant it.

Colloquy.—O most sweet Jesus, who in the cloud of the Blessed Sacrament of the Altar enterest daily into Thy faithful; enter into this dark Egypt of my heart, and throw down those idols of earthly affections which it adores, that from henceforth, I may only love what Thou lovest, and abhor what Thou abhorrest. Amen.

3. This flight of our Saviour Christ into Egypt, on account of the persecution of Herod, likewise represents the primitive Church flying from the persecution of the Jews, and *going over to the Gentiles*, carrying with it the faith and the law of Christ. And generally, if one man persecute Him with his sins, He is wont to fly, and to seek out another that will receive Him; and therefore if Christ have been born in my soul, I am to endeavour not to persecute Him with my passions and lukewarmness, lest He forsake me, and go to another, that will receive my "crown." (8)

POINT II.

The Angel of our Lord appeared in sleep to Joseph, saying : "Arise and *take the child and His mother and fly into Egypt*, and be there until I shall tell thee : for it will come to pass that Herod will seek the child to destroy Him." (9)

Upon this revelation I am to consider *who imposes* this obedience :—*who imitates it:*—upon *whom* it is imposed; and *with what words.*

1. *He that principally imposes* this commandment, is the eternal Father, to manifest the providence He has over His Only-begotten Son: for although He had determined

(8) Apoc. iii. 11.　　　　(9) Matt. ii. 13.

that He should die by men, yet as that hour was not yet come, He took care to defend Him; in token that He has the like care of the rest of His adopted sons, for the love that He bears to this His *natural* Son.

2. *He that declared this ordinance* was an angel, in the name of Almighty God Himself; for His divine Majesty will have us accustomed to obey Him and His ministers, whose office is not only to do His divine will, but to declare it to others in His name, and therefore He said; of them : "He that heareth you, heareth me." (10) And for this reason likewise He said by Malachias the prophet; "the lips of the priest shall keep knowledge and they shall seek the law at his mouth, because He is the angel of the Lord of Hosts." (11)

3. Hence it is, that this obedience was intimated *to St. Joseph*, and not to the Blessed Virgin, because Joseph was head of that family, and God's will was, that the Blessed Virgin should obey St. Joseph in all that he said he had heard of the angel, and should suffer herself to be governed by him. And so she did : for as she was humble and obedient, she stood not upon this, that the advice was not given to her, but to her husband; neither did she vainly boast that God, or His angels should speak to her; like the other Mary who said : "Hath the Lord spoken by Moses only, hath He not also spoken to us in like manner?" (12) wherein I am to learn this manner of humility and obedience of our blessed Lady, desiring to be governed by others, and that greater account should be made of others than of me, holding it for a great happiness to know the will of Almighty God, and to fulfil it, whether I know it by revelation from God, or from His

(10) Luc. x. 16.

(11) Mala. ii. 7.   (12) Num. xii. 2.

angels, or by the speech and ordinance of men. For although the first seems more glorious, yet in the second, more humility is exercised, as we subject our judgment and will, not only to God, but to man also for God's sake. And so the Blessed Virgin was no less resplendent in obeying St. Joseph, than St. Joseph was in obeying the angel, and the angel in obeying God.

Colloquy.—O eternal God, grant me that I may subject myself "to every human creature,"(13) for Thy love, obeying what Thou commandest me by men, as Thou in heaven art obeyed by angels,—fulfilling Thy will upon earth, with that devotion with which it is fulfilled in heaven. Amen.

POINT III.

Then I will consider the *words in which* the angel declared the commandment of our Lord, which were grave, brief, authoritative, and with circumstances very suitable to make proof of the obedience of the saint to whom they were delivered. For in this way God usually commands men who are perfect, to try them by giving them an occasion of demonstrating their obedience : as another angel used the like words in the obedience which he intimated to Abraham, "to go forth out of" his "own country;" (14) and to sacrifice his son Isaac. And for this reason he does not use circumlocutions, or preambles, which the world commonly uses, nor does He request, but commands :— " Arise," says He, " take the child and His mother, and fly into Egypt, and be there until I shall tell thee," &c.

1. In these words we are to consider the *circumstances that make this command difficult,* and declare the value of the obedience.

i. First, it was intimated *by night,* St. Joseph being at

(13) 2 Pet. ii. 13.   (14) Gen. xii. 1, et xxii. 2.

rest and asleep, when men usually have the greatest horror of trouble ; to signify that in the midst of our ease and prosperity, we are to be prepared for afflictions, and that *at all times* we are to be ready, whenever God shall command us, even to the leaving our bed and our rest to obey Him; as He proved Samuel, calling him three or four times in the night, (15) and making him arise out of the bed in which he was sleeping, to exercise him in obedience, and in the abnegation of his own will.

ii. Secondly, the angel commanded him to take *only the blessed child* and *His mother*, leaving the company of all others, and the furniture, and other temporal things that he had in his house, to be able the more freely to fly and escape from the cruel intention of king Herod, and to get away with less noise and disturbance ; figuring what I ought to do when Almighty God commands me to fly from the world and from sin, that is, to abandon all temporal things that may hinder me, contenting myself to carry with me God only. But if I carry the child Jesus and His mother, what shall be wanting to me ?

Colloquy.—O most sweet Jesus, to fly with Thee is no affliction; to forsake all, Thou remaining with me, is no torment; for having Thee wheresoever I be, I shall live contented, and in every place shall be rich. O my soul, take the Son and His mother, and put thyself under Their protection, serving Them very truly; for where those two are, there is no solitariness, and when They accompany Thee, there is no dread of peril.

iii. Thirdly, He assigned to him the *province* where he was to go, namely, into Egypt, a country of barbarous people, and enemies to the Hebrews. For it is the will of God that His elect, especially such as are religious

(15) 1 Reg. iii. 3.

persons, should dwell where He pleases, and not where they, through their own vain liking, desire to dwell ; persuading themselves that wherever God shall place them, they will be secure, contented, and bettered, although it seem to be a place full of trouble and peril ; and contrariwise, where they desire to be, they shall perhaps be with great danger, although it seems to them to be a place very secure ; for neither the place nor the corner gives true security to the soul, but only the protection of God, and with His protection I shall be secure in Egypt for my obedience to Him, without which I shall perish in Egypt through my own self will. And, therefore, the prophet David says, that " blessed is the man whose help is from God: in his heart he hath disposed to ascend by steps in the vale of tears, in the place which he hath set:" (16) as if he should say:—he disposed himself to grow up, not in the place where he chose to put himself, but where he was put by the disposition of God who appointed him to it.

iv. Fourthly, he *left him in suspense as to how long time he should stay* in Egypt, saying to him:—" Be there until I shall tell thee." For it is not the pleasure of God, as holy Judith said, (17) that we should " set a time " how long such things shall continue, as He disposes, and especially in matter of afflictions and discomfits, of offices and employments, that He imposes upon us; but His will is that we should leave this care to Him, resigning ourselves to be where He pleases, and as long as He pleases, be it little or much ; for God knows much better what is fitting for us than we ourselves : and He greatly desires that we should rely upon His providence and government: for in saying, "Be there until I shall tell thee," He gives manifestly to understand, that He will have a care to tell him

(16) Ps lxxxiii. 6, 7.   (17) Judith viii. 13.

16

in due time.   And what can be more certain and assured, than for me to be without care in matters concerning myself, when God and His angels take charge of them ?

Colloquy.—O most provident God, why should I not cast all my care upon Thee, when I know Thou hast so great a care over me ?" (18)

2. Moreover, He *gave Him a reason* for the obedience He imposed upon him, saying,—" for it will come to pass that Herod will seek the child to destroy Him."   In this He confirms the care He has over those who are His, by cutting off dangers before they happen, and inspiring them with a means to free themselves from them.   True it is that sometimes our Lord imposes a commandment on His servants without giving them a reason for what He commands, as He did to Abraham in the cases before mentioned ; that they may learn to obey Him, not for any reason given, nor for their own advantage, but merely because He commands it.   For though faith relies not principally upon reason, but upon the revelation of God ; yet, God's revelation presupposed, reason helps to believe with more sweetness, and to fortify our faith the more.   So, likewise, perfect obedience, although it is not principally to rely more upon reason than God's commandment and His will ; yet this principal motive presupposed, our Lord gives sometimes a reason for what He commands, as He gave to St. Joseph, that He may be obeyed with more sweetness; and, if I cannot attain to understand the reason, yet I am to subject my judgment to it as this holy man did, as we shall presently see.

3. From these considerations I must gather, that if I desire to be perfect, I must show it by having such a disposition, that my superiors and confessors may command

(18) 1 Pet. v. 7.

mc whatever they shall judge suitable, and in what manner they shall please, without suspicion or defect in what ever they may impose upon me ; as St. Paul said to Philemon: "Trusting in thy obedience, I have written to thee, knowing that thou wilt also do more than I say."(19)

POINT IV.

Joseph no sooner heard this commandment, than he "*arose*, took the child and His mother by night, and retired into Egypt."

In which I should ponder the most *perfect obedience* of St. Joseph, in order to imitate it; for he had those *four degrees* of perfection which this virtue can comprehend.

i. First, he had great *submission of judgment*, subjecting himself without reply to God's order; and although he might have alleged to our Lord, that by other more sweet and easy means, He might have delivered him, or at least, if he must needs fly, that it might not be to Egypt, but to Arabia, or Samaria, yet he made no such reply, but *subjected* his judgment and silently obeyed, adoring God's ordinance without any questioning, or show of curiosity in desiring to know more than what the angel had delivered, literally fulfilling the counsel of the Wise man, which says, "Seek not the things that are too high for thee, but the things God hath commanded thee ; think on them always, and in many of His works be not curious." (20)

ii. He had a *great promptness of will* in a matter that was very hard; as it was to abandon his country, and his house, and the conversation of his friends, and to depart like a banished man into a strange country, and in great poverty; and yet, for all this, he was better pleased to accomplish the will of God than his own will, and with

(19) Philemon 21.   (20) Eccl. iii. 22.

more perfection than Abraham; who, though he departed from his country and kindred to obey God,—yet carried with him a great multitude of servants, with much riches and temporal good.

iii. Thirdly, in the *execution he was very punctual;* for he stayed not in his bed to sleep out the rest of his sleep, but forthwith arose; and, imparting the revelation to the Blessed Virgin, they began their journey, leaving all that they had, and departed *by night* to fulfil their obedience with more perfection, by flying in secret; for, to this purpose the night is more proper.

iv. Fourthly, I will consider with *what joy and content they travelled*, although their journey was troublesome and tedious, and devoid of temporal conveniences, which yet they felt not much, through the greatness of their interior alacrity, which was grounded upon two things:—the first, because it was the will of our Lord God, which they held for their greatest consolation;—the second, because they carried with them Jesus, whose company was sufficient to comfort them in any loneliness or abandonment whatever, without looking back, or procuring any other relief which travellers usually seek after.

Colloquy.—O omnipotent God, that gavest to these Thy beloved saints such obedience; by their merits, I beseech Thee, to assist me, that I may obey Thee with subjection of my judgment, with promptness of will, with readiness in execution, and with alacrity of heart, to fulfil Thy will alone, relying upon Thy providence, that it will have a care of me, if in this manner I obey Thee. Amen.

POINT V.

Fifthly, I am to consider how *they remained in Egypt until the death* of the tyrant *Herod;* which was five or seven years after; pondering the special things that hap·pened during that time.

i. The great poverty in which they lived, supporting themselves by the labour of their hands, among a strange and barbarous people, and yet bearing all this very joyfully for the two reasons before-mentioned.

ii. Whence proceeded the great calmness that they there had; insomuch, that they neither desired the death of Herod, nor were they afflicted with the delay of their return, but remitted all to God's providence.

iii. Being also as zealous as they were of the glory of God, they lived there in continual grief on account of the idolatry and perdition of that nation; so that of each of them might be said, that which St. Peter said of Lot, when he was in Sodom: "for in sight and hearing he was just, dwelling among them who from day to day vex the just with unjust works." (21) So it is likely, that the sacred Virgin and St. Joseph were "vexed" in spirit for the sins of that people,—yet always in the midst of them, preserved their purity and sanctity, shining like lights of heaven in the midst of that wicked nation. And it is to be believed that the sanctity, modesty, and celestial conversation of our Blessed Lady the Virgin, and St. Joseph, mollified the hearts of that barbarous people, and caused in them admiration and respect; and some by their example were converted to God, and came to favour them with alms, and with gifts, which they, being poor, accepted for their sustenance.

Colloquy.—O happy he, that might be present in this banishment, to accompany and serve the child and His mother. Aid me, O my God, with Thy grace, that in my exile I may live in joyfulness of

(21) 2 Pet. ii. 8.

heart, conforming myself to Thy will, and giving good example to such as live with me, that many through my means, may serve Thee with perfection. Amen.

MEDITATION XXVIII.

ON THE MURDER OF THE HOLY INNOCENTS; AND THE RETURN FROM EGYPT,

POINT I.

First, I am to consider how king Herod, fearing lest that King whom the sages had spoken of, should deprive him of his kingdom; and " perceiving that he was deluded by" them, cruelly *commanded to be murdered all the male* "*children* that were in Bethlehem, and in all the borders thereof, from two years old and under." (1)

1. In which is first to be considered, *what an abominable vice is ambition*, and the desire of reigning and commanding, whence ensued such horrible misdeeds, the chief of all which was the desire to take away the life of Christ, to usurp His kingdom, and to reign by himself. As also how natural it is to ambitious men to be suspicious, and timorous, suspecting lest others should deprive them of their greatness, and fearing where there is no need of fear, as the tyrant Herod was afraid without cause;—for our Lord Christ came not to "take away temporal kingdoms," but " to give celestial."

2. Secondly, I will consider the *great grief that our Saviour Christ had being in Egypt;* on account of the murder of the holy innocents for His sake; for it is to be believed that the sword which wounded the body of each of them pierced His soul with an agony of compassion through the exceeding love with which He loved them,

(1) Matt. ii. 16.

suffering so many martyrdoms in His spirit, as they altogether suffered in body.

Colloquy.—O most glorious King of Martyrs, who on this day conqueredst in them, and sufferedst with them; have compassion on my weakness, and aid me with Thy grace, vanquishing in me all whatsoever is contrary to Thee.   Amen.

3. Thirdly, I will consider *the great spiritual good,* which grew to these children by the *temporal death which they suffered,* being assured thereby of their eternal salvation; and therefore that was a loving providence which Christ used towards them, although at the cost of the life of their body, which is of less worth than that of the soul. And for this reason our Saviour Christ rejoiced at that glorious death of His martyrs, by which they became partakers of so glorious and eternal a life; that being fulfilled here, which holy Job says of Almighty God, that He laughed "at the pains of the innocent," (2) because He is delighted with the good that comes to them thereby.

Colloquy.—I would, O my God, that I might suffer for Thy sake, that my pains might be Thy joy and delight, taking me away by death, like those children, before "wickedness alter my understanding, or deceit beguile my soul;" (3) for I rather desire to die, than to live to offend Thee.   Amen.

POINT II.

And when Herod was dead, behold an angel of the Lord appeared in sleep to Joseph in Egypt, saying : "Arise, and take the child, and His Mother, and go *into the land of Israel,* for they are dead that sought the life of the child." (4)

1. Here is first to be considered, how *Herod,* seeking to

(2) Job ix. 23.   (3) Sap. iv. 11.   (4) Matt. ii. 20.

take away the life of Christ, *died without compassing his intent*, and died a disastrous death, both of body and soul; for the justice of God, though it dissembles for a time, chastises in the end; and though punishment of the wicked be deferred, yet it comes at last; and when men least think, then death seizes on them, when they pay for all their wickedness together. What profit had Herod by his ambition, and cruelty, and extreme care to preserve his kingdom?—for he lost all in one day, and withal lost his soul, bewailing this irremediable loss, as the rest of the damned bewail it, who say : "What hath our pride profited us? or what advantage hath the boasting of riches brought us? all these things are passed away like a shadow," (5) and now in our wickedness we are consumed, paying the penalty we deserved by it.

2. Secondly, I will consider the *providence of God, in sending* forthwith His angel to signify this news to St. Joseph, and to free him from his exile, commanding him to return to his country. O how confirmed was he by this in the confidence he had in God! and how contented was he to see the care He had of them! Whence I will gather, how securely I may be without solicitude for the success of my own affairs, casting my care into the hands of God, in which are my "lots," (6) and my times, my prosperities, and adversities, He taking it in charge, to dispose them as shall be most expedient for my good.

Colloquy.—O Father, most careful of Thy children, I cast all my care upon Thee, because Thou art so careful of me. One only desire I have to serve Thee, that Thou mayest desire to heal me. Amen.

3. Thirdly, I will consider, that as well in this revelation, as in the other, the angel *calls not* the blessed Virgin *by her name*, nor does he say to St. Joseph, take thy wife,

(5) Sap. v. 8.   (6) Ps. xxx. 16.

and the child : but "take the child and *His Mother;*" to teach us that the most glorious name of our blessed Lady is, Mother of God. By this name the angel and the Evangelist call her, and by this name *we* ought to call her, reverencing the greatness of that name, and rejoicing in it.

Colloquy.—O Mother of God, be thou happy in this name, and make us the worthy children of Him who holds thee for His mother. Amen.

POINT III.

Joseph, obeying the command of the angel, departed towards the land of Israel, and fearing to go into Judea, being warned in his sleep, retired into the quarters of Galilee; and "*dwelt in a city called Nazareth,* that it might be fulfilled which was said by the prophet, that He shall be called a Nazarite." (7)

1. Here is first to be considered *the grief of all the people* of that city where these saints had lived, by reason of their departure from them, through the great relish that they had of their holy conversation, and because it is credible that they left many whom they had converted to the true faith.

2. Secondly, I will consider how *St. Joseph* in all his doubts *had recourse to the remedy of prayer,* always turning himself to God, and how ready God was to hear him, and to free him from his doubts. Hence I will draw desires likewise to have recourse to God in all mine with prayer and confidence. For if I truly desire to be assured of God's holy will, God will give me light to know it.

3. Thirdly, I will consider that *name of our Saviour Christ,* "*Nazarite,*" which He took of the city where He was conceived and brought up, which implies *holy,* or

(7) Matt. ii. 22, 23.

flourishing; signifying by this name that He was to be excellently holy, and the holy of holies, flourishing in all kind of flowers of admirable virtues, and wholly dedicated to God, without having any other employment in this mortal life than in things belonging to His Divine service; giving us an example of being spiritual Nazarites, resplendent in virtue, in imitation of Him.

Colloquy.—O most sweet Jesus, with all my heart, I desire to imitate Thee, to observe the laws of the spiritual Nazarites, separating myself from whatever is created, that may make me "drunk" with inordinate love, and not touching any dead thing that may defile my soul, nor admitting any " razor to pass over" my " head," (8) that may cut off the high thoughts, and affections of my spirit, preserving them all entirely for Thy service. O most flourishing, and most holy Nazarite, aid me to compass my intention, seeing without Thy aid, I can neither begin, or attain the desired end of it.   Amen.

MEDITATION XXIX.

ON THE COMING OF OUR SAVIOUR CHRIST TO THE TEMPLE OF JERUSALEM AND HIS REMAINING THERE AMONG THE DOCTORS.

POINT I.

First, I am to consider the *custom* of St. Joseph, and of the Blessed Virgin with her Son, *to go up "every year" to the temple* of " Jerusalem," to celebrate the "Pasch" (1) of the Lamb, and *with what spirit* they all three went up.

1. St. Joseph went up with the *spirit of obedience,* for the law obliged men to go up "three times every year" to the temple of Jerusalem, (2) especially to celebrate the principal pasch of the Lamb.

, (8) Num. vi. 3, et 5.   (1) Luc. ii. 41.   (2) Exod. xxiii. 14.

2. The Blessed Virgin, although this law obliged not women,—(3) went with St. Joseph in a spirit of devotion to celebrate that feast, and to glorify God therein.

3. The *Child Jesus* went with a spirit of obedience to His parents, who wished to take Him with them, but much more with a *spirit of love to His celestial Father*, to glorify Him in His temple. And all three went with a spirit of thanksgiving, which was the end of the law, to give thanks to God for His benefits received; and therefore marvellous was the sanctity they shewed in this action,—great reverence at their entry into the temple,—great devotion therein,—and a great spirit in all that they did. For, although they had a custom to make these journeys, yet they made them not only for custom's sake, with a little more or a little less; but every time with a new spirit and interior feeling, as if that time had been the first. And here I am to imitate these saints, endeavouring to observe the good customs of the Church, and to make a custom of all things that are virtues; and yet so, that I do them not only for custom, or because others do the like, but with that spirit that they require.

Here it is to be noted, that St. Joseph is called the father of Christ, because he was *held* for His father.

POINT II.

Secondly, I am to consider how the child Jesus "*when He was twelve years old*," having gone up to the temple of Jerusalem with His parents, when they returned to Nazareth, "*remained in the temple*, and His parents knew it not;" (4) pondering some reasons He had for so doing.

1. First, He remained in the temple, to *signify how willing*, so far forth as lay in Him, *He was always* in the house of His celestial Father, employing Himself there in

<hr>

(3) Deut. xvi. 12.   (4) Luc. ii. 42, 43.

things belonging to His service, much better than the child Samuel. And this testimony He gave at *twelve years old*, when other men only *begin* to have more perfect use of reason ; to instruct us how much it imports to attach ourselves to these exercises of virtue from our tender youth, according to that of the prophet Jeremias: "It is good for a man when he hath borne the yoke from his youth." (5)

2. Secondly, with a divine prudence, *He would not ask leave of His parents* to remain alone in the temple, that He might take away occasion of seeming disobedient; if they had denied Him, He had not obeyed them; and because if they had remained with Him, it might have been an impediment to execute freely what He intended for the glory of His heavenly Father; and, therefore, He determined to leave them, and say nothing, teaching us by this example two things of very much importance :—

i. How regardless He was of the flesh, and *how regardless we are all to be* of all that *concerns flesh and blood*, and of carnal love to our parents, friends, and acquaintance, leaving them, whenever it is necessary, to attend more carefully to the business of our heavenly Father.

ii. That when I presume that my parents or friends would hinder me from accomplishing the will of God whether it be by ignorance or right zeal, or through malice or wrong zeal, *it is better to leave them*, and say nothing, although they grieve and lament, and reprehend me afterwards for it, treading all this under foot with a manly courage to fulfil the will of God, according to that which is written:—"He who hath said to his father and to his mother, I do not know you, and to his brethren, I know you not,—these kept Thy word, and observed Thy covenant." (6)　Otherwise, our Saviour Christ will say to

(5) Lam. iii. 27.　　　　　　(6) Deut. xxxiii. 9.

me:—" He that loveth father or mother more than me, is not worthy of me." (7)

Colloquy.—O most sweet child, I am confounded, to see how I am tied to flesh and blood, omitting to do the will of Thy heavenly Father, for fear of displeasing my carnal parents or friends. Give me, O Lord, a manly heart, to leave them all for Thy love, choosing to obey God rather than men, (8) and to " grieve" the human spirit, rather than the " holy Spirit of God." (9)   Amen.

POINT III.

Thirdly, I am to consider how our Lord, Christ with that zeal which He had for the salvation of souls, would then *make some demonstration of the wisdom, and grace* wherewith He was replenished, discovering something of them to these doctors of the law.

1. This He did with admirable *modesty, humility, discretion,* and zeal for the love of God, manifesting these virtues in a manner accommodated to His age.

i. He showed *modesty in His countenance,* and in the gravity of His words, and gestures; which was so great, that it moved the doctors to admit Him, to dispute with them.

ii. *Humility,*—because being able to be *master* of all, He entered among them as a *disciple,* asking and hearing as one that would learn.

iii. *Discretion,*—in answering marvellously to whatever they asked Him; insomuch that they all admired His prudence.

iv. *Zeal,*—since He ordained all this, not for vain ostentation of His own wisdom, but for the glory of God, and good of souls : and especially to confound the proud

(7) Matt. x. 37..   (8) Act. iv. 29.   (9) Eph. iv. 30.

learned men that were there, and to illuminate learned men that were humble, and to open their eyes that they might know that He was already about the work of their redemption.

Colloquy.—O good Jesus, a child in years, but a man in wisdom; a lamb in meekness but a shepherd in discretion, I rejoice to see Thee as a shepherd with this greater flock, giving them the pasture of eternal life, fulfilling that which is written; " a little child shall lead them :" (10) O that I had been present to hear Thy questions, and to enjoy Thy admirable answers! Repeat them, O Lord, to my heart, that I may enjoy the fruit thereof. Amen.

2. From this consideration, I am likewise to gather a great desire, to *imitate these four virtues* of our Saviour Christ, confounding myself in His presence for the want I have of them; especially to see my own so little modesty, and humility : and that in words and gestures, I would make a show of more knowledge than I have; and that being ignorant, I disdain to learn what I know not, and presume to teach others what I have not learned.

POINT IV.

Fourthly, is to be considered, *what* this most blessed *child might do those three days* that He was in the Temple without His parents.

1. How beside the time that He spent with the doctors the rest He might spend in *perpetual watching* and *prayer* before the eternal Father, for the salvation of the world, and of the people that entered therein.

2. It is also to be believed, that He remained there *in the night, taking the ground for His bed,* and some bench for

(10) Is. xi. 6.

IIis bolster; and that He ate of such alms as were given Him, or passed the time without eating; for of all these temporal matters He made but small reckoning. It is likewise certain, that it was a great torment to Him to see the irreverence of some who entered there, and the sins that they there committed, for He had then so fervent a zeal, as when St. John testified of Him that of the psalm; "the zeal of Thy house hath eaten me," (11) although at that time IIe dissembled it.   Out of all this I will draw affections and resolutions of imitation in that, wherein I ought to imitate Him, and to compassionate His poverty and solitariness, although He made small reckoning of His earthly parents, being in the house of His celestial Father.

MEDITATION XXX.

ON THE CONDUCT OF THE BLESSED VIRGIN ON SEEING SHE HAD LOST HER SON,
UNTIL SHE FOUND HIM.

POINT I.

St. Joseph and the Blessed Virgin having travelled "a day's journey" from Jerusalem, on their way to Nazareth; and thinking that the child " was in another company," (1) for they went in several companies, at night *they missed the child*, and seeking among their kinsfolk and acquaintance, they found Him not.

1. In which I must consider the *design of Almighty God* in ordaining to afflict these saints without any fault of theirs, and on the occasion of a good work which they did to honour IIim, and in a thing which might most of all

(11) Joan. ii. 17.   (1) Luc. ii. 43, etc.

grieve them, which was the loss of such a child.   All
which He *contrived in order to exercise* them in *patience,
humility*, and fervent diligence, and in other virtues that
were resplendent in the Blessed Virgin, and in St. Joseph,
in this case, for our example.

i. Their *patience* was resplendent, because they were
not troubled, nor lost the tranquillity of their souls, nor
complained of our Lord; but enduring this loss by yield-
ing to God's ordinance, though it was an exceeding great
loss.

ii. Their *humility*,—because, like good people, they feared
a fault or a negligence where none was, or at least they
attributed this to their own unworthiness; they feared
lest our Lord would already leave them, and follow some
other course of life, or lest they themselves had omitted
their duty in looking after Him, and they confessed themselves to be unworthy of His company.

iii. Their *diligence*,—because they went forthwith to seek
Him, full of solicitude and pain to comply with their obligation, and love urged them on; and though they sought
Him among their kinsfolk and acquaintance; yet, for all
this, they found Him not, for if Christ would have been
with any of His kinsfolk, He would soonest have been
with His mother.

iv. To these three things was added the fourth of *fervent
and long* prayer.   And especially I will ponder what a sad
night that was to the Blessed Virgin,—how solitary she
was without her son,—and how she spent it wholly in
meditating and mourning like a dove, praying with great
zeal, and beseeching the eternal Father not so soon to deprive her of the care of her son, but to look after Him
wherever He was, and not long to defer the restoring Him
again.

Colloquy.—O Sovereign Virgin, thou art entered into the perils of the sea, nor is there any remedy for thee but to pray; the loss of thy beloved has been to thee a bitter and tempestuous sea, the waves of sorrow have entered into thy heart, and afflicted it with many cares; the darkness of night has stopped thy passage, and thou art as it were overwhelmed in the depth of sorrow; thou findest no ease upon earth, and therefore with the cables of prayer, thou dost presently cast forth the anchor of thy hope into heaven, hoping for remedy from thence, and thy hope shall not be deceived; for the heavenly pilot, who is thy Father, knows not how to leave or abandon; nor does He forsake for ever those that hope in Him.

2. With this result, and the cause of it, I am to lift up my spirit to consider the *mystery that it signifies,* pondering how our *Lord God* many times *absents* and *hides Himself from men,* they not knowing nor perceiving it, according to that of holy Job :—" If He come to me I shall not see Him, and if He depart I shall not understand; although I should be simple, even this my soul shall be ignorant." (2) And this ignorance usually lasts all day, until it be discovered at night, as in this case it happened to our Blessed Lady the Virgin and to St. Joseph; and it happens divers ways.

i. It happens *through hidden mortal sins,* when they are committed with culpable ignorance, or through the illusion of the Devil under the cloak of virtue. And then God absents Himself, man not knowing it; and this ignorance sometimes lasts the whole day of his life, until the night of death, when man, thinking he possesses God, finds himself without Him. Upon which the Wise man says: "There is a way that seemeth to a man right, and the end thereof leads to death." (3)   And this absence is most terrible,

(2) Job ix. 11, et 21.   (3) Prov. xvi. 25.

17

because after it follows the *eternal* absence. I am therefore to beseech our Lord not to absent Himself from me in this manner, and say to Him with David:—"From my secret sins cleanse me, O Lord, and my youthful ones do not remember." (4)

ii. Other times it happens through a *secret pride* and *vain glory,* which consume substantial devotion, and deprive the soul of the favourable presence of God. But this is not known during the day of prosperity, for vain glory is accustomed to relish good things; but the night of adversity and humiliation coming, man begins to perceive the absence of God, and the want of true virtue, and finds himself dejected and pusillanimous.

iii. Sometimes, again, it happens through the *secret providence* of *our Lord God,* who absents Himself, and deprives us of sensible devotion to exercise us in humility, and this usually happens upon solemn festival days, and in the exercises of good exterior work ; and although we sometimes perceive not this during our exterior employments, yet we afterwards perceive it in our recollectedness. In this case, it is always most secure to presume that this absence is through my sins, and in chastisement of my negligences and omissions, although I know them not, saying, with the royal prophet David:—"Before I was humbled I offended, and in Thy truth Thou didst humble me ;" (5) because, for my sins, I justly merited this humiliation. But yet, all this, notwithstanding, I should persuade myself, that when I lack the grace of devotion, and the favourable visitations of God, whether it be through my fault or no,—that all happens, by the disposing of God's providence, for my greater good, according to that of the prophet David;—"It is good for me that

(4) Ps. xviii. 13, et xxiv. 7.   (5) Ps. cxviii. 67, 75.

Thou hast humbled me, that I may learn Thy justifications." (6)

3. In all these cases, I am to exercise those four virtues which were resplendent in the Blessed Virgin and in St. Joseph,—striking deep roots of humility,—arming myself with patience,—animating myself to seek God with diligence, and soliciting Him with fervent prayers; for it is written :—" Ask, and it shall be given you; seek, and you shall find." (7)

Colloquy.—O sweet Jesus, who didst speak generally to all, "whoever seeks shall find," grant me such fervour in asking for Thy visitation, that I may obtain it; and aid me to seek in such manner that I may find Thee, for ever and ever.   Amen.

POINT II.

The next day in the morning, St. Joseph and the Blessed Virgin "returned into Jerusalem," to seek the child Jesus, and the third day entering into the Temple, "they found Him sitting in the midst of the doctors, hearing them and asking them questions :" (8) at which they were greatly astonished.

Upon this point I am often to consider the *time* and *place* where the Blessed Virgin found the child :—the *company* and business wherein He was employed;—and the *joy she had* when she saw Him : gathering out of all this the spirit included therein.

1. First, *the time* was the *third day after He was lost*, in which time the sacred Virgin suffered as many hours, more or less, of affliction and desolateness, as she did from the Passion to the Resurrection, when He appeared to her alive and glorious.   And the mystery herein contained is,

(6) Ps. cxviii. 70.   (7) Luc. xi. 9.   (8) Luc. ii. 45.

to signify to us, that when the soul loses God, and the grace of devotion, she does not find Him immediately; rather He is wont to hide Himself for some time, either to chastise her for having lost Him, if she were in fault; or to exercise her in patience and humility: and that with this delay, her care and diligence to seek Him may increase, and that it may be made worthy to find Him more speedily, and with more abundance of grace. And this is signified by the number of *three* days, to encourage our hope that we be not dismayed by thinking that our remedy will be long deferred, according to that saying of the just in affliction:—" He will revive us after two days: on the third day He will raise us up, and we shall live in His sight." (9)

2. Secondly, the *place* where He was found was the Temple and house of God, which is the house of prayer and of recollection, dedicated to worship and works of divine service : to signify that Christ our Lord is not found in flesh and blood, nor among the pamperings and vanities of the world, but within the Catholic Church, and within the living temple of our heart, making it a house of prayer, and exercising it in exercises of sanctity. For hereupon it is said in the book of Canticles, (10) that the spouse found not her beloved, which is Almighty God, in the bed and quietness of the pampering of the flesh; nor in the streets and places of the traffic of the world, but in the renunciation of all this: leaving the comfort of the creatures to find out the Creator. Therefore, O my soul, look where thou seekest Almighty God, if thou hast a desire to find Him ; for, as holy Job says: He is not "found in the land of them that live in delights." (11)

3. Thirdly, I am to consider what *company* He was in,

(9) Osee vi. 3.　　(10) Cant. iii. 1, 2.　　(11) Job xxviii. 13.

and what He *did* at such *time* as the Virgin entered into the Temple: for by special providence He was then "in the midst of the doctors, hearing them, and asking them questions:" that she might thereby understand the cause why He left her, and remained in the Temple; and.that I may understand that our Saviour Christ is found among the doctors of the Church, (12) who by their teaching and direction, are a means to find Him : and that they might understand that Christ is in the midst of them, hearing what they speak and teach, to chastise them if they speak evil, and likewise to aid them to speak well, if through their fault He be not diverted.

4. Fourthly, I will consider the great *joy of our Blessed Lady* the Virgin, when she saw her son, and found Him whom she had lost, and sought with such sorrow. She seemed as if this third day she was raised from death to life ; and as Anna, the mother of Tobias, who bewailed the absence or her son (13) with disconsolate tears, when she saw him wept for pure joy: so. it is to be believed that her joy was in all full measure as her pain, that being fulfilled of the prophet David :—"According to the multitude of my sorrows in my heart, thy comforts have given joy to my soul." (14)

Colloquy.—O Sovereign Virgin, I rejoice at the joy that thou didst feel at this hour at the sight of thy son. "Hope deferred afflicted thy soul," (15) but the fulfilling of thy desire, was to thee a tree of life, since then thou didst find Him that is the tree of life to all. Obtain for me, most Blessed Virgin, so to seek Him, that I may find Him, that I may enjoy the life which proceeds from that tree. Amen.

5. But withal I will consider the *modesty* with which

(12) Cant. iii. 3, 4.   (13) Tob. x. 4.   (14) Ps. xciii. 19.
(15) Prov. xiii. 12.

the Blessed Virgin accompanied this joy : for though she saw her son in the midst of the doctors affording admiration and astonishment to all, yet she used not such gestures and behaviour, as other women use to do, boasting of.having such children : but wondering to see Him there, she reverenced what she saw; whereby she teaches us to unite together modesty and alacrity, according to the saying of St. Paul :—" Rejoice in the Lord always; again, I say rejoice." "Let your modesty be known to all men; The Lord is nigh." (16)   As if he should say: "So rejoice that you lose not modesty, for our Lord is near you, and beholds you, and in His presence there ought to be no immodest joy."

POINT III.

The Blessed Virgin seeing her son, said to Him with an affectionate expostulation : "Son why hast Thou done so to us? behold Thy father and I have sought Thee sorrowing." (17)   All these words are full of mystery, and therefore it will not be amiss to consider well each one by itself.

1. We are to consider that word : "Fili cur fecisti nobis sic?" "Son, why hast Thou done so to us?" by which her intention was not to ask, or demand of Him the cause of what He had done, for this would have been an inexcusable curiosity : but only to *declare the grief of her heart:* and therefore holy men use this manner of speaking to our Lord when they are afflicted, and it is a manner of prayer, in which they calmly ask a remedy of their affliction.   For on the one side, they attribute their affliction to His divine providence, who ordained or permitted it for their good : and on the other side they confess that to Him it belongs to remedy and prevent it.   In

(16) Phil. iv. 4.   (17) Luc. ii. 48.

this manner I may pray, saying sometimes to our Lord with Job: "Why hast Thou set me opposite to Thee, and I am become burdensome to myself? why dost Thou not remove my sin, and why dost Thou not take away my iniquity? (18)   Why hidest Thou Thy face, and thinkest me Thine enemy?" (19) at other times, I may say with our Saviour Christ Himself nailed on the cross: "My God, my God, why hast Thou forsaken me?" (20) Neither was it without mystery, that the Blessed Virgin said not:—"Son, why hast Thou done so to *me?*" but "to *us?*" for it is the property of holy people, when they suffer any necessity that is common to many, not to complain of their own affliction only, nor to ask remedy for themselves alone, but to grieve for the affliction of all, and to ask remedy for all: for charity seeks not only its own good, but the good of many, saying with the royal prophet :—"Why turnest Thou Thy face away from us? and forgettest our want and our trouble?" (21)   But in these expostulations we are to endeavour not to lose our love and confidence in Almighty God; and therefore we are to join with them some word to express this, as the Blessed Virgin used this word, "Son;" and our Saviour Christ upon the cross this word, "My God, my God," which are words of confidence and love.

2. Secondly, I am to consider that word, "Pater tuus, et ego." "*Thy father and I:*" in which is resplendent the *humility* of the Blessed Virgin, not only in naming St. Joseph before herself, for the respect she had of him; but also in calling him before all, the father of Christ, whereby they might imagine that He was conceived by the work of man; which was to her own humiliation; but the holy Virgin being humble, more esteemed her husband's honour

(18) Job vii. 20. 21.   (19) Job. xiii. 24.   (20) Matt. xxvii. 46.
(21) Ps. xliii. 24.

than her own, in giving him so honourable a name, teaching us by her example how to honour our neighbours, though it be to our own disparagement.

3. Thirdly, I am to consider that word,—" Dolentes quarebamus te;" "*have sought Thee sorrowing.*" Wherein we are advised *to seek* Almighty God *with sorrow* proceeding from love, such was the sorrow of the Blessed Virgin: for true love causes all these effects; viz. *sorrow* and tears for the absence of its beloved : *purity of intention* in seeking Him with sincerity, not for its own interest or sensible pleasure, but to be united to Him: *diligence* in all the means, and exercises ordained to find Him with *perseverance* in them, until it compass its intent, according to that of the prophet David:—" Seek ye the Lord and be strengthened in Him, seek His face evermore." (22)   And so that of the prophet Isaiah: (23) If you seek our Lord, seek Him well, that is, seek Him in truth, as such a Lord deserves to be sought, and you shall find Him ; for He has said : " You shall seek me, and shall find me : when you shall seek me with all your heart." (24)   And if I find Him not, it is because I fail in some of these things, and, therefore, making reflection upon them, I will consider which of them it is, to amend myself, and to procure it.

4. Finally, I am to consider the *brevity* and *succinctness* of the Blessed Virgin's *speeches,* in which she not only avoided superfluous words, but also smothered in silence some that might seem necessary to declare her mind more amply, and embracing them all under that short word, " Sic," "*why hast Thou done so ?*" in which is confirmed the care of our Blessed Lady to guard her tongue, and to measure her words; as at other times has been considered:

(22) Ps. civ. 4.   (23) Is. xxi. 12.   (24) Jer. xxix. 13.

but at this time somewhat more especially, because she declared how she had mortified and restrained the violence of speaking, which in such cases issues from the heart.

POINT IV.

To this question of the Blessed Virgin, our Saviour Christ answered:—" How is it that you sought me? did you not know that I must be about my Father's business." (25)

This answer was no less grave and admirable, than any of those which our Lord made to the demands of the doctors : and therefore it is to be considered as given by the infinite wisdom of Almighty God.

1. And first, I will consider that word, " Quid est, quod me quærebatis ?"   " How is it that you sought me ?" or for what cause ? which word at the first view seems dry, harsh, sharp, and reprehensive, as if He had said: Wherefore sought you me with such sorrow, seeing that I, being what I am, could not be lost ?   And this He said that it might be understood, that He was *more than man :* and that the Blessed Virgin might make demonstration of her heroic patience and humility, silently suffering this dis-tasteful answer, and receiving it with great reverence and love.   And by the way Christ our Lord teaches us that such as govern religious persons who are desirous of per-fection, are sometimes to exercise them with sharp answers, and with reprehending them when there is no cause, to discover what humility and patience they have, and to make profit of it : (26) for to be silent when I am repre-hended for a fault is not much, seeing my own conscience also reprehends me : but to be silent when my conscience excuses me, is a token of heroic virtue.

2. Secondly, I will consider the word which He said :

<hr>

(25) Luc. ii. 49.   (26) S. Joa. Clim. gradu iv.

"*Did you not know that I must be about my Father's busi-ness?*" As if He had said:—"Since you know me, and know who I am, you likewise know that I am to be about those things which appertain to the honour of my heavenly Father : for I have no father on earth." Wherein Christ our Lord taught us, that His whole business and employ-ment was wholly to attend to the service of His heavenly Father, without diverting to any other thing, confirming that which afterwards He said, that He "came down from heaven not to do" His "own will, but the will of Him that sent Him :" (27) and that He "must work the works of Him that sent" Him, "whilst it" was "day." (28) In imitation of this our Lord, I am to endeavour that my whole employment be not in the things of this world, nor of flesh, nor of self love, but in the things which are of God, and for God, confounding myself to see how far I have been from observing this advice, employing myself wholly in my own business, and careless of that of God.

Colloquy.—O good Jesus, seeing Thou wast so stead-fastly set about the things that were Thy Father's, Thou heldest it for a rule, that such as knew Thee should find Thee employed in them: Aid me, I be-seech Thee, that I may never find myself without them, but ever employ myself in loving, and accom-plishing them. It is just, O Lord, that my memory, understanding, and will, my senses, and all that I am, should be employed always about Thee, and in that which concerns Thy honour, seeing Thou always em-ployest Thyself to my profit.

POINT V.

1. Fifthly, I will consider how having said this, without further reply, *the child returned with His mother*, and St.

(27) Joan. vi. 38.   (28) Joan. ix. 4.

Joseph to Nazareth.   And it is to be believed that by the way, the Blessed Virgin would ask Him about all that had passed during those three days, and that the child related all to her.   And she, as St. Luke said, treasured up, and "kept all these" words "in her heart," (29) recording, ruminating, and pondering them to her great consolation and profit.   Whence I will learn to *store* in my memory *whatever* Almighty *God* shall *teach* me, to make my profit of it : for otherwise that of the prophet will happen to me—that eating much, I shall always be weak; and gathering together great riches, I shall always be poor, because I "put them into a bag with holes." (30)

2. Finally, I will consider how *wary* and circumspect the Blessed Virgin was thenceforth *not to lose sight* of her son, being afraid from what was passed, lest such another accident should happen.   And the like circumspection ought I to have not to lose Christ, nor His gifts, taking advice from what has happened in times past.

Colloquy.—O most sacred Virgin, I rejoice at thy joy when thou didst find thy Son, and at thy gladness to have Him always in thy company; aid me, that I may never lose Him, nor ever depart from Him until with thee I come to enjoy Him in His eternal glory. Amen.

MEDITATION XXXI.

ON THE LIFE THAT OUR SAVIOUR CHRIST LED IN NAZARETH UNTIL HE WAS THIRTY YEARS OLD.

POINT I.

I am first to consider how our Saviour Christ all this

(29) Luc. ii. 51.   (30) Agg. i. 6.

time, according to St. Luke, (1) "Proficiebat sapientia, ætate, et gratia apud Deum, et homines." "And Jesus advanced in wisdom, and age, and grace, with God and men." Concerning which I must first consider:—

1. How, although Christ our Lord from the first instant of His conception, was so full of immense wisdom and sanctity, that He could not increase in them, yet He increased in the exercise of them, giving daily greater demonstrations of knowledge and virtue, of wisdom and sanctity : like the sun, which though in itself it increases not, yet the light that proceeds from it when it rises in the morning, goes on always increasing until it is mid-day. This our Lord ordained, to teach us by His example, what a desire He has that His children should daily increase, and progress in virtue. For between the sons of the terrestrial Adam, and those of celestial Adam, there is this difference; that they "from" their "youth" are prone to evil; (2) as they increase in years, they increase in vices; that *and* of the prophet David (3) being fulfilled in them, "The pride of them that hate Thee, ascendeth continually." But these, as the prophet Jeremiah (4) says, "from" their "youth" upwards carry "the yoke" of God's law, and exalt themselves above themselves : for as they increase in years, they increase in virtues, exalting daily their spirit above themselves, and above what they before had, that "forgetting the things that are behind," (5) they may extend themselves to other things that are greater, until they arrive at perfection. This so singular favour our Saviour Christ did to His Blessed Mother, and to His fore-runner St. John, as has been said : and this He has done to other eminent saints, who from their infancy

(1) Luc. ii. 52.   (2) Gen. viii. 21.   (3) Ps. lxxiii. 23.

(4) Thren. iii. 27.   (5) Phil. iii. 13.

began to serve Almighty God, and proceeded forward like the light of the morning, increasing "even to day." (6)

2. But particularizing this more amply, I may likewise consider *different sorts* of men that *begin to serve* Almighty God either in their childhood, or in some other part of their age.

i. Some there are that instead of *going forward turn back*, leaving off the virtuous life that they began : of whom our Saviour Christ said: (7)—"No man putting his hand to the plough, and looking back, is fit for the king-dom of God :" and then consequently he must be apt for hell. And therefore I am to tremble at turning back in this manner, taking warning, as Christ our Lord (8) counselled, by Lot's wife, who turning back to look upon Sodom, from whence she had departed, was turned into a statue of salt, and into a mark-stone to terrify those that prosecute not the way of virtue.

ii. Others there are that begin with *fervent zeal*, but instead of increasing therein, they *decrease*, either omitting some virtuous exercises, or the fervour of zeal with which they did them. And these, although they be just, yet are in great danger of destruction,—like that bishop whom our Saviour Christ (9) praised for his good life, but yet had "somewhat against" him, because he had "left" his "first charity," that is the fervour of charity which he used to have. And then He adds :—"Be mindful there-fore from whence thou art fallen, and do penance and do the first works. Or else I will come to take an account of thee, and will deprive thee of the dignity thou hast :" as if He should say:—"Take heed, for to lose thy fervour, is to fall from high to low, which if thou repairest not

(6) Prov. iv. 18.   (7) Luc. ix. 62.   (8) Luc. xvii. 32.

(9) Apoc. ii. 4.

thou deservest not to be in so high a place as I have placed thee in."

iii. There are others that begin and go forward slowly without *desire of increasing*, or passing farther, and these although outwardly they seem not to decay, yet inwardly ordinarily turn back, and finally will altogether sink : for as the holy Fathers say, (10) in the way to heaven, there is no stopping, but one must either go forward, or turn backward.

iv. Finally, there are *others* who as soon as they begin, with the aid of our Lord, as the prophet David says : (11) *resolve "in" their "heart," to "ascend by steps,"* so long as they live in this "vale of tears :" and "the" celestial "lawgiver" helping them with His copious benediction, they fulfil their resolutions ascending "from virtue to virtue," until they see "the God of gods in Sion." And these are the true imitators of Christ Jesus, whom it is reasonable that I should imitate, confounding myself for those many times that I have turned back in the way of virtue, or that I have fallen from the first fervour that I begun with, or that I have walked on a lukewarm life, as if I had been tired : encouraging myself henceforward greatly to increase in zeal, saying to our Saviour Christ:—

Colloquy.—O Sun of justice, illustrate and inflame my soul in such sort, that her paths may be like the light of the morning, which " goeth forwards and increaseth even to perfect day." (12) O Sovereign lawgiver, give me thine abundant benediction, that as Thou desirest, I may increase in virtue and sanctity, ascending from one degree to another, until I clearly behold Thee in Thy celestial Sion, world without end. Amen.

(10) S. Bern. Epist. xci. S. Greg. 51. in 1. Reg. ii.
S. Aug. serm. xv. de verbis Apost. et alii.
(11) Ps. lxxxiii. 6. (12) Prov. iv. 18.

POINT II.

Secondly, I am to consider before what persons, and in what things, Christ our Lord increased in the manner aforesaid.

1. The Evangelist St. Luke says, that *He increased with God and men*, teaching us by His example to avoid two vicious extremes.

i. The one is, of *zealous indiscreet persons*, who presume to increase before God only, making no account of men, nor of their edification or dis-edification, or scandal, not remembering that he that loves Almighty God, ought likewise to love his neighbour ; and that he so ought to seek his own profit, that it be not to the hurt of others; attending, as St. Paul says, (13) to the edification of all.

ii. Another extreme is of *hypocrites*, such as feign zeal, who lay all their care in increasing before men, doing whatsoever may help them to increase in opinion of sanctity before them, without attending to the true augmentation which the prophet David (14) calls augmentation in the heart.   But Christ our Lord by His example teaches us to embrace both, not permitting the one to prejudice the other, proposing first the increasing before Almighty God with true increasing in His eyes : and secondly, increasing before men, doing likewise, as St. Paul says, (15) that which is good before them, not that they may honour or praise us, but that they may glorify Almighty God, and may be edified and profited.   And if doing what for my part I ought to do, some, through their own fault, be dis-edified or scandalized, yet for all this I will not cease to increase before God, and before those that are wise and holy, and deserve the name of men.

2. Secondly, St. Luke says, that " *Christ our Lord*

13) Rom. xiv. 19.   (14) Ps. lxxxiii. 6.
(15) Rom. xii. 17.   2 Cor. viii. 21.

increased in wisdom and grace:" for in these two things true augmentation ought to consist.—i. In *wisdom* and in the acts proceeding from it, which are meditation and contemplation of celestial things : (16) prudence and discretion in actions and affairs ; the estimation of all things in that degree which they merit, much esteeming eternal things, and temporal things but little, and consequently so speaking of them, that our words may be seasoned with this wisdom.—ii. We are to increase in *grace,* and in the acts of virtues that make us gracious and holy before Almighty God, and amiable before men ; in which our Saviour Christ exercised Himself at this time : such are the heroic acts of the love of God, of the fervent zeal for His glory and the salvation of souls ; a vehement sorrow for the offences done against God, and for the souls that perish, and continual prayer that they perish not. In this He was so gracious and pleasing to Almighty God, that as He Himself says by the prophet Isaiah, (17) His soul delighted in Him. Besides this He edified men with rare examples of modesty, humility, patience, meekness, and subjection ; for which He was pleasing to those persons with whom He conversed. For as the same prophet Isaiah says, (18) His conversation was neither " sad," nor harsh, " nor troublesome," nor offensive, nor distasteful to others.

Colloquy.—O most sweet Jesus, seeing Thou art full of wisdom, and grace, and that from Thy fulness the just receive augmentation both in the one and in the other ; replenish me abundantly with both, and aid me daily to increase in them, Amen.

3. Lastly, to animate myself I will consider how the *most holy Virgin made her profit* of these two examples of

<hr>

(16) Coloss. iii. 2; iv. 2.   (17) Is. xlii. 1.
(18) Is. xlii. 4. Matt. xii. 19.

her son : for contemplating them, she also in imitation of Him increased in wisdom and grace before Almighty God, and before men ; our Saviour Christ rejoicing to behold the holy emulation that His mother had of Him.

Colloquy.—O most blessed mother, aid me with thy intercession, that I may increase as thou increasedst, imitating Him whom thou didst imitate.

POINT III.

Thirdly, I will consider how all this time our Saviour Christ, as the same Evangelist says, *was subject to His mother* (19) *and St. Joseph*, obeying them in all that they commanded Him.

Here I must consider *who it is that obeys* and subjects Himself;—*to whom,—in what things,—and in what manner.*

1. He that obeys is *Almighty God* infinite, the Creator and supreme governor of the world, whom all are obliged to obey, and be subject to.   And although it was not much that as man He should obey His eternal Father, yet it is admirable that He should subject Himself to obey His mother, and a poor artizan, the Creator subjecting Himself to the creatures, the Lord to His servants, and the king to His vassals : by which I may confound my own pride and rebellion.

Colloquy.—O vile worm, why dost not thou subject thyself to man for God, seeing that God subjects Himself to man for thee?   If God obeys the voice of a man, (20) why dost not thou, wretched man, obey the voice of God?   O Sun of justice, that movest Thyself and stayest at the voice of these two persons, to whom for my love Thou didst subject Thyself, grant me that I may subject myself to those whom Thou hast left me in Thy place delighting to deny my own will, to accomplish theirs.   Amen.

(19) Luc. ii. 51.   (20) Josue x. 12, 13.

18

2. Then will I consider the *things wherein He obeyed*, that is to say, in such base things as are used to be done in the house of a poor carpenter, and in that manner that children use to serve in the house of their parents when they are· poor. And this did our Saviour Christ with great humility and punctuality, with astonishing promptness, alacrity, and with all that perfection which perfect obedience requires: which equally embraces great, and little, easy and difficult, honourable and contemptible. For seeing that God Himself humbled Himself to be obedient in things that were so base, all things in its estimation are very high, and esteems nothing base in the house of God, if He commands it : for if God commands, it is sufficient to make the execution honourable, as the Archangel Raphael held it for an high honour, (21) to serve Tobias in things very base, because God commanded it.

3. Hence I will collect that the excellence of spiritual life consists not so much in doing works of themselves very glorious, such as are to preach, to govern, or to teach, as in doing those works that God commands, though of themselves they be base, *in an excellent manner :*—that is, with great love of God, with a pure intention of His glory, with great promptitude and alacrity of heart, and a fervent desire in all these things to please Him. And in this sense it is that the Wise man says;—"in all thy works keep the pre-eminence," (22) doing them in such a way, that in the eyes of Almighty God they may be very excellent. And so Christ our Lord, as to the manner of working with a spirit of sanctity, was no less excellent in the work of sawing than in the work of preaching, or performing some miracle. And our Blessed Lady the Virgin showed no less the excellency of her sanctity when she spun, than when she served her son, or suffered anything

(21) Tob. v. 15, et 20. (22) Ecclus. xxxiii. 23.

for His sake. And in this I am to imitate our Saviour Christ and His blessed mother, if by the shortest way I would attain to the greatest perfection.

POINT IV.

Fourthly, I will consider how Christ our Lord, until He was thirty years old, *exercised* the *trade of a carpenter:* as may be collected from the speech of those of His own country, according to the report of St. Mark the Evangelist : " Is not this the carpenter the son of Mary?" (23)

1. Here I will consider the reasons that our Saviour Christ had for choosing this trade of life, and for *continuing* it even till after the death of St. Joseph, if it be true that he died before Christ had attained to thirty years of age.

i. The first was, to *avoid idleness*, and to give us an *example* of *labouring* and being ever employed : for idleness, as the Wise man says, is the origin of all mischief. (24)

ii. The second was of His own free will to *subject Himself* to the *malediction* that Almighty God imposed upon Adam, when He said to him:—" In the sweat of thy brow thou shalt eat thy bread." And, therefore, all this time, He gained His food with the labour of His hands : whence St. Paul and other saints took example of labouring, to eat of their own labours.

iii. The third was, *to exercise humility*, employing Himself in a vile and contemptible occupation ; for Christ our Lord, in the judgment of the world and of His own countrymen, did not follow this occupation of His own will, (as some noble and wise gentlemen are wont to learn from mechanical trade for their pleasure,) but from mere necessity, and to get His living ; and so He was then

(23) Marc. vi. 3.   (24) Ecclus. xxxiii. 29.

treated by gentlemen, and those of the higher classes, as at this day such mechanical artificers are treated.

2. Out of all this collect affections of admiration and imitation, considering also the spirit wherewith our Saviour Christ exercised this office, labouring with the body, and praying with the heart, to imitate Him when I shall labour in any bodily works;, as did those valiant soldiers the Machabees, of whom the Scripture says, that they fought with their hands, and prayed with their hearts, and therefore obtained a glorious victory. For as St. Augustine said in a tract that he wrote on this subject to certain monks, "It standeth well together, when the hand laboureth, and the heart and the tongue prayeth." (25)

POINT V.

1. Fifthly, I will consider how our Saviour·Christ containing in Himself the treasures of the wisdom and knowledge of Almighty God, and all the graces, and gifts, and power to do miracles that before have been recounted, yet *during* all this time of *thirty years, would give a rare example of humility*, covering all this with an extraordinary silence, without either preaching, or teaching, or coming to the disputations and assemblies of the learned, or to the schools and universities; as is collected from what the Jews said of Him :—"How doth this man know letters, having never learned?" (26) Whence it arose, that some of His countrymen, held Him in their opinion for an idiot. And therefore when they saw that He began to preach, St. Mark takes notice, "when His friends had heard of it, they went out to lay hold on Him. For they said, He is become mad," (27) or possessed with some devil, not being to believe that such words and works could proceed from a man, whom they had always known to exercise the lowly trade of a carpenter.

(25) De Oper. Monach.   (26) Joan vii. 15.   (27) Marc iii. 21.

2. By this so rare an example, I may learn *silently to cover my gifts and talents*, when there is no need of publishing them for the glory of Almighty God. As also not easily to trust myself, in seeking before my time to manifest my own qualities to honour myself, delighting rather not to be known, or to be held for an ignorant fool, if God shall so permit it. And finally to lay deep roots in humility and silence, seeing through all this my Redeemer was willing to pass, who having great care of the salvation of souls, repressed this desire, keeping silence for so long a time: for though He might have preached at five-and-twenty, or before, yet He would not: for by this example of mortification and silence, He preached and taught us the secure way of humility. (28) And withal He advises us, that none should begin to be a preacher, or master, till he come to a mature age, by which time he may have learned in silence, what he ought to manifest by words, laying deep roots of humility in secret, before he adventure to manifest himself in public. And His thus keeping silence for thirty years, to preach only for three, which is but the tenth of thirty, is not without a mystery : but that we might understand how much more time we ought to give to the exercises that are directed to the benefit of others, that without hurting ourselves we may do good to others.

Colloquy.—O Sovereign master, whose silence preaches to me no less than Thy word, I confess my pride to be so great, that being ignorant I would be held to be wise, and that through vanity, I would manifest the little wisdom that I have ; teach me, O Lord, to walk in the way of humility, following Thy footsteps, that humbling myself with Thee, I may reign with Thee, world without end. Amen.

(28) S. Greg. hem 2. in Ezech i.

APPENDIX:

CONTAINING MEDITATIONS

ON THE

SACRED HEART OF JESUS CHRIST,

BEING THOSE TAKEN FROM A NOVENA IN PREPARATION FOR THE FEAST OF THE SAME,

BY FATHER C. BORGO, S. J.

TRANSLATED FROM THE ITALIAN.*

"Sicut dilexit me Pater et ego dilexi vos. Manete in dilectione mea." Jo. xv. 9.

MEDITATION

    i.—On the ends for which the B. Sacrament was instituted.
    ii.—In honour of the Sacred Heart for its life of beatitude.
    iii.   ,,   ,,   life of grace.
    iv.   ,,   ,,   life of sacrifice.
    v.   ,,   ,,   life of humiliation.
    vi.   ,,   ,,   life of love.
    vii.   ,,   ,,   active life.
    viii.   ,,   ,,   hidden life.
    ix.   ,,   ,,   glorious life.
    x.   ,,   ,,   life of consummated sacrifice.
    xi. (*For the Vigil of Feast.*)—Priceless value of the sacred Heart.
    xii. (*For the Feast of the sacred Heart.*)—The love of the sacred
        Heart and our ingratitude.
    Acts of consecration and reparation to the sacred Heart.

---

    * These meditations were first published in Italian in 1778; they passed through several editions. The present translation was made from the edition of 1824.

MEDITATION I.

ON THE ENDS OF THE INSTITUTION OF THE MOST HOLY SACRAMENT.

(For the Day preceding the Novena.)

Preparatory prayer.—Faith in God's presence.

Offering of the meditation.—Petition for attention, light, and affection.

First Prelude.—Imagine you behold Jesus Christ in the act of instituting the divine Sacrament. View Him at table with His apostles, with that bread in His hand which He blesses and substantially changes into His divine body.—Observe how he raises to heaven those divine eyes brightened with a light of more than ordinary sweetness :—see how that divine countenance is more than usually inflamed. He appears truly in an ecstasy of love.

Second Prelude.—Beg Him to give you an extraordinary light, that you may understand well the *ends of His love* in this Sacrament, and grace to be penetrated deeply with them, that you may also concur to the accomplishment of these ends.

POINT I.

1. Jesus Christ instituted the divine Sacrament that He might fully *satisfy His desire of communicating to us all His riches.* So many other ways of communicating His divine gifts to men had not yet contented Him. Ponder well, Religious soul, this insatiable desire of His most liberal Heart.

i. This is not simply a new gift that He offers to the souls He loves; *it is a compendium of all His gifts;* every kind of grace is included in it. Whatever wants a soul may have in this life, it can here find a means of supplying and satisfying them all. Tempted, afflicted, timid, weak, blind, poor, sick, dying souls, here, if you know how to make use of them, you may find 'all the helps which are found separated in so many other means; in friends, advisers, masters, books, examples, considerations,' in all the devotions of Christianity. In each of these kinds of advantages bestowed by the Heart of Jesus numberless souls have found means of sanctifying themselves. In other means we may often want the opportunity, or that facility and frequency we require. But in this Sacrament Jesus Christ is always present and ready, everywhere and for every one. What a reproach this of your long tepidity in the service of God! What a reprehension of your indolence and neglect of so universal a remedy!

ii. But this is not simply a compendium of the other divine gifts; it is also *a gift entirely new, and the greatest of all* the gifts to which the infinite charity of your Redeemer has given birth. Here He gives you the plant itself, the parent of so many fruits, He gives you Himself. In Himself He gives you everything, without reserving anything to Himself. He gives you His sacred humanity, with all the merits of His mortal life; He gives you His divinity, with all the infinite treasures of His wisdom, power and goodness. He puts no other limit to His desire of enriching you than the limit which you put yourself, your disposition, and your capacity.

2. Ponder well this excess of love, O soul that art so sensible to all human courtesy. The gifts of men appease you when irritated, rouse you when indifferent, engage and conquer you. Only towards your God your ungrateful heart changes its nature. Be confounded, repent, melt into sorrow, and resolve once for all what you ought to think, to feel and to do in order to give contentment to

the divine Heart, insatiable in its desires of imparting good.

POINT II.

1. Jesus Christ instituted the divine Sacrament *to unite Himself to our souls.* This is the object of His most liberal love. Behold Him here, that merchant in the Gospel, who sells all his property to purchase a pearl he believes to be rare and precious. O Jesus, Son of God, can then we and the possession of our hearts be so valuable in your eyes? Vile and ungrateful soul, think of this mystery! So ardently does the Only-begotten Son of the Father long to become one thing with you by the most intimate union that can exist between the eternal God and a mortal creature. And by an effort of power and of wisdom He has found a means of making Himself as it were one with you, by becoming your food, so as to be wholly and in truth the property of the creature, provided the creature consents to be wholly His by a reciprocal and loving return. Reason would shudder to think of it, if faith did not oblige us to believe it. Yes, my Jesus and my God, I believe it.

2. But do I properly conceive as I ought how it is that *I am so insensible* to such love? O how late have I known Thee and myself! As I admire Thee, so am I horrified at myself. How often hast Thou thus lovingly united Thyself to my soul! But to what a monster hast thou found *Thyself* united, O divine lover! To what a monster of unworthiness, uncleanness, coldness, and ingratitude! This my soul has so often found itself in the bosom of a happiness it has not known; to enjoy which, even for once only, all my blood would have been well shed! O blind, foolish, unhappy and guilty soul of mine, what moments have you lost! what delights you have not had the taste

to relish! The Seraphim themselves envied you; and I.........Ah! my vile senses, ah deceitful world, ah! treacherous passions, what have you given me in exchange?

3. Here pause a little, Religious soul, and *compare* this infinite and loving *possession of God with those occasions of your tepidity* that deprive you of the knowledge and relish of so great a good. Make generous resolutions, beg great light and great graces, and conclude with an entire renunciation of your self-love, and with an absolute offering of your heart to the desires, designs, and burning affection of the most amiable and loving heart of your divine Spouse.

MEDITATION II.

THE DIVINE HEART OF JESUS CHRIST IN THE MOST HOLY SACRAMENT LIVES A LIFE OF BEATITUDE.

(For the First Day of the Novena.)

This is a truth imperceptible to your self-love, which, in the most holy Sacrament, sees the Heart of Jesus Christ in a total privation of all the sensible blessings of earth.

Preparatory prayer.—Faith in God's presence.

Offering of the meditation.—Petition for attention, light, and affection.

First Prelude.—Imagine you see Jesus Christ in the most holy Sacrament, opening His divine breast, and showing you His Heart as on a throne of sweetest light and of living fire.

Second Prelude.—Beg of Him to give you a share of that sweet light and of that divine fire, to undeceive and inflame your heart.

POINT I.

Seek in the Heart of Jesus Christ the idea you ought to form of the greatness, beauty, and felicity of *temporal* blessings.

1. That divine Heart *enjoys in that narrow ciborium an infinite happiness,* without however tasting any of that which the world esteems, and which your self-love believes so necessary to your contentment. Silence and solitude surround Him, instead of earthly pleasures. His lodging is often in poverty and filth, instead of gems and gold. For the few moments that He is not left alone, He generally has before Him rude people and persons of low esteem. How often does He find Himself in the midst of those who offend Him, and of His enemies! How often does it happen that He is insulted, derided, profaned! What a wretched situation is His in the eyes of your self-love! If you had to remain in that tabernacle as He remains, were it only for a week, you would die of melancholy. That divine Heart, however, in such solitude, in such company, in the midst of such contempt, loses nothing of its happiness, which is always infinite.

2. And how often do *you lose your tranquillity!* And for what a *trifle* do you lose it! O blind and feeble heart! By your attachment to sensible things you have made your happiness depend upon them, because in these things it is that you have hitherto sought happiness. Ah! your heart is of the same nature as that of Jesus Christ. Like His divine Heart, your heart was never made for these pleasures that thus allure the senses. Be confounded at your past folly. O Heart infinitely blest, make me know the deceitfulness of the pleasures which my self-love suggests and requires. Give me an utter contempt for all that the world esteems and loves.—Examine what desire

of self-love allures you most, and against this particularly direct your resolutions and prayers.

POINT II.

1. Study in the Heart of Jesus Christ the idea you ought to form of the greatness, beauty, and happiness, of *spiritual* blessings.

i. *The love and possession of God constitute* the happiness of the divine Heart of Jesus Christ. As that Heart is personally united to the Divinity, its happiness is infinite, because its love and union with the Divinity are infinite. Behold the reason why its happiness is not at all disturbed by the absence of these temporal blessings, which to you appear so great. As far as regards its happiness, that poor ciborium is equal to the throne of glory which it enjoys in heaven. After having fixed your eyes on the sun for a short time, you no longer see anything else; in everything you continue to see the sun, because the intense impression of that great light makes your eyes insensible to the weaker light of other objects.

ii. O *happy insensibility* to all the goods of this life! How necessary is this insensibility for you to make your heart happy, even in this life! Say once more to yourself, "My heart is of the same nature as is the Heart of Jesus Christ: that only which makes Him happy can make me happy also." Call to mind those days, or at least those hours of your life, when your heart was most inflamed with love of your God. O sweet and yet bitter recollection! What was then wanting to your happiness? Compare the tranquillity of your heart then with that which it enjoys at present. Compassionate yourself, envy yourself, be indignant with yourself.

2. O infinitely content and happy Heart of my Lord, when wilt Thou have pity on me? Foolish soul, and why

do you not *take pity on yourself?* Thus does that Heart answer you from that tabernacle. What reply will you make? Ask pardon for having allowed that holy love for His Heart, the sweetness and peace of which He has formerly made you taste, to be extinguished by your dissipation. Make great, but practical and particular, resolutions to disengage yourself from that which is the *special impediment* to the increase of divine love in you, and consequently the impediment also to the acquisition and increase of the happiness of your heart even in this life.

MEDITATION III.

ON THE LIFE OF GRACE OF THE SACRED HEART IN THE MOST HOLY SACRAMENT.

(For the Second Day of the Novena.)

He who lives in a foreign country to trade or to learn some science, is said to be leading there a life of traffic or of study. Jesus Christ wished to remain on this earth, although it no longer suited His state of glory, in order that He might promote the interests of divine grace. Thus the life that He leads here amidst us in the Sacrament, may be called a life of grace.—We will meditate the sentiment of His divine Heart on this subject, and the sentiments He requires from our hearts on it.

Preparatory prayer.—As usual.

First Prelude.—Imagine you behold Jesus Christ in the most holy Sacrament, who with His breast open, shows you His divine Heart, from which bursts a torrent of most clear water, signifying the graces He desires to shower upon all who present themselves.

Second Prelude.—Present yourself before Him as a poor

unclean leper, and languishing with thirst, and beg of Him to cure, cleanse, and restore you by His grace.

POINT I.

Jesus Christ in the Blessed Sacrament lives a *life of grace*. What are the sentiments with which this life inspires His Heart?

i. What were *His sentiments during His mortal life*, when He healed the sick, and for this purpose sought them out Himself; when He gave sight to the blind, raised the dead to life, and conferred His numerous miraculous favours? All these sentiments of pity, tenderness, mercy, and liberality, He now feels at the same moment in this state, which is a compendium of all His wonders. With what sentiments did He encounter so much fatigue, want, and torment! All this charity and infinite love He now feels in this state in which He continues to renew every day the work of our redemption.

ii. A great flame confined in a narrow furnace, how does it gain strength and rage! You may imagine the same of this divine Heart. Think, to speak after our way of understanding things, that this infinitely loving Heart *is in a kind of inexpressible suffering, through the excessive fulness of the graces it contains*, and to which it cannot give vent through want of persons to receive them. One day Jesus said to a beloved soul as He showed her His Heart, as in an abyss of fire,—"My Heart, my daughter, can no longer support its desire to communicate itself to souls. Do thou assist me, my daughter, to lessen this fire. Publish and cause it to be published over all the world, that I will set no limits to my graces, for those souls that come to seek them in this my Heart."

2. Now you are one of these cold souls, *so reserved* with the Heart of this loving God. Have you ever well

pondered and understood these sentiments of His Heart? What do you think of Him, now that you know them? what do you think of yourself? O Heart of infinite liberality and charity, why have I not known Thee before? Why have I hitherto been so destitute of grace, so diffident with Thee, so timid in praying to Thee, so reserved in my requests?—Admiration, thanksgiving, confidence, resolutions.

POINT II.

1. What *sentiments does the Heart of Jesus Christ require from you* by this life of grace, in which He remains for you in this Sacrament?

i. First, you ought practically to make this divine Heart *your only place of refuge in all the wants of your heart.* You have not done so hitherto, since this loving Heart has been the last to which you have had recourse. Had you practically believed that in this divine Heart there was a true remedy for all your temptations, fits of melancholy, doubts and weaknesses, you would not have sought it from creatures, from your senses, and even from your passions.—Examine yourself with sincerity on the wrongs you have done in this to the most tender and powerful of all hearts, and begin immediately to repair them.

ii. Secondly, you ought to have recourse to this divine Heart *with a sincere and strong desire of the graces of which you stand in need.* Ah! that divine Heart is perfectly acquainted with your most secret sentiments, and sees how weak is your desire to love Him, even in the very act of begging the grace of His love; that you fear to have the grace effectually to break that attachment to creatures; that while you beg the grace with your lips, you have a secret horror of self-hatred, of love of contempt, of an entire renunciation of the indulgence of your senses. Your best means of deserving the graces of Jesus Christ is by the sincerity and greatness of your desires. Compare your desires with those which you have meditated in the Heart of Jesus Christ. Blush, seek pardon, and begin by asking as a first grace such a desire of being cured by His graces, as may be worthy of the desire He has to communicate them to you.

iii. Thirdly, you ought to have recourse to the Heart of Jesus Christ *with an humble, but loving confidence;* that is, with a kind of affectionate familiarity which, in this Sacrament, God allows and wishes you to have with Him. O soul! unmindful of your happy lot! I might almost call this forgetfulness a greater wonder than the love of this Heart for man; for this is the God of majesty and glory, before whom the Seraphim tremble in heaven, who here on earth wishes to converse confidently with us. You give the closest confidence of your heart to creatures sometimes more vile than yourself, and who perhaps, dishonour and betray you; and are reserved and close of heart with God, who condescends to abase Himself so much for you. Ah! it is not humility that influences you; it is the little love you entertain for Him, and the superficial nature of the persuasion which you have of His excessive love for you. O divine Heart, infinitely amiable and loving, it shall be so no more!

2. Open your whole heart to the heart of Jesus, relate to it your pains, your wounds, your wants. He knows not how to resist a heart that is wretched, be it but anxious and confiding.

MEDITATION IV.

JESUS CHRIST IN THE MOST HOLY SACRAMENT LEADS A LIFE OF SACRIFICE.

(*For the Third Day of the Novena.*)

The sacrifice of the cross lasted a few hours. Jesus Christ renews it every moment in the Eucharist, since the holy Mass is celebrated every moment in some part or other of the world. Thus the life of Jesus Christ in the Sacrament may be called a continual life of sacrifice; in which He Himself is both priest and victim. We will then meditate,—first, what share the heart of Jesus has in this Sacrifice of itself: and—secondly, what a strong invitation this is to our heart to sacrifice itself for Jesus.

Preparatory prayer.—As usual.

First Prelude.—View Jesus Christ in the Sacrament as a lamb placed on the altar to be sacrificed, and flames issuing from His Heart, with which, like a victim, it is consumed.

Second Prelude.—Beg of Him to make you understand well the value of His Sacrifice, and to give you courage to imitate Him by the sacrifice of your whole self to His love.

POINT I.

1. The love of Jesus Christ for His divine Father, and for us was the principal cause of the Sacrifice of the cross; but the envy and hatred of His enemies and executioners had also a share in it. But *here it is love alone that does everything.* This new sacrifice is, then, entirely the invention and work of His loving Heart alone. The essential interest of the divine glory and of man's redemption, was already infinitely satisfied by the sacrifice of the cross.

i. Why then is it thus *continually* and for so long a time renewed? Ah! what sufficed to satisfy the infinite justice of the Father was not, however, sufficient to satisfy the infinite love of the loving Heart of the Son. In order to be sacrificed on the cross, it was sufficient that He left His enemies in ignorance of His Majesty, for had they known Him to be the God of glory, they would never have crucified Him; but in order to sacrifice Himself again in the Blessed Sacrament, it is necessary for Him to conceal His humanity itself from His dearest friends.

ii. And then why not content Himself with this renewal of His Sacrifice *once in the year*, as He is satisfied that the memory of His other mysteries should be renewed in the .Church once a year? Or why not at least provide in this His new sacrifice for His own divine honour? Why accomplish it with a concealment that exposes Him to many irreverences and sacrileges? And then, why—Ah! how infinite are the difficulties that His greatness and our unworthiness opposed to this Sacrifice; nothing could overcome them but the excessive love of a heart insatiable in loving us.

2. Do you understand now, my cold, blind, ungrateful soul, the share the Heart of Jesus Christ has in His continual sacrifice of Himself for us in the Blessed Sacrament?—Admiration, thanksgiving, and desire of correspondence.

POINT II.

1. The *life of sacrifice* that the Heart of Jesus Christ lives for you in the Blessed Sacrament, is *an invitation that urges you to enter upon a similar life of sacrifice for Him.* If you desire to answer the call, you have nothing to do but to imitate Him. It is His love for you that every day sacrifices Him : love Him, and you too will easily

sacrifice yourselves for Jesus. Ah! consider attentively that these repugnances to trifling sacrifices are a sign of your little love for Him. What other reason is there why retirement, poverty, and obedience, are disagreeable to you? What other reason is there why it costs you so much to subdue a resentment, an affection, a dislike? During so many years of religious life, you have never, alas! tasted a drop of that ineffable joy which souls that love Jesus Christ experience in suffering. Unhappy soul! do this at least: begin to sacrifice yourself, in order to learn how to love Him.

2. *Every little sacrifice produces a new degree of love in us,* which moves us and strengthens us for a more noble sacrifice. Provided only the soul perseveres with some constancy in her little efforts, the loving heart of Jesus Christ loses patience in thus inflaming her heart by slow degrees. A day suddenly comes when He purposely puts her in the occasion of making an heroic sacrifice to Him, and provided only she has resolution to attempt it, He enkindles in her heart one of those flames of His love, which animates her to some great action that becomes the beginning of her sanctity. This is the ordinary way of the sanctification of souls. Consider it well, as it is less difficult than it appears.

3. *Compare the sacrifices of Jesus Christ with those you have an opportunity of making at present.* If yours are at present small, what a shame to refuse to make them! If they are great, ah! happy soul! this is the day, on which Jesus Christ wishes to begin your sanctification, and consequently this is a happy day for you. Fix your eyes on that tabernacle where dwells your only good, your Spouse, your God sacrificed for you; and speak to that adorable Heart with that confidence and familiarity you have learnt from yesterday's meditation, and resolve.

MEDITATION V.

(For the Fourth Day of the Novena.)

"Learn of me, who am meek and humble of heart," are the words of Jesus Christ, and He repeats them by His actions in the *life of humiliation* which He has embraced in the Blessed Sacrament. In this Blessed Sacrament we will meditate His entire humility, and its most remarkable circumstances.

Preparatory prayer.—As usual.

First Prelude.—Observe with a little attention the total absence of majesty Jesus Christ shews in that tabernacle, and conceiving as well as you can the majesty which surrounds Him in heaven, conclude what an infinite difference there must be.

Second Prelude.—Beg of Him to let you fully comprehend the secret intentions of His Heart in a state so unworthy of His greatness, and the grace of an effectual love of Him by imitation.

POINT I.

1. Self-abasement and the love of everything that can contribute to it, form the character of humility. Observe the abasement of Jesus Christ in the Eucharist. *He totally conceals everything that gives honour.* What mark do you see of His divinity? Splendour, majesty, the attending bands of angels and throne of glory—where are they? What appearance betrays itself of that power which supports the whole world? of that wisdom that governs it? of that sovereignty which reigns in heaven and on

earth? Could He hide Himself more, if He feared to be honoured in this Sacrament as the God that He is? Could He even debase Himself more, if He really desired to be disregarded and despised? His abode is nothing but a narrow lodging of wood, or at most of stone, and although a few altars are kept becomingly, numberless others, on which He remains, are so destitute, wretched and dirty, that the dwelling of an artizan is neater. He could have made it a precept in Christianity that the gold and finest jewels of the cities should be devoted to His tabernacles as formerly in the ancient Temple built by Solomon. But though He knew what would happen to Him, He has abandoned Himself in this respect to the indolence, the avarice, and the irreligion of ungrateful men. What a complete example of the sincerest humility of heart! It is not necessity, it is His Heart that generously chooses such humiliations and such a contemptible appearance and state. Here then is a Heart that loves humility with a sincerity beyond suspicion.

2. And this is the humility He wishes you to imitate. Examine your words and the acts of humility which you also sometimes perform; are they thus *voluntary and loving?* Are you as indifferent as the Heart of Jesus Christ in the Blessed Sacrament whether you are treated with honour or contempt? Do you resign your honour as He does, into the hands of others? Ah! what a model! what a school! what a difference between the two Spouses you and your Lord, and yet the one but a slave, the other a king! Resolve and pray.

POINT II.

1. Consider two striking circumstances of the humility of the Heart of Jesus Christ in the Blessed Sacrament.

i. First, a heart less fond of humility than that of

Jesus Christ might have believed that, *for the greater glory of God*, He should have set bounds to His debasement in this adorable Sacrament. This God present in the Blessed Sacrament would have been more easily known and respected there, if He had at least from time to time, let *some sensible sign* of His hidden majesty betray itself. But not so, thought the Heart of Jesus Christ. He wished that the example of His humility in the Blessed Sacrament should be perfect to the last degree. Reflect religious soul, that it is sometimes your secret vanity that thus deceives you. If I remain silent, if I yield, honour, innocence and justice are lost. Ah! do you not know that the highest honour of innocence is, to be innocently undervalued, and that the greatest glory of justice, is to be unjustly oppressed? This is the beloved maxim of the humble Heart of Jesus Christ, and to many souls, even in Religious houses, and even in objects in themselves small, this maxim frequently gives opportunities of great and heroic acts.

ii. Secondly, a heart less fond of humility than the Heart of Jesus Christ, might have believed that to let itself be sensibly known by men, a little at least, was likely *to produce more fruit in souls*. O loving incarnate love! what heart amongst us could have resisted even a fleeting glimpse only seen by us once in life in a sensible manner, of the sweet and heavenly beauty, were it only of Thy adorable humanity. But not so thought the Heart of Jesus Christ. He the infinite wisdom, thought it *most for our good* to give us in the Blessed Sacrament the greatest example of His humility.

2. Ah! then, pride, vain esteem of yourself, your natural haughtiness has been considered, O Religious soul, by Jesus Christ as His and your greatest enemy. Jesus Christ, to undeceive us by His own example in a thing of

so much consequence, has even renounced the more easy acquisition of our tender love. But, O Heart wonderfully humble! O my sovereign, infinitely adorable, and infinitely humbled! more dear art Thou to me precisely as Thou art more humbled for my instruction. "Quanto pro me vilior, tanto mihi carior."—Examine your particular circumstances, make particular resolutions, and beg with a great heart for great helps.

MEDITATION VI.

IN HONOUR OF THE LIFE OF LOVE OF THE SACRED HEART IN THE BLESSED SACRAMENT.

(For the Fifth Day of the Novena.)

Since this life of love of Jesus Christ ought to be in a particular manner the especial subject of meditation for the day of the feast of the sacred Heart, we will take for to-day one small specimen of it from the single circumstance of Jesus Christ having wished *to remain always with us* in the Blessed Sacrament.

Preparatory prayer.—As usual.

First Prelude.—Fixing a loving and attentive eye on the holy tabernacle, try to make the most lively act of faith of the real presence of Jesus Christ, and imagine you hear Him address to you the sweet promise He formerly made to His apostles.—" Ecce ego vobiscum sum usque ad consummationem sæculi."—" Behold I am, and establish myself among you to the end of the world."

Second Prelude.—Beg of Him to make you feel all the tenderness of His loving Heart in this His continual presence in the Sacrament, and all the gratitude you owe Him for this His loving invention.

POINT I.

1. Jesus Christ could work our sanctification by communicating Himself to us figuratively, not really. But
great love is not satisfied with giving assistance only at a
distance, *it loves personal presence.* But why could not
Jesus Christ content Himself with being really present in
the Blessed Sacrament only during the holy Sacrifice of
the Mass? By this alone He would have made many
personal visits every day to His beloved souls. No! this
did not seem enough to His Heart; He would always remain under the Sacramental species, that is, He would
become absolutely and perpetually our fellow citizen and
familiar companion. Then He might have contented
Himself with remaining in one city of every province, or
at the most in only one temple of each city. No! He
would be in every street. In the wide expanse of heaven,
His humanity is only found in one place, on earth the
same humanity assumes a kind of immensity, and where-
ever is to be found some small number of Christians, there
it also is found. Oh! how very true is the saying of
some saints, that the Heart of Jesus Christ is enamoured
of men.

2. But reflect, moreover, that this His remaining always
and ever among men *costs Him one of the greatest miracles
of Omnipotence,* for such is the renewal of His sacred
humanity in so many places;—and still more, that it costs
Him an infinite number of *insults,* because it has been the
very occasion of His receiving them. Ah! how little,
perhaps, your desire of being with Him corresponds with
the desire of His loving Heart to be with you. Examine
yourself. Does He require anything difficult or incon-
venient from His friends to visit Him? What expense,
considerations, and trouble, to pay court to the kings of

the earth! How many ceremonies, purifications, and observances were formerly necessary for approaching the tabernacle of the ancient Ark! But neither poverty, nor deformity, nor meanness of state, of person, or of dress, hinders our approaching this loving God. It is sufficient to love Him, to have a right to be received by Him with boundless affability, and to treat Him as an equal, a friend, a confidant. O incomprehensible love! What condescension! What tenderness! But, oh! what secret remorse for you, O Religious soul, who have been so easily deterred from visiting Him by every slight reason.

POINT II.

1. Consider other circumstances of His love in remaining with us. He delights in it so much, that if we cannot go to Him, *He causes Himself to be carried to us*, and in this the proofs of His tender love are excessive. And whither does He often let Himself be carried? Where you would dread and shudder to enter. Into the vilest and poorest cottages, into the most loathsome abodes, and most horrid prisons. Neglect not to reflect, also, *by what hands* He sometimes lets Himself be carried. O dreadful unworthiness, even among His ministers! But the tender heart of this loving God seems not to perceive it. In the ancient times of Christianity, the Christians were allowed to take the Blessed Sacrament from the sacred table, and carry it with them, and they brought it to their homes, and bore it with them where they pleased in their journeys. And if the Church, indignant at the irreverences that languid faith and cold charity began in process of time to commit, had not forbidden it, Jesus Christ would allow Himself to be thus treated even at present. What say you, Religious soul, to these reflections? Have you

ever yet well comprehended all the love this divine heart displays in continually remaining with us ?

2. But observe a more astonishing condescension. However strongly He desires always to be with you, *He does not, however, hinder your human duties and interests.* Yes, go to your labours, duties, and business. Jesus Christ is content to remain alone, waiting your moments of liberty which may restore you to Him. He does not even wish to disturb your suitable recreations. Yes, willingly He lets you go at your ease to meals, to recreation, and to lawful diversions. He is quite a wonderful lover ! He seems to be careful in contenting Himself, not to burthen or distress you in anything. Besides so many hours of the day, He remains solitary in His ciborium the live-long night ; and while you sleep, His heart watches for you to guard you :—watches and prays to His divine Father for you ;—watches and defends your person from so many dangers ;—watches, and faithfully guards your houses. Oh ! if you are not touched with a love so tender, so discreet, so dissembling, so constant, so condescending, so beneficent, confess either that you have no faith, or that you have a heart unworthy to live. Reprove yourself, then, severely, bewail your forgetfulness, and determine what you ought to do in future, that you may correspond to such loving-kindness in Jesus Christ, as has made Him sacrifice Himself to remain always with you.

MEDITATION VII.

IN HONOUR OF THE ACTIVE LIFE OF THE SACRED HEART IN THE BLESSED
SACRAMENT.

(For the Sixth Day of the Novena.)

If you really love Jesus Christ, it is impossible that your heart should not feel concerned in the interests of His. Now that loving Heart is never idle in the Blessed Sacrament, it exerts itself there with an activity equal to its love.   Consider, therefore, to-day:—i. First, the employments of the active life of Jesus Christ in the Blessed Sacrament, and why you ought therefore to act with Him. —ii. Secondly, His way of acting, and in this the model you may imitate in your actions.

Preparatory prayer.—As usual.

First Prelude.—Imagine you behold Jesus Christ in the Blessed Sacrament in the figure of the Good Shepherd, carrying in His breast a mangled and dying sheep, and healing and reviving it by pressing it close to His open Heart.

Second Prelude.—Beg of Him to inspire you with an ardent zeal to concur as far as you can in making Him known and loved.

POINT I.

1. The glory of His divine Father and the good of souls are the motives that detain Jesus Christ in the Blessed Sacrament.   These are the interests of that loving Heart, which consequently *remains there in continual movement to promote those interests.*   From those silent tabernacles Jesus Christ rules and directs His Church. At that divine table, as a shepherd, He nourishes and

gives life to His sheep, that is, to good souls, and makes Himself at that same table their master, their physician, and their protector.—There, like an attentive and loving guide and tutor, He instructs and comforts weak and tender souls.—There, He reproves with more force as He does it with more pity, and calls to His love, not only the sick, but souls that are dying, and even dead, whilst both by paternal threats and the sweetest promises, He revives, cures, and renovates them. In a word, all the good we receive comes to us from this source. His Heart is the immense ocean of light, affection, health, and spiritual riches, which pours itself through the whole mystical body of the Church.

2. Now, religious soul, if you wish to belong to this adorable and amiable Heart, you should clothe yourself with its spirit, *concern yourself in its concerns, interest yourself in its interests.* You are the slave of Jesus Christ, purchased by Him, and at how great a price ! You are under obligation to bear as far as you can the burden which He carries.—You are His daughter: you ought to take to heart as much as possible the affairs of your great Father.—You are His spouse: what a disgrace if, content with enjoying the quiet repose of His love, you do not use all your efforts to concur to His glory! Nothing then can exempt you from procuring, as far as you can, the glory of God and the good of souls. You will afterwards see how you can really do this; meanwhile, be convinced that it is your duty. Review now the thoughts, the words, and the actions of your life; and observe, if you direct some of them at least to the great end, that your patron, your father, and your spouse, may be glorified in the world. Ah! consider it is impossible truly to love Jesus Christ without doing something for Him. Make then your resolution. Happy that religious com-

munity, in which such a resolution is made at the same time by all.

POINT II.

1. The active lif e of the divine Heart in the Sacrament is a model of the active life that you too should lead. The great works which Jesus performs here for the divine glory, *He performs without the noise of that external ministry which He exercised in His mortal life*, as a model for apostolic men. Here He does all by peaceful interior graces, insinuating thoughts and counsels, inspiring with most patient sweetness salutary emotions into our hearts, and giving in secret the most opportune and copious aids to all who approach Him.

Behold, O spouse of Jesus Christ, the share in the apostolate which may be yours. Without assuming the tone of a preacher, *a pious conversation, a prudent counsel, a friendly entreaty,—sometimes an affectionate word, a mild and compassionate look* with your equals, may gain much for your God. Ah! many know how to weave secret nets, and even from a distance, that they may insinuate themselves into the confidence of others, and sometimes for an evil end. Why should not the love of Jesus Christ be equally ingenious in enabling us to re-unite two souls that have been asunder, to prevent some one neglect of rule, to deliver from danger some simple and unguarded soul?

2. The second means of which Jesus Christ makes use, in His active life in the Blessed Sacrament *is example.* The secret life of Jesus Christ in the Blessed Sacrament is the compendium of all the divine examples which He gave in His mortal life; and many are the souls which are thus conducted, and in a most singular manner, to the most sublime perfection. But your good example has in some measure an advantage over that of Jesus Christ

in the Blessed Sacrament; because His example does not engage all, because all do not consider it; whereas all your sisters must see yours even against their will. Be assured that the greatest difficulty to introduce an improvement in a monastery, is to find one who will be the first to put it in practice. Aspire to so noble a glory, when an occasion presents itself, and to so high a merit with the Heart of your God.

3. Finally, the third means of which Jesus Christ makes use in His active life in the Blessed Sacrament, *is prayer*. In this Sacrament He is always present as an advocate and victim, that He may offer for us to His Father both His mediation and Himself. This most sweet and efficacious device for glorifying God can never be wanting to us. You should always join this to all your other means, and when they are attended with any hindrance or difficulty, this will supply the deficiency. Ah! · if you knew what immense troops of souls there are in heaven gained by the prayers of holy virgins! And do you unite your heart likewise to the Heart of Jesus, making yourself a secret victim with Him for the salvation of souls. Let all the good you do and all the evil you suffer, amongst your other ends, be directed to this also. Make, then, now for ever an offering of yourself to the active heart of Jesus Christ, and you may promise yourself that you will certainly obtain by this means the greatest favours of His love.

MEDITATION VIII.

IN HONOUR OF THE HIDDEN LIFE OF THE SACRED HEART IN THE BLESSED
SACRAMENT.

(For the Seventh Day of the Novena.)

The hidden life of Jesus Christ is one of the most sublime examples given us by our God in the blessed Sacrament. Enter upon this meditation with a docile heart, desirous of the impressions of grace. You will meditate,—

i. First, *what this hidden life is* to which you are invited, by the example of your Spouse, in the blessed Sacrament.

ii. Secondly, *the very great advantages* you may safely promise yourself from it.

Preparatory prayer.—As usual.

First Prelude.—Present yourself to Jesus Christ with all possible recollection. Separate yourself in thought from all the world. Imagine yourself alone with your divine master, as in the desert to which He retired for forty days, to receive from Him lessons, not indeed common to all Christians, but peculiarly belonging to your state.

Second Prelude.—Beg Him, then, with great fervour, to conceal nothing from you of the sublime perfection to which He has already called you, by calling you to religion, and to join to great lights the strongest graces.

POINT I.

1. Who, seeing Jesus Christ in His present state, would say that it is He who moves and governs the heavens, the stars, the angels, mankind, and all creatures? Of so extensive and noble an exercise of His providence, wisdom,

and power, here nothing appears. In fact, He is here for no other purpose but for the secret interests of His heart with souls. All is silence, solitude, humility, patience, concealment, secret and interior life. Taking your view from this range of admirable examples here before you, consider what is that hidden life in which He so much desires you to imitate Him.

i. *The foundation of this hidden life is the internal spirit,* which ought to animate your every action ; which never acts by chance, nor for human ends, but which in all things ever looks up to God ; which does not estimate things from appearances, but only from the substance, and for which everything is vanity and without substance, which is not the will of God,—which never seeks to do much, but to do well ; to which nothing appears little that pleases God, and which consequently springs from the pure love of God, and seeks the pure love of God as well for its guide, as for the only reward of its actions. It will be easy for you to consider and understand how necessary this internal spirit is for your perfection. Begin here your practical resolutions ; because, if you do not begin with the care of acquiring this internal spirit, you will never arrive at that hidden life in Jesus Christ, of which the saints, after the example of St. Paul, say so many great things.

ii. In this hidden life, then, the religious soul, having by help of the internal spirit entirely banished the world from her heart, *loves to hide from it as much as she can all her actions as well as herself.* She is not at all so deluded as to retire by a false spirit from her proper duties and observances, but if the common duties of the rules and of charity do not interfere, she has a special love for solitude, silence, and recollection. She fears to see and to be seen by the world, in order that human respects may not by any chance secretly insinuate themselves into her actions, or the circumstances of her actions. She desires and seeks no other witnesses of her virtue and her sufferings but God, and therefore she renounces all vain consolations from the world, and exerts her utmost to conceal from it all sign of her interior joys, as well as of her secret sufferings. She has an infinite dread of singularity, the ordinary consequence of delusions. In virtue itself, although she loves and aims at greater perfection, she avoids as far as possible all unnecessary display. She would not wish that any one should think of her ; she never interferes in anything that does not concern her, and if she can, she always chooses in all things whatever is most obscure and disregarded by others. Obedience alone holds the key of her spirit ; and as long as this virtue does not oblige her, she knows how to live in a Religious house for whole years, without giving occasion to others to speak of her.

2. Compare the picture of this life with that of Jesus Christ in the Blessed Sacrament. It is exactly the same. Compare it with your daily life, and *see what is wanting.* And even if you find everything wanting, take the greatest care not to lose courage. Beg of the divinely hidden Heart of your Spouse to inflame yours with a desire full of courage and of confidence.

POINT II.

1. The *fruits* of this hidden life are as precious as the life is excellent.

i. First, it is a sure and compendious means of arriving at a great purity of conscience, and a great *disengagement from the world and from ourselves.* Consider the origin of your defects ; for the most part they arise from the occasions that exterior objects present to your senses, and to your past bad habits. Thus it is with your faults of impatience, curiosity, vanity, etc. The pursuit of this hidden life making you fond of retirement, of attending to yourself, and of not interfering in things that do not concern you, at least preserves you from very many occasions. Moreover, the study of this life insensibly accustoms us often to reflect upon ourselves, our intentions, and the motions of our hearts, and by this reflection are prevented those frequent defects which you only perceive, I may say, after you have fallen. Hence, by little and little, our attachment to the world and to ourselves becomes weakened, because the habit of thinking of, and so also the habit of taking pleasure in the objects of our former attachment, natural inclinations, and disordered customs gradually diminishes.

ii.   Secondly, *the serene peace and quiet of the superior part of the soul* at least, are certain fruits of this hidden life. Think of all the things mentioned above, and you have immediately as many causes of this interior quiet. "Whence come," said St. James the Apostle, "the many storms of your poor heart? Do they not arise from your passions?" (St. James iv.) Whatever food, then, you take from your passions by the study of this *hidden life*, so many steps do you make towards that constant quiet of spirit which you are seeking.

iii. Thirdly, this life is most necessary for *the acquisition of the spirit of prayer.* This spirit of prayer cannot be attained by a soul full of self, occupied with countless frivolities, and dissipated during the rest of the day. Here, then, is a sure method of ending once for all your complaints about prayer. Prayer follows in conformity with the rest of your day. How often have you not experienced the truth of this!

iv. Fourthly, *interior sweetnesses and the most choice favours of heaven*, in the ordinary providence of God, are annexed to this hidden life. One who does not practise it, believes it to be a melancholy life: one who practises it, finds it (and will not be long before he begins to find it,) to have joys infinitely superior to those which the world can give. Recall what you have heard and read, of so many holy souls.

2. And now what say you to advantages so great as these? Inflame your desire, and with it *overcome the repugnance of your blind self-love.* Make a purpose to think often of this, by reviewing every day your resolutions. Offer them to the divine Heart, beg His grace, and resolve to make every day some brief examen, on the purposes formed during this meditation.

MEDITATION IX.

IN HONOUR OF THE GLORIOUS LIFE OF THE SACRED HEART IN THE SACRAMENT.

(For the Eighth Day o, the Novena.)

The *Glories* of the Life of the Sacred Heart of Jesus Christ in the Blessed Sacrament are many. But to-day you will honour that particular glory of the Sacred Heart, for which it dwells so wonderfully in the Blessed Sacrament. This glory of the Sacred Heart which is quite its own, manifests itself in this Sacrament :—

i. First, by reducing souls through the force of love alone, to a total annihilation of self;

ii. Secondly, by raising them through the strength of the same love to an elevation in itself, which is wholly divine.

Preparatory prayer.—As usual.

First Prelude.—Imagine that you see in the open breast of Jesus Christ, His divine Heart full of such a fire of love, that it seems like a burning furnace, in which the hearts of His elect souls melt and dissolve more quickly than wax, and are purified and refined like gold.

Second Prelude.—Offer with great courage your heart likewise to these divine flames, giving yourself freely to your divine Saviour, for all that He would wish to do with you.

POINT I.

1. The *glory* of the divine Heart manifests itself in that *great power of love, with which it inspires souls in the Blessed Sacrament*, and with which it triumphs in such feeble creatures, and annihilates so many and such strong enemies. Call to mind for awhile the many great victories of which you have read in so many admirable young virgins, weak in nature like you, having to contend, like you, with dangers, engagements, repugnances, and instability. It was, above all, in this Sacrament of love, that those most stupendous changes were wrought in them. Think how often you have shrunk at reading of those so heroic acts of patience, of charity, of obedience, of mortification, and hatred of themselves. How have you not been astonished at those examples of silent, meek, and joyful constancy in the midst of long and most undeserved persecutions, of lingering and painful maladies, of most terrible and obstinate temptations! And how did such feeble creatures ever attain to such complete loss of all pity for themselves, of all feeling of repugnance to acts most difficult to perform, of every sense of sympathy with the·most innocent and sweet calls of humanity? Ah! from this Sacrament they drew such strength, and this strength was the *strength of love.*

2. Behold, then, that glory of the divine Heart which is all its own, and by which it made itself loved by these

souls in so high a degree. If you love Jesus Christ, you now know how to glorify Him. What are the thoughts which rise within you, when you feel the greatest desire to correspond with His love? Count all as illusion that does not aid you to despise yourself, to contradict your own will, and submit blindly and lovingly to the divine will. *Die wholly to your own self-love;* this is the final triumph to which the divine Heart aspires in all the graces, which it offers to you in this Sacrament of love. Resolve, then, to bring to Jesus Christ in every visit to the Blessed Sacrament, and much more at every communion, *some victory gained over yourself.* This is the most solid way of corresponding with His grace, for this is the peculiar interest of the Sacred Heart in the Blessed Sacrament.

POINT II.

1. That *glory* of the sacred Heart in the Blessed Sacrament, which is all its own, manifests itself also *in raising souls by the strength of love, to an elevation in itself*, which is wholly divine. The marvellous victory that love gains in the soul, and which you have considered in the first point, works in them a change, or rather a transformation, into something quite different from what they were. They live no more except in Jesus Christ, or rather it is Jesus Christ that lives in them, as St. Paul declared of himself, and therefore, even before putting off the infirmities of this mortal life, they live a life which is entirely superhuman and divine. Observe how it appears in them externally. What angelic modesty! What unalterable gentleness! What amiable meekness! What exactness, prudence and sanctity breathe in their every action! Could you enter into their minds, you would seem to be entering a kingdom of light—that unspeakable light which shines

in paradise. The justness of their ideas, and the sublime intelligence which they have of God and His mysteries, is inexplicable. Could you enter into their hearts, how great would be your astonishment to observe the purity and strength, the peace and sanctity of their affections. Their soul is made the throne of grace and divine love, and these reign paramount. A Gertrude, a Catherine of Sienna, a Teresa, and so many souls, which, like theirs, were enriched with the interior treasures of Jesus Christ, will make you understand how great is the glory of this our God, the lover of souls, in raising them from such a low abasement to so high a state.

2. Feed yourself for awhile on these wonderful objects of admiration as a holy recreation of spirit. But in order that you may not lose courage for yourself, recollect, that in the house of God our Father there are many mansions; which means that although you cannot for humility aspire to such high gifts, yet by the obligation of your state, *you must aim at a certain measure proper even for you.* Renounce readily all that is extraordinary in these gifts, but aspire to the gift of great self-denial, of a great contempt of the world, of great patience, great recollection, etc. To these gifts you have a right, and if you desire them truly, this divine Heart cannot refuse them to you, and they will work in you a change, which will elevate you high above your present misery, and thus will glorify exceedingly in your exaltation, the strength of the love of Jesus Christ. How long will you then remain so lukewarm? How long will your mind and heart continue to be fixed upon this vile, miserable, dull earth? Ah! in how many poor servants of His—souls who are dwelling in the world, Jesus Christ by His love, works out His glory; and in you, His spouse, shall He find nothing but dishonour? Rouse yourself, resolve, and prepare yourself

in such a manner that the coming feast of this divine Heart, and the communion you will make on that day, may be the beginning of a new happiness to you and of glory to Jesus Christ.

MEDITATION X.

IN HONOUR OF THE LIFE OF CONSUMMATED SACRIFICE OF JESUS CHRIST IN THE BLESSED SACRAMENT.

(For the Ninth Day of the Novena.)

In the most noble kind of sacrifice, that is in the *Holocaust*, the victim was to be entirely consumed. Such was the Sacrifice of Jesus Christ on the cross, of which Sacrifice the Sacrament of the altar, is the renewal and memorial. And therefore the life of Jesus Christ in the Sacrament may be called a *life of consummated sacrifice.* In order to inflame you to imitate in this Sacrifice your divine Saviour, you will meditate :—

i. First, what sort of consummation of your sacrifice He desires.

ii. Secondly, the constancy and continuance which are necessary to your sacrifice when consummated.

Preparatory prayer.—As usual.

First Prelude.—Look on Jesus Christ in the Sacrament, laid on the altar as a lamb for sacrifice; and with flames issuing from His Heart, by which He is consumed as a victim.

Second Prelude.—Beg Him to make you understand the value of His sacrifice, and to give you courage to imitate Him with the entire sacrifice of yourself to His love.

POINT I.

1. Consider that Jesus Christ was not content to sacrifice Himself for you in an ordinary manner, but He

sacrificed Himself *in all that He could sacrifice for you!* What more remained for Him on the cross to give, either in His goods, His honour, or His life? Conclude the devout review of what He has given for you with this reflection. After death, His Heart alone remained untouched by that cruel treatment which had carried its rage to His very vitals, which were in many places laid open and wounded. But His Heart, too, would have part in that sacrifice, or rather we may say that it was in that divine Heart that the last consummation of the sacrifice was to be fulfilled. Accordingly it also was to be laid open and pierced.

2. Now *such ought to be your sacrifice to His love.* Count over the sacrifices you have ever made for Him. How many have you only begun? Infinite in number are those which you have offered Him with a mere inefficacious desire. You, however, are none the more His after all this; for in this matter, so far as the object is concerned at which we must aim, he does nothing who does not all. Consider well the reason of this. He gives nothing of any worth to God, who does not give Him his heart, for this God values more than all the rest together; and he does not give his heart truly who does not give it *all without reserve.* So then, the consummation which Jesus Christ desires in your sacrifice, consists in a sincere and total abandonment of yourself to Him, with a determined resolution to leave yourself to be guided at His pleasure. In this state of complete sacrifice, you ought not to consider yourself any more as your own in anything; but to think that God does as He wills with His own, when He gives you either what is bitter or what is sweet.

3. Here renew again the consideration of the infinite generosity with which Jesus Christ has given Himself for you, and *given Himself entirely.* Ah! what need had He

to be wholly yours in order to be happy? whereas it is impossible for you to be happy, even here, without being *wholly* His. Make a serious examen of conscience, but let it be a brief one nevertheless, for your conscience will quickly tell you the truth as to what has been that one thing which has been principally wanting in the sacrifices our Lord has required of you. Ah! most ordinarily it is some one thing only which makes our sacrifice imperfect, and this our self-love always reserves. To this one point apply the lights, the affections which our Lord gives you. O divine Heart, divinely prodigal of Thyself, help me to accomplish by Thy grace that to which Thy example invites me.

POINT II.

1. Jesus Christ *has never retracted in the least part the entire gift He has made of Himself*—nay, rather, every time that He renews His sacrifice in the holy mass, He renews the complete surrender He has made of Himself. What constancy ! What continuance of most noble love ! Now turn again your thoughts to the sacrifices you have so often made to Jesus Christ. Alas! of the greatest part of them, there does not, perhaps, remain a vestige in your heart. Do you recollect those burning resolves of a recollected, observant, patient life?—those sacrifices of your affections, of your dislikes, of your regards, your human respects—those good beginnings of study, of diligence, of exactness in prayer and spiritual things—where are hey now ? Who has snatched them from you ? Ah ! faithless and inconstant heart, be witness against your-self in the bitterness of your confusion and your sorrow. But this confusion and this sorrow, shall they be once more useless? Reflect how infinite would have been the loss for mankind if Jesus Christ, as His foolish and im-

pious enemies instigated Him to do, had come down from the cross! If that loving Heart had closed that sacred wound, which is so precious a fountain of sweetness, of courage, and of love for souls, what a beloved object and incitement would have been taken away from the hopes of weak and timid souls !

2. Draw near, then, to this adorable fountain of life in a transport of extreme, but holy, despair. If Thou dost not help me, omnipotent Heart of my Jesus, so often deluded by me, I have no other resource in my misery. Here excite your grief as much as is in your power, and at the same time, as if you would fan the flame, rouse and provoke your desire to be now and henceforth true and faithful; and cry aloud from the bottom of your desolate heart, *that this time you must not be refused the grace of persevering constancy* in your good purposes. Know that nothing can give greater pleasure to this divine Heart than the sight of your longing desire. Let this reflection revive your confidence. If you know how to desire earnestly enough, you will certainly obtain your wish. Call to the aid of your prayers the most sweet Mother of this most sweet Heart, and conclude the meditation with an offering which may embrace and renew all those which you have hitherto made.

VIGIL.

(PREPARATION FOR THE FEAST OF THE SACRED HEART OF JESUS CHRIST.)

Since the end for which Jesus Christ Himself taught this devotion to His sacred Heart, was to inflame the hearts of all the faithful with love for Him, and to engage all who love Him to repair by the most perfect love they are capable of, and by their tender and reverent worship, the wrongs which He so especially receives in

His most holy Sacrament, from the coldness and faults of those souls which persevere in ingratitude towards Him—in accordance with this end the same intention must animate all you do in honour of the sacred Heart on this feast.

On the evening of the Vigil, if you are able and can obtain permission, spend some reasonable time—half-an-hour, perhaps—certainly not more, that it may not interfere with public duties, and with the morning rising—before Jesus in the Sacrament. In this visit dispose your heart to the sentiments which ought to animate your devotion on the feast with the following meditation.

MEDITATION XI.

ON THE PRICELESS VALUE OF THE MOST SACRED HEART OF JESUS.

In order that you may attain to the best knowledge you can of this most holy Heart, consider in it,—i. first, the divinity to which it is united ;—ii. secondly, the love of which it has been, and is, the seat,—iii. thirdly, the grief of which it was once the centre.

Preparatory prayer.—As usual.

First Prelude.—Imagine that you see in the blessed Sacrament Jesus Christ as He revealed Himself to the Venerable Mother, M. Alacoque, showing her His divine Heart, wounded and wholly surrounded with flames, encircled by a crown of thorns, and with a cross planted upon it.

Second Prelude.—Beg of your Sovereign and your divine Spouse to give you a special light to know the incomprehensible value of this His Heart, and to dispose you to honour it with the sentiments of veneration and of love which He expects from you.

POINT I.

The *divinity to which the sacred Heart of Jesus Christ is united.*—

1. In the Incarnation the divine nature united itself personally, not only to the soul, but also to the adorable body of Jesus Christ, so that in this personal union *His Heart also became one with the divinity of the Eternal Word* of the Father; and was therefore, and will be eternally, a divine Heart, and the Heart of God. God, therefore, is the principle of the subsistence of this Heart; and the life which this Heart lives is not merely human, but also divine. To the divinity, therefore, as to the final term, are referred all the supreme honours which we pay to it, and which all the faithful ought to pay it. Observe the religious worship and solemn adorations even, which the Church pays and commands to be paid to the adorable body of the Man-God. The same exactly His adorable Heart merits, and for the same reason. When, therefore, you prostrate yourself, Religious soul, before a holy picture of this Heart of your spouse, understand to how exalted an object you offer your homage, and take care to animate it with feelings of that most profound veneration which is due to the divinity of so noble a 'spouse.

2. But oh! from this intimate union with the divine nature, *how many, how great treasures enrich the Heart of the Man-God!* These treasures of grace, and of sanctity cannot be greater, because they are divine. O Heart pure with the very purity of God—Heart holy with the very holiness of God—Heart charitable with the very charity of God—Heart strong with the very strength of God! O Heart, sweet, liberal, faithful, generous with the very sweetness, liberality, fidelity, and generosity of God! O Heart adorable, then, and amiable, as God Himself is

adorable and amiable!   To-day, perhaps for the first time, I begin to conceive what Thou art!   Ah! my Sovereign and my spouse, make my heart a worthy offering to Thine! Yes, Religious soul, this is what God Himself expects. The Heart of your Spouse is made so noble, so pure, so holy, so faithful, so courageous, in order that it may be a perfect model for your wretched heart.

3. *Compare, then, attentively, the Heart of Jesus Christ with your own* in these divine gifts.   O God! what an infinite difference!   Observe where this difference is greatest, and what the cause may be.   Every human heart has its weakness, and it is in this precisely that you must especially propose to yourself, the example of this most holy Heart.   What is there wanting in Thee, O divine Heart, of the qualities of which I stand most in need?   O living Temple of the divinity, my heart is in darkness, and in Thee the fulness of wisdom inhabits corporally—my heart is weak, Thine is the throne of omnipotence—my heart is fearful and afflicted, oppressed, and craving after happiness, but despairing to find it; in Thee alone, and in imitating Thee is my true happiness to be sought, and in Thee for the future I will seek it.

POINT II.

The love of which the Sacred Heart of Jesus Christ has been, and is, *the seat.*

1. The heart which is so active a member in us, is still more so in Jesus Christ.   For in Him that Heart was, and is, the seat of His love, not only for His divine Father, but oh, how much more wonderful, for us also!

Enter, O cold Religious soul, on this consideration with an ardent desire of understanding well the secret history of love in this divine Heart.   For love and life had there the same beginning, and for you that divine Heart learnt at once those emotions which form the occupation and the labour of a heart that loves. Go in thought to the crib, and there enter the Heart of that infant God, that little Heart whose new-born love is already so great, that truly it may be said of the divine infant, "He exulted as a giant in the beginning of His course:" and His course is the course of love. And oh! in all His life, what resistless, what laborious, yet unwearied strides! Mark the emotions, the pains of the heart of one of us, when a prey to the violence of love. Remove from this most lively passion that which partakes of moral imperfection in us, and all that remains, the Heart of your divine spouse has really and sensibly experienced for you. We call love a fire, because it kindles in the heart a flame that can be felt; a flame so devouring, where love is great, that Saints have needed cold winds and freezing water to temper its heat. And in such a state the Heart of Jesus lived for you during so many years. Oh, how quick is the heart's correspondence with the emotions of a soul that loves! What throbbings and impetuous sallies does a great desire not cause in the heart? Distance dries up the very life of the heart in which it burns: ingratitude pierces and wounds it as would a sword: compassion wrings and straitens it; loss will make it languish and die.

2. And you—ever present to the mind of your most loving Redeemer, with all the various and melancholy vicissitudes of your life foreseen—*you have made this incredibly loving Heart of His pass, in its affection for you, through all these anxieties.* Oh! may you one day at least be as holy as He desires! Oh! that I could show you the pain, not grievous indeed, but sweet, which its love for you gave to that most amiable heart—how it swelled, and throbbed, and burnt with sweet yet ardent transports of joy in its affections for you! It is true that Heart, in the

midst of this sensibility, is infinitely, imperturbably happy; but for the pure, the faithful, the affectionate soul, that sensibility is glorified, not lost. You may yet be an object of those divine emotions of pleasure, of that divine fire, which even in its glory still inflames the Heart of Jesus. And now what think you of this idea, though so feeble, of the effects of the love which glows for you in that divine Heart? And does not this give the exact history of the merits of this Heart towards you, and yet unacknowledged by you? And what does so pleasing and so amiable a devotion require at your hands? Draw from these considerations sentiments of admiration, praise, and thanksgiving: but above all inflame your desires, and resolve that henceforth the love of this Heart shall be the continual business of your heart.

POINT III.

The grief which once centred in the holy Heart of Jesus Christ.

1. " No," said the devout Thomas à Kempis, "there is no life of love without pain :" and thus the life of Jesus' Heart especially was nothing but cross and martyrdom. Consider only its share in the Passion. Recall, O Religious soul, the horror and the pity which you have sometimes felt when meditating on the impious and cruel outrages offered to the adorable body of Jesus Christ, and know that all these together were the least of His pains. *The most terrible was the unseen martyrdom of the Heart.* It first was assailed in the garden, it was at last broken and crushed, when He breathed forth His soul on the cross. In us, too, the heart is the seat, not of love alone, but of grief, so that no evil really pains us, but when and inasmuch as the heart admits it ; but oh ! never hope to understand the share which the Heart of Jesus bore in

His Passion. You have heard of its fear, its weariness, its sadness, at the apprehension of the tortures it was to suffer, at its abandonment and loss of every comfort, and from its hatred of sin and the ingratitude of man. But reflect that all these woes exteriorly came in succession one after another ; but the Heart felt them all at once. Reflect that if the physical nature of the body of Christ was exquisitely sensible, much more sensible was the moral organization of His Heart ; and thus that every torment touched the affections of His Heart more than it did any part of His body : that, in fine, the eagerness of His executioners to strike, was but the eagerness of human malice ; but that in the Passion of His Heart a far more eager executioner—His own chosen and most barbarous executioner—was *His own unchanging love.*

2. Who, then, can imagine the *languor,—the heaviness, —the fainting,—the heart-rendings,—the anguish,—the spasms,—the burning fever,—the death-like chill.* Oh ! where are there words to express even what we comprehend, and how very little do we comprehend in comparison of that which we believe ! Jesus Christ Himself would give us a visible proof of the invisible martyrdom of His Heart, but nothing less sufficed than the portentous miracle of a bloody sweat. O loving Heart, O suffering Heart of my Jesus, what do I owe Thee ? If I owe love for love, truly I owe Thee pain for pain. But how can I, so weak, so tender towards myself, offer Thee such a return, unless Thou give me a share of Thy courage ? Give me, O Jesus, give me love, a great love; for love will teach me to suffer, will help me to suffer, will make it dear to me to suffer in union with Thy most Holy Heart.

FOR THE DAY OF THE FEAST.

As this is the Feast of the Heart of Jesus Christ, it is also the Feast of His love : and the end for which He wished it should be instituted, was, that He might draw from our cold hearts a return and compensation for His love. And that He may obtain this end more easily, He presents His sacred Heart to us as the object of our feast, as it is really in itself, and as it is the symbol of His divine charity. To the worship, then, and adoration of this Heart, infinitely worthy of our adoration and our homage, you should especially consecrate this day in the spirit of this devotion, and that spirit is to excite your love to a correspondence with the love of the Son of God for you, and for all men, and to make some reparation and amends to a God so loving and so little loved, for your ingratitude and that of all mankind.

Hasten, then, to consecrate the first moment of your day by an offering of your heart, and of all the good you may do, to the most amiable Heart of your divine Spouse for the end already spoken of, and continually renew this oblation throughout the day. All the day should be a perpetual act of love, of sympathy, and honour to Jesus Christ. Be as silent and as recollected as you can, and animate even your external actions with the same intentions. Entertain yourself with Jesus Christ in the Blessed Sacrament, as assiduously as your duties and your strength will permit. Offer your holy communion in reparation for the coldness, the unworthiness of your former communions, and of those of all Christians : and make your preparation the most diligent, and your thanksgiving the most affectionate that you ever offered.

But, for the love of Jesus Christ, do not run to-day into the too common error of so many souls, which grow weary of making acts of virtue, because they do not experience sensible peace and devotion. If you take too much notice of this, you will perhaps do nothing to-day. Labour therefore with an open heart, and a good will, and omit nothing which you would do if you were in a state of devotion.

MEDITATION XII.

ON THE LOVE OF THE SACRED HEART, AND OUR INGRATITUDE.

(For the Feast of the Sacred Heart.)

Preparatory prayer.—As usual.

First Prelude.—Imagine that you see Jesus Christ in the Blessed Sacrament, as the Venerable Mother M. Alacoque saw Him, shewing her His Heart, wounded, surrounded by flames, encircled with thorns, and surmounted by a cross; and explaining the mystical meaning of these symbols, which signify His love and His sufferings for ungrateful man.

Second Prelude.—Beseech Him to make you know and feel, how equally incomprehensible are these two excesses of so great a love in Himself, and such great ingratitude in us ; that thus you may resolve to make satisfaction to the best of your power to this Heart so loving and so little loved.

POINT I.

1. What are the continual *sentiments of the divine Heart towards man* in this Sacrament? They are sentiments of *the most lively and most sincere love.*

i. What the mid-day is to the sun, such is the Blessed Sacrament to the love of Jesus Christ for us—the culminating point of its light and heat. What is Jesus Christ doing in the Blessed Sacrament? He is loving us. Behold an answer which says everything, and satisfies all that can be asked about Him! Why does He come to you? Because He loves us. How does He remain with you? As a God who loves. What does He desire for you? That which love desires. Why does He so multiply Himself? Why is He so enduring with you? Why does He thus hide Himself? Because He loves, because He loves. On the cross love shared its empire with, or rather was subservient to, justice. Here love reigns alone, and all is subservient to it. Wisdom, power, providence, immensity, employ themselves to this end, that love may have its final satisfaction. Blind man, see what the Heart of your God is for you.

ii. And do you not *experience this* every day?—Sinful souls, how does He receive you here? His complaints, His lamentations, His reproaches, His very terrors, are but emotions of love. Tepid and imperfect souls, has He ever driven you from Him? Does He not on the contrary, offer you light, and medicine, and comfort, and encouragement?—But you, O pure and fervent souls, ah! it is yours to testify to the world what this divine Heart is in the Blessed Sacrament! What condescension! What forgetfulness of its own greatness! What artifices! What interior speeches! What caresses! What torrents of delights!

2. Linger here, O Religious soul, and apply all these reflections to yourself. Take up the place which once perhaps belonged to you, and then that which now belongs to you, whether among sinners, or the imperfect, or the fervent. The affections which you should call forth are those especially of admiration, praise, and thanksgiving. Ah! perhaps in all your life you have never returned

express thanks to this divine Heart, for this excess of love.

POINT II.

1. What are *the feelings of most men towards Jesus Christ in the Sacrament of the Altar?*

i. See how many *do not even know that there is a God who has reduced Himself to this state* for love of them, and Jesus Christ meanwhile is actually employed in loving all in His Sacrament. And of these blind ones some wilfully close their eyes, though invited to become acquainted with their Lord, and to consider Him.

ii. And is not this, O Jesus, the most monstrous contempt of all Thy love ? Ah ! no—*this is not the worst* of the cruel treatments which the greater part of Christians offer to the loving Heart of their God in this Sacrament. Full well do they know, ungrateful creatures, and profess to believe His immense love in the blessed Sacrament. But how do they correspond?

2. Ah ! Religious soul, now review in thought the infidelities, the irreverences, the dishonour, the sacrileges, the insults which Jesus Christ suffers from Christians in this Sacrament. Consider the circumstances of time, manner, number, persons, which aggravate these wrongs. Excite yourself to a great, a holy indignation, at the sight of such outrages, and then reflect upon your own behaviour. What, have you, too, ill-treated your divine Lover ! Run over your past life. Good God ! And perhaps your ingratitude has gone on increasing with your years ! O terrible thought, if the purity, the devotion, the fervour of your first communions have been continually relaxing ! At such a sight, O throw yourself in spirit at the foot of this throne of love, burying yourself in confusion. Beg light to recognize and detest yourself, and plenteous grace to form suitable resolutions.

POINT III.

1. What are the feelings of this divine Heart with regard *to the unworthy return made to it by men?*

i. That we may come to understand them, let us first consider *what they justly might be.* How did this same God treat the Hebrew nation, when ungrateful for the favour of His abode with them in the ancient Temple? He repudiated the Temple, rased it to its very foundations, and protested that He departed from their nation for ever. Surely the Christian, so much more highly favoured, would deserve no less; but God's love is far greater than our offences. What patience, what charity, what invincible sweetness! Here Jesus is still the meek Lamb, dumb beneath the knife that slays it.

ii. True, *He has sometimes given vent to His feelings* in secret with souls which He loved ; but His complaints are but stronger proofs of His love. Hear how He spoke to the Venerable Mother M. Alacoque, of the forgetfulness of men:—"This is a greater torment to me than any which I suffered in my Passion. If men did but render me love for love, I should count as nothing all that I have yet done for them, and would willingly do even more if it were possible ; but the desire I have to benefit them meets with no return but coldness and repulse !" What feeling do these tender complaints of the Son of God excite in you ? " But that which most afflicts me," He said to her on another occasion, "is, that I should be so treated by hearts consecrated to me."

2. Ah! here Jesus Christ speaks of you, Religious soul, cold, unfaithful, insensible to the outrages offered to Him. To preserve always in yourself a tender *gratitude* for such great love, a lively *sorrow* for such ingratitude, an *efficacious desire to make reparation* by service and love on your

part,—these are the affections which you should excite. These three affections form the distinguishing character of a heart devoted to the adorable Heart of Jesus. Resolve, offer, beg grace, and thus dispose yourself to make a gift, an entire sacrifice of yourself.

The thanksgiving after your holy Communion should be finished with the *act of consecration*, or an offering of your heart to the love of Jesus Christ ; in which, remember, you are to have no intention of a vow ; and then let the *act of atonement* or *reparation* follow, for your own ingratitude, as well as that of all mankind.

ACT OF CONSECRATION TO THE SACRED HEART OF JESUS CHRIST.

Adorable Heart of my most amiable Jesus, seat of all virtues, inexhaustible source of all graces, what fitness canst Thou ever have found in me, to win Thee to such an extent, that Thou should love me with this excess of love; while my heart, defiled as it is with countless faults, has reserved nothing for Thee but indifference and hardness? The most generous remonstrances made to me by Thy love, then, even while I loved Thee not, make me hope that Thou wilt graciously accept this offer of my love. Vouchsafe, then, most amiable Saviour, to accept the desire which I have of consecrating myself entirely to the honour and glory of Thy most sacred Heart; accept the donation which I make of all that I am. To Thee I consecrate my person, my life, my actions, pains and sufferings. My wish is to be in future a victim consecrated to Thy glory, soon to be set on fire by Thy love, and one day, according to Thy good pleasure, to be entirely consumed by its holy flames. I offer Thee, then, my Lord and my God, my heart, with all the sentiments it can ever have, since I purpose that, throughout my whole life, the sentiments of my heart shall be perfectly uniform with the sentiments of Thy most sacred Heart. Behold me, therefore, O Lord, wholly devoted to Thy Heart, behold me wholly Thine. Ah! my good God, how great are Thy mercies towards me! My God, God of Majesty, and who am I that Thou shouldst deign to accept the sacrifice of my heart? It shall be wholly Thine in future, this heart of mine, and creatures shall have no part in it, since they deserve none.

Be Thou, for the future, amiable Jesus, my Father, my Patron, my All, since I wish to live no longer but for Thee. Accept, O adorable Saviour of mankind, the sacrifice which the most ungrateful of men makes to Thy heart, to repair the wrongs which he has not ceased hitherto to offer to it, by corresponding so ill with its love. I acknowledge that I give little; but I give at least all that I can to Thy sacred Heart, and I know that it is my heart which it desires; and when I consecrate to it this heart of mine, I give it never more to take it back.

Teach me, most amiable Saviour, a perfect forgetfulness of myself, this being the only road which can give me the entrance which I so earnestly desire, into Thy adorable Heart; and as from henceforth I shall do all for Thee, make what I shall do worthy of Thee. Teach me what I ought to do, to arrive at the purity of Thy love; or rather give me this love, yes, give it to me most ardent and most generous. Give me that profound humility without which no one can be pleasing to Thee: and accomplish in me all Thy holy wishes as well in time as for all eternity. Amen.

AN ACT OF REPARATION IN HONOUR OF THE SACRED HEART OF JESUS.

My most amiable and most adorable Jesus, ever full of love for us, ever moved by our miseries, ever most desirous to share Thy treasures with us, and to give Thyself wholly to us: Jesus, my Saviour and my God, who by an excess of the most ardent and wonderful love that ever was, would make Thyself a victim in the adorable Eucharist, in which a million times a day Thou offerest Thyself in sacrifice for us, what must be Thy sentiments in this state, when in return for all this Thou findest in the hearts of the greater part of men, nothing but hardness, forgetfulness, ingratitude and contempt.

Was it not enough, my Saviour, to have trod for our salvation that path so full of suffering for Thyself, when Thou mightest have given us proof of Thy excessive love at so much less a cost? Was it not enough to have once abandoned Thyself to that cruel agony and deadly weight of sorrow, occasioned by the horrid picture of our sins which Thou tookest upon Thee? Why expose Thyself every day to all the indignities of which the blackest malice of men and fiends is capable? Ah! my God and my most amiable Redeemer, what were the sentiments of Thy most holy Heart at the sight of such ingratitude, and of all our sins? What, alas! was the bitterness in which Thy heart was plunged at such outrages, and such sacrileges?

Moved, therefore, to bitter sorrow for all these indignities, behold me prostrate and annihilated in Thy presence, humbly offering Thee this reparation of honour before the face of heaven and earth, for the irreverences and outrages suffered by Thee upon our altars since the first institution of this adorable Sacrament. With a heart humbled and pierced with grief, I ask pardon of Thee a thousand, thousand times, for all these base wrongs. O my God, why can I not wash with my tears, or even with my blood, those places where Thy sacred Heart has been so fearfully despised, where the most precious pledges of Thy divine love have been received with such strange contempt? Why is it not allowed me to repair such sacrileges and such profanations by some new homage, humiliation, and self-annihilation? Why might I not be for one moment only master of the hearts of all men, to recompense in some manner with the sacrifice I would make to Thee, the forgetfulness and insensibility of all those who would not know Thee, or knowing Thee, have loved Thee so little?

But, O adorable Saviour, that which covers me with confusion, and which ought to make me lament most, is, that I have been myself one of these ungrateful creatures. You, O my God, who behold the very depths of this heart of mine, behold also the grief which I feel for my ingratitude, and at seeing Thee treated with such indignity! Behold the disposition in which I am to do and suffer all to repair it! See me, then, O Lord, with my heart broken with grief, humbled, beaten to the ground, and ready to receive at Thy hands all that Thou shalt be pleased to exact in reparation for such outrages. Strike, Lord, strike, I shall bless, I shall kiss, a hundred times, the hand which inflicts so just a chastisement. Why am I not worthy to be the victim to repair such wrongs? Why can I not bathe with my blood those places where Thy most sacred body has been dragged along and trampled under foot? O! how happy should I be if, by all imaginable torments, I could make reparation for such outrages, such contempt, such impieties! I do not merit so great a grace, but accept at least my desire. Accept, eternal Father, this reparation of honour in union with that which the most sacred Heart made to Thee upon Calvary, and that which the Virgin Mother made at the foot of the cross of her Son! And in conformity with the prayer which that divine Heart offered to Thee, pardon me these wrongs and irreverences which I have committed, and by Thy grace give effect to my will, and to the resolution which I make to love Thee with all fervour, and to honour Thee in all possible ways, my Sovereign, my Saviour, and my Judge, since I believe that Thou art really present in the adorable Eucharist; and for the future I will show, also, by the respect with which I will stand before it, and by the frequency of my visits to adore it, that I believe Thee to be really present. And as I make profession of giving especial honour to Thy sacred Heart, I will choose it as my sojourn during the rest of my life. Grant me the grace which I ask of Thee, that at the moment of my death I may breathe forth my last sigh in this same most sacred Heart. Amen.

END OF THE MEDITATIONS ON THE SACRED HEART.

END OF VOL II.

RICHARDSON AND SON, LONDON, DUBLIN, AND DERBY.